A Thousand Thoughts in Flight:

Diaries, 1974–1996

Maria Gabriela Llansol

TRANSLATED

FROM THE PORTUGUESE

BY AUDREY YOUNG

DEEP
VELLUM

DALLAS, TEXAS

Deep Vellum Publishing
3000 Commerce Street, Dallas, Texas 75226
deepvellum.org · @deepvellum

Deep Vellum is a 501c3 nonprofit literary arts organization founded in 2013
with the mission to bring the world into conversation through literature.

Support for this publication has been provided in part by
grants from the National Endowment for the Arts, the Texas Commission on the Arts,
the City of Dallas Office of Arts and Culture, the Communities Foundation of Texas,
and the Addy Foundation. Funded by the DGLAB/Culture and the Camões, IP –
Portugal.

Paperback ISBN: 9781646053056
Ebook ISBN: 9781646053209

LIBRARY OF CONGRESS CATALOGING-IN-PUBLICATION DATA

Library of Congress Cataloging-in-Publication Data

Names: Llansol, Maria Gabriela, author. |
Young, Audrey (Translator),
translator.
Title: A thousand thoughts in flight : diaries, 1974-1996 / Maria Gabriela
Llansol ; translated from the Portuguese by Audrey Young.
Description: Dallas, Texas : Deep Vellum, 2024.
Identifiers: LCCN 2024008861 (print) | LCCN 2024008862 (ebook) | ISBN
9781646053056 (trade paperback) | ISBN 9781646053209 (ebook)
Subjects: LCSH: Llansol, Maria Gabriela--Diaries. | Authors,
Portuguese--20th century--Diaries. | LCGFT: Diaries.
Classification: LCC PQ9274.L36 Z46 2024 (print) | LCC PQ9274.L36 (ebook)
| DDC 869.8/42--dc23/eng/20240325
LC record available at https://lccn.loc.gov/2024008861
LC ebook record available at https://lccn.loc.gov/2024008862

Cover art and design by Emily Mahon
Interior layout and typesetting by Andrea García Flores

PRINTED IN CANADA

Contents

Llansol:
The Unending Diary

JOÃO BARRENTO

A reflection on the practice and place of Maria Gabriela Llansol's diary writing—the nature, structure, and content of her diaries, as well as their connection with the rest of her work—inevitably leads to something like a general theory of Llansol's writing. It is often thought that the diaries might be a good entry point into her work, and for more than one reason. Indeed, the pieces published here are not substantially different from much of the rest of her work and the distinctive hybridity of her writing. Her diaries (a microcosm of her entire body of work) give us immediate access to the modes of writing specific to that work. And as we know so well today, all of Llansol's works originated in the uninterrupted diaries that are her writing notebooks, which are thus conceived as part of a sequence that she herself saw as a single, uninterrupted book.

But in order to truly understand this aspect of her writing, it is essential to identify what may be a paradox, one I will endeavor to elucidate as I proceed: although Llansol was a writer who kept diaries, her writing is not "diary writing" in the most conventional sense of the term and "genre." The diaries published during her

7

lifetime—the three you find here—are never simply circumstantial accounts; they were *osmotic* diaries: their genesis, their development, and their final form are inseparable from Llansol's other books, which always accompany them and are interwoven with them. And this osmosis becomes even more apparent in the posthumous diaries now being published in Portuguese—the "Books of Hours"—in which the great constellations of her work are all present. The handwritten notebooks where everything is conceived indeed form a rhizomatic network of boundless entries, from the reflective to the informative, from the introspective to the critical, from the contemplative to the ironic, from the properly "diaristic" to the fictional, from simple lists to records of dreams, all of which are present in them since the late 1960s. The handwritten notebook thus becomes the true seminal place and the original chaos out of which emerges all of Llansol's writing, her thinking, the ethics and aesthetics that inform this work, often in its final form. When speaking about this unending diary that is her day-to-day writing in the notebooks—singular and diverse and with no immediate purpose—Llansol often mentions that it is a question of privileging the compulsion to write and the unpredictable outcome of the transit from notebook to book, along pathways that the published diaries allow us to better understand.

The decision to "create readable volumes" out of the diaries using her handwritten, numbered and dated notebooks, which since 1974 accompanied the passing of her days and the genesis of her books in a disparate but insistent way, emerged during the final phase of her twenty-year exile in Belgium. But the writing in these notebooks (like that in the three diaries presented here) was never undertaken by Llansol in a systematic way or with any definite purpose, apart from certain stages during the intense preparation of specific books, when there is a greater degree of discipline in the diary entries, and even a rigorous planning of the structure of the work—although it is never seen as definitive, as is evident from the titles, which frequently change. The inherently fragmentary, non-narrative, and non-sequential nature of this writing means that there are no essential differences between the "storehouse"—impressions, images, visions, readings—of the notebooks and the rhizome of the books. Her writing is singular and diverse, a way of "absorbing the experience of time," of all the times, tonalities, and gradations of the boundless experience of an author with multiple registers, ever-mutating, always different, and yet very similar.

But what exactly is a diary by Llansol, a diary for Llansol? In the first posthumous Book of Hours, we come across a striking sentence: "Good writers keep bad diaries." The distinction drawn is between "writing well" and not wanting to write "well," the decision to write outside the norm, as is the case with Llansol when she arrives at the great inflection point in her writing: between orderly, defensive writing and a writing that takes risks; and it can also mean contrasting the "writer" (author[ity]) with someone who simply writes (the "writing being"), transforming body and world into writing as the days elapse—this is the diary for Llansol, day-to-day writing, not necessarily following the most common rules of the diary genre. Writing seen as "the double of living," always more attentive to the "folds of the world" than to the circumstances of the days, which can transport us into a bright, fragrant, musical atmosphere, as well as a dark, heavy or acrid one—but never into an artificial space. The function of the diary for Llansol is thus to be a mirror of the fragmentary dynamism of the world and of the "I" (as in any of her books). Of the world refracted through the filter of an "I," of course, but an "I"

9

that prefers to become a *we*, to shift into the *third person*, to become impersonal, clearing away the excess of oneself, even when saying "I." Because "a diary can be more objective than a personal life."

In its unstable and hybrid typology, in its polyphony of voices, the diary for Llansol is neither a circumstantial account, nor an archive of memories, nor (merely) a writing workshop or a breviary of reflections—it is all of these things, just as it is pure autobiography with a total rejection of the autobiographical. Because the "I" that speaks always does so in the name of "an absolute and subjectless speaking" (as the great essayist Eduardo Lourenço once wrote).

The gaze upon the world—the small and the large, the inner and the outer, the visible and the invisible—of someone who writes in this way, explains the paradoxical statement above: Llansol is *not* a writer of diaries, yet she did nothing else all her life other than write a diary! It is the gaze of someone who, by immersing herself in the most enigmatic and incandescent aspects of the everyday, knows that this everyday—one of common experiences, of reading, of small and large gestures and epiphanies—can transport us outside the narrowest orbit of existence. It is the "dog's eye" that Llansol speaks of in *Inquiry into the Four Confidences*, which, as has been said, is a gaze "that seeks the light which emerges somewhere between the ethics of responsibility, the uncompromising pursuit of beauty, and the soaring, just expression." There it is: the perfect radiographic image of Maria Gabriela Llansol's singular and unending diary-book.

Llansol wrote her diaries largely in Portuguese, with the occasional French word or quotation. In this edition, Arno Pro has been used for the text in Portuguese, while Signifier has been used for the text in French.

1.

Finita

ALPEDRINHA, SUMMER 1939

Copied into a small notebook with a heart drawn on the cover:
I want to be humble in your eyes, and under your "omnipotent"
hand.

Copied into the same notebook, sewn with needle and thread:
give me reason and understanding.

Then, after two blank pages:
God.

A few more blank pages:
a drawing of the Portuguese flag.

A second notebook is sewn to the first:
I lay down in this bed, to sleep and to rest. If the enemy
comes...

Then, there are more texts, copied by another child with better handwriting, and fewer errors.

After a few pages, the completion, in ink, of a text written in pencil by the same child, now older:
I entrust them to the three delights that are within, that everything may go well for them.

A few pages later and, this time, written by my own hand:
the Lady makes stockings with thread made of light.

Undoubtedly, a year or two later, which can be seen by the improved handwriting:
forgiveness for my grave sins.

At the end of the notebook,
Lisbon, 11 December 1943,
I am twelve years old:
my prayer is very simple:
be merciful to me.

Six days later, Augusto was born.

Today I finished *The Book of Communities*. And another book is already emerging, *The Remaining Life*, which will be the true book of the battle. I don't want to write today about one nor the other.

Only that the first one finishes:

It was the end of the text

The next morning the dialogue with the new being began again, a silent dialogue of glances, caresses, absences, thoughts, smiles, and fear.

and the other begins:

the new being was a monster; they aspersed themselves with perfume.

I sense this new being is the one that John of the Cross, Suso, Eckhart, Friedrich Nietzche, Müntzer, Heart of the Bear, Pegasus carried within themselves, in the sorrows and joys of the unexpressed, willingly and unwillingly, when a greater will so desired,

and they came, in History, to lay it down before the Princes, as a sign of contradiction and a mark of the end.

Augusto rereads to me, in the meantime, a fragment studied with Christine, by Friedrich Nietzsche:

"The European princes should really ask themselves whether they can do without our support. We immoralists — today we are the only power which needs no allies to reach victory: that makes us by far the strongest among the strong. We do not even need lies: what other power could dispense with them? A strong seduction fights for us, perhaps the strongest there is: the seduction of truth ... of 'truth'? Who put that word into our mouths? [...] No, we don't need even that, we would gain power and victory even without truth. The magic that fights for us [...] is the *magic of the extreme*, the seduction that every extreme exercises: we immoralists, we are extreme [...]"

It leaves me perplexed,
I am exhausted.

I speak with Christine about the fragment by Friedrich Nietzsche, which Augusto read to me a few days ago. I am always unsettled by him, so abrupt is his thinking. Musil, who meditated on him to write *The Man Without Qualities*, so often, sitting there with us, would ask:

— But what does he want? His critique does not allow any possible politics...

Christine laughs when Friedrich Nietzsche speaks of "we immoralists," for there was no we, there was only him, despite the appearance of Many. Why use "immoralists" to refer to those who situate themselves beyond good and evil, in a place whose name they do not know, until the arrival of the poet who knows how to name it?

What to call the world that does not recognize the distinction between truth and appearance (which has been our perspective since Plato)? And who will be able to live in it?

— *You have passed beyond the silence of dusk* — she said.
She let herself fall backward, meditating.

I write in these notebooks so that the experience of time can, in fact, be absorbed. I thought that one day, reading these texts, which come from my tension of dissipating and accumulating in metamorphoses, might offer me clues to the *eternal return of the mutual.*

I believe that where there is pleasure, knowledge is near. The same could only be said of the kind of darkness from which light is born.

In short: I write in these notebooks so that my body does not stray from the rising line which runs toward old age, as I conceive it: an immense reflection, a loosening obtained from contrasts, a concentration on the present, in which all times imaginable are unfolding forever. This state is the ideal moment for writing.

And I also returned to this account to fend off the book about the School — *The Experience of The Namur Street School;* I could only write about my perception of the groups for a few moments; a group is the equivalent to "dispositions necessary to serve."

For example:

I put a handkerchief sodden with perfume into my bag, which then came into contact with a letter from my mother, written in blue ink, staining the paper. One of them is so enticing that I'm going to save it. But I can barely reread the letter; only a few words are still legible.

When I am not writing *The Remaining Life,* which I began today, I will write here. I am certain that a few legible words will pass from one to the other.

I am, regretfully, nearly finished with *Fragments d'un Journal*, by Mircea Eliade, and next I am going to read *Fictions*, by Borges. I do not know what encounter awaits me; to begin with, there is a kind of portal within the book: Ibarra's preface. I think about Saint John of the Cross, and about the two rr's as in two columns; about the Spanish language, which my grandmother no longer spoke. Between two columns, I return to the page and, a surprise: "What do you want me to tell you about myself? I don't know anything about myself; I don't even know the date of my own death." Extremely pretentious, or else, entirely true; why not grant others the sincerity with which I read them? It needed to be elucidated. And then, immediately following this question, the great rhythm: "I owe the discovery of Uqbar to the conjunction of a mirror and an encyclopedia."

When it is already late in the evening in terms of desire and I forget all the messages for which you make me messenger... I am now writing *The Remaining Life.* Today, Christine told me about the vision she had. She confided to me that she doesn't understand why we must move toward the necessity of our death.

I read to her:

when Ana de Peñalosa entered the boat that was moored at the far end of the room, someone put a pane of glass under her writing hand. In one of these musings, surprised because she did not think it possible, Ana de Peñalosa lost her sex.

Fearful; but the most beautiful part of the house had been preserved. Its musical part. The desire to live in a house I can no longer lose overtakes me again.

Where to find such a place?

A house in the middle of the bare earth, drawn by horses to our, my, death. For Augusto will have a death all his own. That house causes me to think of reflections, and water; when I think, I often think about a pool of water, where I am slowly sinking. In actuality, without that movable house, where to steer my profusion?

The moment of departure, however, had not yet arrived; in the deepness of the window, the sun of Copernicus shone with a mathematical calculation. Ana de Peñalosa ran her fingers through its heat. For the text, it was the ephemeral sign of departure. She drew back the curtain, but dawn had not broken, she imagined that the normal course of time had encountered an obstacle. She could not make out the sutures of the dawn, but the Siamese cat, on her lap, was still alive on his four paws.

In reality, only
an insistent language is a
true language.

If you knew how many shadows will remain living among us, emerging from your maternal body, how many shadows will be reduced to nothing, at night and along the walls, and in the morning will come and lie in your arms, at the moment you confide your dreams to me... I write in The Remaining Life.

At Christine's house, Fokouli revealed that he was full of gifts. On the 6th, we returned from Portugal, where we hadn't been since 1965; and I long to know the future, as I long to understand the past. Why does it seem to me that in Portugal, today, the poor and the rich are now able to hate one another overtly?; on the streets, at night, and in the intimacy of the houses, there is the scent of a violent reckoning.

The smell of a perverted message.

I would like to warn them to keep their distance from Justice.

We sat down on the floor.

Following the silence, we listen to Gregorian chants, and gaze at a burning candle.

But then I invent that we touch the flames with the palms of our hands, so that our knowledge of the *mutual* is set aflame.

Then, I read *L'idéal historique* and Augusto reads Eckhart.

Finally, I serve tea, and honey.

And I am reminded of the impression, which I have long held, about what dominates gender relations between men and women,
on the margins of the mutual:
vassalization and crime.

When woman dominates, fecundity absorbs affection, and names are kept alive or not, insofar as they serve that earthly invading desire.

Fecundity and crime go hand in hand.

When man dominates, conquest turns men into warriors of the beyond, and woman is ever the first vassal, paying tribute for the safekeeping of the conquered lands.

Conquest and slavery are two names of the same agent.

And are sex and writing not two names of the same action?

If I strive to open up a path to a text that does not *represent* (and therefore, before all else, speaks), what sex will I be speaking?

"I will open up a path to *one*, whose source is neither aggression, nor imposture."

There is within me a woman who has sex, and another who does not.

"Perhaps it is indeed a question of two types of thought, joined by nostalgia."

An exceptional time, although harsh, under certain circumstances; I bend over the books I will write, over the outcome of a human house, in a garden, with the mutual desire to live alongside people who know how to move toward

_____ .

There was a shadow,
impossible to capture in a portrait;
when the light was gone,
the shadow fell to the ground.

How to explain that this was how she wanted to live with
Eckhart; to detect, as she draws back a curtain, the plausible sound
of his voice, to see on the white wall not even his shadow; then
having closed the door, to come across the Sermons, rest her hand
atop it as on an abandoned coffer of clairvoyant thoughts; remain
lying there accompanied by the light until Nietzsche came and
Müntzer explained in her ear the duration of the message that was
ambiguous, but so timely.

And long for us to be sociable and hermits.
To live among one another as if we were obeying an undemanding Rule, with neither passion, nor devotion. To, as hermits, live the gestalt that we are, whose creation unfurls over us, without deluging us, out of sheer pleasure. The Possible of creational indifference, reflected inattention, compassionate selfishness, and solidarity, out of a joy for life.

The lace cloth on the table, at Christine's house. Roses, lace connecting the roses. Perhaps it was this, making lace, that I first desired. In its place, I began to write. I have the feeling that, once again, there will be a moment when I would have rather devised this texture than become involved with writing.

Why didn't I?

Why did I become involved in precisely *this* writing? When did I stop writing stories, in order to piece together the movements of the subtle Being in your lives? When must I have become aware that only close to that place, following the edges of that movement, would life perhaps be able to grasp the sources of Joy? At what moment did I know that only by creating *nonexistent realities*, as Augusto calls them, would we open up access to those sources?

I am perplexed when I see that, outside the text, those realities are fleeting. And that if we lose them, we will be reduced to chaos, absent any cartography.

How the world appears in states of language...

How they emerged in forms, making themselves...

How we can return there, making and unmaking...

Am I to conclude that I was born, in the image of all women, to make lace? The other, that of Ariadne? That of the threads of gold which Ana de Peñalosa weaves, writing, so that we do not lose the lost meaning of the battle? And the long absence of her sons not an exile, but rather, "They set out on a discovery"?

I was talking to Christine, who said to me, and this was all I
heard
    the cycle of the Renaissance   is not yet finished;
    there is still time to return to its beginnings, and rewrite a
new meaning for it.

    There was such a certainty in her that I found myself more
at ease,
averting my gaze from
hers
to the table
covered in lace.

A visit to the house we are supposed to rent in Jodoigne. The owner, an old woman, tells us we won't be able to visit the house that evening because there aren't any lamps. We see the large building, and the courtyard, with a small abandoned garden, through the bars of the gate, closed with an iron chain:

_____ *the house still inaudible, yet to be uttered by the murmur of the subsequent life; she observed that, scattered across the ground, Müntzer, John of the Cross, the light, and the animals they had swept along with them, were waiting to be invited to dwell within the walls; she asked the plants, and the beautiful secluded, or anonymous books, to guide her. But where, since the house persisted in being the appearance of nothingness? Pegasus, in the shape of a horse, swiftly ran toward it. Müntzer and John of the Cross, turned into lumps of earth, agreed that the garden revealed a disconcerting poverty of inspiration. I declared that the hour of departure had arrived and that, together, we would make the garden of mutual desire. We awaited the thousand details that would construct the cosmogony of the house.*

We set out under the impetus of Genesis, as ten years earlier we set out on Augusto's desertion, and our subsequent arrival here, in the wake of Exodus.

I start to move objects, papers, books, organizing them into groups. I begin this task well in advance, for one should not deride eras that are beginning. It was not an infantile desire by the Zen Master, when he sought the original face, the one before birth. An encounter with his-own-self-instant; participating in the desire or in the happenstance that would produce it.

All the children I have analyzed have that desire, which psychoanalysis called the primal scene. In them, to refuse that curiosity is the affirmative principle of thinking, distancing oneself, even there, from knowledge. Thinking, in that instant, is the price of not knowing. But I *know* there is also an instant when one should not deride the era that is beginning. The instant when I must halt my thinking, as a precautionary measure for breath and vision, and risk reason in that encounter with myself, at the moment I was desired when my father *saw* me as a boy.

If I never risk reason, I will never *know*.
I will never know how to think.

Christine came to help me put objects and books into their respective boxes, all afternoon. Only when she was gone did I notice she had left a letter *there*, addressed to us, in which she is

inconsolable about our departure. And yet, it is only twenty-five
kilometers from Louvain to Jodoigne… I had the urge to run,
to follow her enticement and tell her
that everything I have written up until this point has been
an attempt to understand how to write the Rule of mutual
desire,
the rule that you say applies to the Community. If we are too
precise, impulses are curtailed; if we do not approach the exact,
the weave is undone and the mutual vanishes.

    And yet, I did not move,
there among the boxes, with the letter I rewrote well in advance,
at a distance. And
I found myself murmuring a passage from *The Book of
Communities*, which at the School had served as a text for the
cycle of "Pegasus the Horse":
the fecundity of the gift is the gift's only retribution
it seems to me, before anything else, that the rules should rest on
their own
that is
that is
that they should be able to remain sleeping,
and be taken as a dream.

Tonight, all the ghosts took the path to Jodoigne to give the departure the appearance of an impassible mountain; from the ghost of writing scattered along the bank of a river to the ghost of quality dissolving into shallow quantities of water; from the ghost of silence lost to the anguish of the scattered furniture whose wood remained afloat; from the flight of the animals to a place where they will no longer be together; from the messenger letters of friends to the terrible ghost of dear friends, with absent letters; from the ghost that tells me *who you are going to be* to the ghost that tells me *who she was with you is no longer here*; from the ghost of the fearsome face-to-face between Augusto and myself, from which was born a harrowing reflection of the absolute; from the record of symphony music that spins, marking the timeless swells of the day; from the most chilling ghost to the ghost that is fainter when morning draws near _____ . *In the nightmare, she traveled in the arms of the fantastic being, which listens to the tenuous noises, a phoenix reborn from its own ashes which had always been enticing,* I wrote, in the middle of the night, in *The Remaining Life.*

Here, that faint ghost rests its attenuated sentences, its blue-colored fears, on my shoulder; it is a ghost of girls, a creator of exiles. Outside the doors, there is a garland which, behind the doors, *will flee from you unendingly.* The faint ghost has a greater fear, as true ghosts have lesser fears. It is the lesser fears that I am more afraid of, for when I am confronted by them, I am defenseless. Because true ghosts have a faint way of indicating their presence. For example, I am moving tomorrow. But what is the *reality* of departing? Of leaving, of abandoning, of moving? In the move, there is the becoming.

(Augusto often reminds me that   those who choose
the word determine reality;
but in this warning I sense, more than anything, voluntarism,
for I do not relinquish the vision of the *eternal return of the*
mutual, which is revealed in the faint way of moving.)

It is scarcely even noticeable. But there is such a discretion
in this presence that is absent, that its existence hollows out an
imperceptible and consistent terrain.

As if the move were not the place for the act of becoming
_____ .

The moment it vanishes, reality goes with it. I am aware of
this retreat, and it produces an unfathomable anguish in me.

Having forgotten, since then, the message delivered by Müntzer,
she sat down on the beach to study the waves, looking for the place
where her sons would gather; but it was an expanse far too vast in
width and depth.

When, for the first time, I was alone in this house in
Jodoigne, with undisturbed time stretching out ahead of me,
the space fragmented by reminiscences, and the furniture
settling into their new places, I remembered that underground,
on the right side of the garden, there is a stream, and that in the
greenhouse, there is an old pump once used for drawing water.

_____ I "come" to this house with the inquiring sense I give
it. To peruse and usher in   certain folds   of historical
events, nearly depleted and effaced. For me, the book is not the
swift object of a reading; it conceals a mutual: a time and
someone. "I write to speak for my ancestors who have fallen
silent." _____ Liliane Wouters.

*Mother of objects, I deliberately left the other side of the page
blank; today I awoke dreaming that I did not live alone in this
house but with my husband, father to Thomas and John; and that
Hadewijch was loved by him, and loved us…*, I wrote today in *The
Remaining Life.*

I listen to Gregorian chants and write the battle in *The Remaining Life*. I know that *the ones I hold dear* are going to lose, have already lost. And yet, I still don't know what it is to lose, what they have lost, at the moment the battle is written. There is a remnant that was left behind, and which, in the form of the *mutual*, is uttered. Although I don't quite understand what is looming in that word.

What is it to lose?

Who loses, what do they leave behind, written on the battlefield?

Absorbed in the question, I gazed, distracted, at the candle flame at my side.

I have seen the flickering of a candle flame so many times. But, in that instant, I saw it differently. I was not sensitive to the color, but to the flaring and wavering of the flame. To its hesitant and persistent way of breathing. As it was dark, the flame, its intensity rising and falling, created more or less illuminated space. And, in this rare coincidence of fluctuations, I felt the equality between flame, sound, and vibration. The same rhythm, the same oscillation, the same creation of space, the same variety of "time," the very same combustion.

I saw that sonorous manifestations are luminous combustions.

Sounds cease because they burn and, in burning, they make matter evanescent.

Sounds transform into smoke; this one will be a cloud.

Cloud and melody are the two faces of matter. Nothing vanishes; everything moves from mountain to mountain, from hand to hand, listening. As if the reverse of history arrived to me in a fold, and I saw it begin to open up ever so slightly, and my hands received only clouds.

And yet, I write...

The lives that will be lost during the battle, as living flames, have illuminated who, what? Me?

And what unnamed aesthetic vitality did they have (or are they having?), those men and women?

What timeline was ruptured there, but not shattered, and enfolds their being?

What cloud continues traveling? Why is it that howls can be heard on the horizon of history, the steady dripping of unfinished actions?

Why are the words for the thoughts
expressed there
only now being born here?
Why do I recall:
"Reginaldo, Reginaldo, /
Page to the much belovèd King / You could very well,
Reginaldo, / Spend the night with me?"
Why were they, like I, confronted with the pestilential odor
of their own texts?

Still for 21 April 1975:

to a gaze that I saw, which I called
the eternal return of the mutual:

a tremulous gaze is lying in my familiarity, a fleeting instant,
between the desire to slake its thirst and the fear of becoming
enamored with the love of eternity;

it reflects back the image of the essential encounter, when souls
touch without rapture in the indecipherable breeze of the
motionless trees;

that tremulous gaze desires and does not implore
an intense fleeting,

a mark with no memory of a sign, drawn there as a meaningless
image;

at the table where love was shared, it called Everything One; in
mute words, it suggested I choose Nothingness, as proof there
had been an unexpected epiphany about the love of eternity in
that place.

I am weary. The work at the School exhausts me. I can no longer bear the constant intrusions of the parents, who never know what they want as a group. I am with the children and I think about the book. I feel the absence of a master for my constant questions.

Someone will have to come.

Christine came to spend a few days with us, and brought me a book by Kierkegaard: *Philosophical Fragments*.

_____ when I get up, I turn on the light at my work table
with crossed legs; then I wander around, putting away the
objects that had been moved during the night;
Kierkegaard is on his way to me, and I to him, but the encounter
has been delayed: "In taking this path, then, love does not
become happy." With *Philosophical Fragments* on my knees, I
wait for a horizon at the top of the mountain.

The first lines I read
are familiar footsteps that leave no echo: "Nature itself comes up
with many terrifying devices and many subterfuges in order to
disturb"; a drifter came, a drifter went, leaving behind only
crumbs. I have the painful certainty that the imperceptible
movements have become so slight that _____; I pick up the
crumbs and place them on the doorstep, thinking that perhaps
the drifter will return and, if he doesn't find me, he will have no
difficulty experiencing the feeling of his own guilt.

As soon as the one I call V. told me about the first milk
from which she drank her first words, I instinctively looked at
her breasts, where an incandescent abecedarium may still be
leaking even now.
  There is a rumor she is dependent on two phalluses, V. I
went in and sat down where she serves food and drinks.
  The soup was heavily seasoned,
and a man was scratching at his beard and hair with his hand,
never taking his eyes off me.
  The window, in eight small panes, fogged over;
I look at the steam from the food being prepared.
  Forgetting the environment into which I had plunged, only
to place importance
on the literal *virtù* that pierces me:_____ ,
we must escape the vicious circle. "The human mind so often
aspires to might and power," in which the soul does not learn to
have a heart.
  When V. took away my plate and replaced it with another, I
thought about the steady line of known biographies; the man I
mentioned was still gazing at me,
and I,
I thought,
always men, and the women who mean the most to us, almost
men themselves,
what a loss.

  From the insistent gaze of the man upon us, he spread out a
glove on the final plate V. had brought:

the glove of Kierkegaard — the Master of Guilt.

It was a plate with no recipient,
and I,
relating the different perceptions which I had had, understood
that Kierkegaard was regarding us as units of thought. I, V., and
the younger girl, *who burned with a great flame* in the kitchen,
merely by looking at the small, stocky man who had intervened.
I wanted to open the door for their journey and immediately let
them board the ship, which was a symbol,
another visible reality. But
Kierkegaard halted my steps — or rather — his glove held my
hand with a particular weight on my fingers.

— The boat is guilt — said the velvet pressure he exerted; I
closed my eyes, I have never heard of a breath that is able to
confront him; he questioned and denied at the most remote
point of the thinking which had been given to me. And
suddenly, out of the shamelessness
of that negative statement,
a body was born for him,
utterly marked by the sign of guilt.
I could envisage its life.
As I returned to my meal, I underlined the images it left me:
the fragments of a tragic thinking ("one's greatest suffering
and one's highest hope" — dixit Friedrich Nietzsche) which
lingered in him and, in a penetratingly tender form,
flecks of guilt in his eyes,
and spots of ink on his knees.

We departed, leaving V. and her younger companion behind.

On the street, he bought a handkerchief, and chose one made of fine cambric. In one corner, he had the initials R.O. embroidered. He wrote the letter that was to accompany the handkerchief, always with a halo of fleeting life around him. At that moment, his feet were cold; his circulation was slow, bound to the second nature that had been left to him: — Father! — The connection between the generations was made through guilt: Kierkegaard found in his life, which he had always imagined to be swift, the fertile time to structure it as a small, mysterious garden, with the discreet and enduring ability to be discordant.

He wrote the letter that would accompany the handkerchief like a man in love and suspicious of other liaisons, such was the rhythm of his surface, always inscribed at the maximum of his instant.

——————— the gulls have returned to my horizon, soaring over the cliff (on this green plain in Brabant, where there are neither cliffs, nor gulls); in their wandering flights, they embody my dispersion, the dispersion of someone who has, against the present wind, a thousand thoughts in flight; I do not know where these images entangled with gulls escape to. They let me assume that the new place is located at the point of dispersion. I anchor these images in oblivion, as they drown on the sand or in the sea, and press upon me a final, vain attempt to enthrall.

I had another thought under my eyes,
"A muddiness of mind in which earthly distinction ferments almost grossly."
In the *gross* morning air, the sun and wind, borne by the momentary darkness of guilt, grapple with one another, in the ancient branches of the northern cherry trees in my new garden,
and out of that conflict is born the unreal gull that succeeds the first ones I had imagined: "Because the truth in which I rest was in me and emerged from me. Not even Socrates would have been capable of giving it to me, no more than the coachman is capable of pulling the horse's load, even though he may help the horse do it by means of the whip."

Sitting in the garden, I await the Master of Guilt. Behind me, the house is covered with hidden gulls that appear to be small rectangles of red clay; I hear them swooping, and making high-pitched aquatic sounds; they are what chase away Kierkegaard's melancholy ideas, and they stretch out in the

44

rain   when he feels better in the curve of love, and in
the swell of his thinking.

The sky is now empty of gulls and I scratch at the earth, not
far from two lizards slowly crawling along the ground, seeking
the warm face of the sun. I am delighted by those true
thermometers. Where they alight, in their magnificent non-
flight, will always be warmer, and in the warmer, insects are
more distracted and accessible.

I return to the book: "Viewed Socratically, any point of
departure in time is eo ipso something accidental, a vanishing
point, an occasion."

I slowly reenter the concentration I need and which, with
great care, I will take possession of, without taking away its
freedom.

Those who know Zarathustra's animals will see that I can
proceed no differently. At the top of the mountain, he was
accompanied by the eagle and the serpent, with whom he
dialogued at the essential moment of the revelation of the
eternal return of the same.

As I await, in a minor key, the Master of Guilt, sitting here
in a valley reduced to a small garden, I must confine myself to
listening attentively to the swift swooping of the gulls and
watching, in a glance,
the slow crawling of the lizards. From this is extracted the
potential spark, on which I concentrate, leaning against the bare
window, as I have seen women do eternally   "then the
moment in time must have such decisive significance."

The aloof lizard and the unreal gull are not symbols, nor metaphors, but images from the text: my rightful companions on this day.

At the hour of the rushes.

He knocked on the door, and said:

— I am a character dear to myself, and dear to you. — J.G., who appeared at the doorway for the first time, and was one of the peasants killed in the battle, made an instinctive movement of retreat, but opened up the darkness to the light he was bringing. It was not yet the hour of the candlelight, and Kierkegaard, as ever, feared that he, or his father, had spat in the face of truth. To punish themselves, they proposed the crucified Christ to one another, which sent Friedrich Nietzsche into a trance of horror; from his earliest childhood, he had known he was enfolded in a garment that had belonged to his father.

It was, in the square, the hour of flags and manifestos, and in its light could be read: "I owe everything to my Father. As a child, they never stopped showing me that sinners had spat in the face of the Christ. To atone for that fault will be my life itself." To Friedrich Nietzsche who, in one of the rooms, conceptually intoned the words before writing them, someone had once expressed their desire that he "achieve a dream worth a life," but for Kierkegaard, the dream would be to reconvert.

I myself have the feeling he is a fold, carrying J.G. Hamann's *Aesthetica in Nuce* in the outer pocket of his long coat, that This One was the peasant killed in the battle, who had welcomed him at the entrance, and who since that instant had begun to serve him: polishing the furniture, shining his shoes, and cleaning his suit. To such an extent that, from that moment on, he was called Kierkegaard's faithful servant.

He welcomed him into the house. His forehead was steeply sloped, and he resembled a circle of tinted candles, with black in the background. His hope was to never desire to speak again. A fond feeling of guilt washed over me — an active feeling that came from the palm of his long, thin hands.

But how were scruples expressed in a man superior to his curved portrait? He had arrived at my house accompanied by a forest tree dressed entirely in black; he, conversely, was absurdly dressed in green, and apologized to me for letting the greenness seep into his entire being; he asked me, "But how are we to raise the defunct languages of nature from the dead?"

I felt J.G. shudder, but I was unable to dwell on that feeling because the tiny man, just before he sat down, continued fulminating:

the Great Work of the Angel and the Disaster
was interrupted.

The sweet light falls away, and the face of the Disaster appears slowly
hesitant,
as if corrupted.
The Angel knows.
It knows that   corrupted   it is not an image of
the face,
but the authentic design of the catastrophe.

Something is changing shape and texture
but so imperceptibly that only other eyes of a new body will be able to make out the vague signs of the shaking which has already begun. The flute of the forest and of life has been broken. The clever satyr broke it with his hooves. A spurt of sound was exiled into the air, yellowing the leaves and volitions; joy

hibernated in boredom, and the satyr embarked upon the zoological mythology of Dionysus.

The Disaster was losing its allies one by one. Without abandoning the cause, it saw the effects proliferating, restless and unruly. It could not depend on the loyalty of the Angel, which alone could hear my voice — continued Kierkegaard — mirroring reality. I hereby present to you man, born from the lost effects of the Disaster. Evil son of the death of the deer, the ivy, the vine, and enthusiasm,
deadly hunter of the satyr,
a beardless figure pursuing nymphs. And the Disaster watched its rival grow, the sharpening of his teeth on the clitoris of the euphoric   nymph-made-woman   with isolated and pestilent openings.

> This is what was proclaimed at the culmination of the rural feast,
>> which only the closed body of the Angel sensed
>> under the sign of trembling and nostalgia.
> This is the story of the guilty man and of Lucifer, the
Angel.

And yet, the Angel cannot lose. In its defeat, the thinking that saddens man and consoles him would be lost. As long as thinking lasts, the Great Work will remain interrupted: as soon as the concept is lost, the Disaster ensues, again and again drawing to itself the sutured parts of man. Over their remains, the rural feast will begin anew. The flute of Dionysus is not only the soul of man, it is also his death: in every sound, there is a risk of rupture.

— My voice returns to the Angel — Kierkegaard

whispered. — I am looking for the potential hope that there is another path, and that man, in overcoming his sorrow, will not incite an even greater Disaster.

The faith of this narrative is not entirely justified: more than once, the Angel and the Disaster have helplessly let the richest parts of their Work be destroyed. Even today, man has not seen them, and he is no different: he no longer thinks he is blind, he still hopes to restore sight
to his eyes.

Ah! If only man would accept his guilt.

He fell silent:
Do not trust the Angel
to impart joy to your thinking.

And I continued writing the folded echo of his voice:
but the figure of Ana de Peñalosa was already taking shape beyond, at the same instant they heard the thunder of the horses' hooves. A fire without sparks swept the field, and time had not yet reached the Temple. At that moment, Hadewijch fled from Nietzsche. "Out of mercy," he said, "we will camp here. I want to write Zarathustra." But it was the first words of the Spiritual Canticle that came out of his mouth as his lost love wandered in the distance;

I have never spoken directly about the new house in which I live, passing through a courtyard for carriages and horses; a difficult garden, a large iron door, ornate and closed. This is Jodoigne. Today, if someone were to arrive from outside, they might be received as a stranger.

Contiguous thoughts / I cannot bear the word History, and yet there are centers of irradiation, unbroken wefts of spiritual geographies, places of recurrence, enduring and abiding humans; all that enters here will be imperceptibly beautiful, or will become beautiful.

Night fell before I was able to set aside the day; I was waiting for it, full of patience, with the sole purpose of welcoming it in the darkness; I am sitting in the garden, with Augusto and Christine.

I thought I was silent, but in reality, I presented my *inmost self*
to the night,
to the garden eased from the green of the day,
and to the animals lying all around.

Thomas Müntzer is not a very learned man, I told them.

Friedrich Nietzsche is beset by memories, which now, at the end of his days, are nothing more than the return of what he irradiated, and also of what he remains attentive to, being, as he is, a singular man,
a much-tormented man,
full of compassion,
very unpleasant
in the eyes of others,
and in his own eyes. Look at the way he observes Saint John of the Cross and gathers all his loves of ardent thinking. The irony with which he sees Thomas Müntzer and all his struggles. The solicitude he shows to Ana de Peñalosa, which extends to all her plants and sorrows. The desire he harbors for Hadewijch, a virgin and a seductress, capable of understanding the subversive aim of his thinking.

Brandishing "a crook," it occurs to me.

Are you sitting in front of your door, Hadewijch? Why do you flee from Friedrich Nietzsche?

Why don't you come inside? It's getting late. Guide Thomas Müntzer, for he doesn't see the brambles, and lead him, with his head, inside, toward the warmth of the fireplace. John of the Cross lit a lamp and held it out to Ana de Peñalosa. Just as Ana was about to take it, John extinguishes it.

Ashes and clouds, I say.

The Master of Guilt has been absent as of late. He is mistaken for the scarecrow dressed in rags in the field. But at night, the birds do not set upon the crops. He refuses to write with us. His opinion about the ultimate aims is truly paradoxical. He has no cats in his house and no one knows whether he lives with a dog that lies at his feet.

As night settles in, as if it had always been Night, the original face appears, the one the Angel and the Disaster declared to one another long before they ceased to be allies:

> Such was their desire,
> such was their spirit,
> such was the universe for them.

I hold out my hand for Augusto's.
When we lived together in the same house, it was the deep-rooted vision of the beguines.

When we think, or when we speak (at this moment, a yellow forsythia petal, in the shape of a flower, fell out from inside the book; it is the truth _____).

Look at Copernicus, standing there, in the snow, awaiting his long and perilous journey.

All is sound.

It would be possible to live here, in this region. When I
look at the ridge of the mountains   a question insinuates
itself into me and, simultaneously, I have a desire:
what if nothing existed?
I long for these mountains to exist for their nothingness.

In the room at the Forest Service Lodge, there is, at the
head of the bed, a blue cup with a wide mouth and narrow base.
As there was forty years ago at the house of my Aunt Alice, a
notary in Vila Pouca de Aguiar. Forty years, an entire period of
oppression that ends with assertions of power, and group
personal languages. Portugal, today, is not the middle of a
journey, it is a departure, accomplished at great cost, for an
erroneous journey. For now, they (we) are unfettered but not
yet free. The institutions, the categories, the authorities, the
epidemic knowledge and ignorance continue to mediate the
relationships between people; there is no sign of ecosystems
being created. There is no talk of abolishing the effects of power,
but rather wresting new forms from the old.

I wait for Augusto and, to avoid becoming bored, I play
with words. Only at first because then I think that the food,
which I am slowly eating, has transformed me. But I feel as
though I am someone traveling in a foreign country, for I do not
feel bound, in any way, to a nation. In Belgium, I feel less as
though I am in a foreign land, perhaps because it is obvious that
no political ties bind me to this country. No country anywhere,
save for the emptiness in which I have given myself over to a
common age. A *common age* that is real because it is imaginary,

and imaginary because it is true. The writing, the animals, are part of that periphery, and it is those beings excluded by men which I embrace.

Working on difficult material moves my tongue; living almost entirely alone gradually draws those who are utterly alone.

For Augusto:

I fall asleep *only* to awaken in a thousand years, when countries and their role still exist, or have already ceased to exist; there was a woman who was called *Quando*, a dog's name, a grammatical name, who had a thousand possibilities for living, or remaining dead. In human organisms such as hers, there is a plurality of functions, but they are not contradictory.

Fire is set in the forests. And on the beaches, many abandoned "swimsuits" (which we will burn, in the place of forests, full of fire beyond measure).

Before going to meet the family in the mountains, we spoke with some of the inhabitants of Cavra, at the entrance to a small store with the dark interior of a house. Despite the light in the countryside, it is dark inside the dwellings. The store sells bread, tobacco, and they tell me they are plagued by rats. I speak to the women, while the men speak to the men. They work in the fields, earn a wage in the gold mines or in the forest service. In their leisure time, they still spin, and make socks from sheep's wool. I have written this text in French because ever since I began traveling around Portugal, I have been fascinated by the school language which, during my childhood, explained the rural world with uncompromising commonplaces. This

Portuguese language, in which I learned to speak about what I had not experienced. In my 4th year notebook, I read, in a dictation: "The Portuguese settler has not found anyone to worthily proclaim his virtues." And I myself wrote, in an essay: "Francisco's mother is a poor washerwoman, who washes her customers' clothing in the crystal-clear water of a stream, every day, from morning to night."

I write today, thirty-five years later, in *The Remaining Life*:

millions of peasants
and solitary lands
flowed side by side
like a river.

There was then a great sorrow, a great fear, a great hatred, on the path, with them. Looking into each other's eyes the intimate light of their eyes fled and the bloody war on the great battlefields manifested itself in the words they uttered or scarcely uttered.

The forest warden's house is on top of the plateau: a small building carefully constructed amidst boulders and three centuries-old trees; the human presence is preceded by three enormous dogs which, as they bark, are rejoicing; two children come up to us, and then an older child. They are beautiful. I sit down beneath an oak tree, as the climb has exhausted me. For several minutes, I see no one else. Only a woman, her face pale and lucid, comes toward me, as if she were the one bearing the message into the depths of the forest. We tell her who we are, that José Velez is the Director General of the Forest Services   and, in other words, that Augusto has come to study the   sociological framework of the vacant lands.

She looks for an echo within us: "There's something wrong with my heart   the air is very strong here   I can't stay still, and I find no relief. When I had my first child, my uterus dropped   my husband isn't at home."
The dogs and children made a ring around us; they are called Leão, Coimbra, Porto, Jorge. Eugénia, her daughter, leads me to a monumental stone, and as I walk through the crevices of the rock, I discover, with the admiration I have always had for fleeting games
china sets
broken pieces of porcelain. The next house, Eugénia's, has taken root in the inmost places of the gigantic, with a dining room, a kitchen, a bedroom. Between two granite arches is the plaything, the most unforgettable I will ever see; a forest doll, which Eugénia's creation had given the appearance of a human being. A single eye — Lord of the head; of the head — a hard

covering, with a rag inside. It was a body bereft of arms, its feet, or legs, absent, but nothing that might have seemed to be missing was abnormal. This caused my imagination, and Eugénia's, to open up to one another, and I thought I might be able to stop writing on my own, with someone else who would awaken ideas and images for me. At this point, her mother says she shouldn't disturb me. "You're bothering her, Eugénia." But she soon understands that her children, and I, have found our pleasure.

When the forest warden arrives, he also expresses himself with sorrow: "There is a great loneliness   and the illnesses?   the difficulties of the work in the forest   the lack of money, and the distance."

It's time for me to leave; I kiss the children, the mother who pushes my fallen hair away from my face. She wishes me a pleasant hour, when my time comes; I think   so it will be   when my time comes to write with another language.

29 AUGUST 1975
back to Lisbon.

The tiles between Santarém and Lisbon, on the pink houses;
now and again, charred olive groves / appearing behind an
enormous wall or cactus; small, sparse flowers burst forth from
tentacles / in the north, the potatoes remain unsold. Once
more, they are buried. / This year, there was a large production
of wine / A cow pasture. The cows are brown / In Cartaxo:
"The workers and peasants united will never be defeated";
"Death to social democracy" / the solitary house on the hillside
of olive trees is part of the house in Jodoigne. The pines and
oaks are pioneer trees. First are born the oaks and, later, the
pines are planted.

I have returned from Portugal. I need to stop, and speak
about it to someone else. But for a while, I continue writing in
French... "knowing that, in addition to the daily signs, there are
others," those that indicate the world, absorbed with Power.

Jade is mistaken when he desires, almost exclusively, the company of humans.

Jade is a dog who was given to us.

It is essential to write to all beings.

The day is so peaceful that it seems as though I am sleeping. I amble through fields that exist autumnally, and give Jodoigne the shape of an orb. I long for the sky and the land. Leão Jade and Fokouli could be described in short pieces of writing that render a portrait, through an accumulation of attempts. I go out in the morning and encounter this foggy, almost warm weather. I feel independent and unrecognizable. Who would be able to say that I am distant if Fokouli jumps into my lap, and Jade sleeps at night at my feet, and enters its shadows in dreams? I am hidden in the midst of men's lives. Why don't we remain silent, or speak, through things? When I, in a short while, open the gate, Leão Jade will say nothing, other than with movements of his body; if I draw closer, I will see through the window Fokouli lying on top of the television, his hanging garden, but if I remain standing in the middle of the courtyard, I will call out to Prunus Triloba, Forsythia, Aspirea, shrubs I planted with the hope of giving them my body, at the hour of my death, and replanting them during the days of my eternity. Beings that do not invade with words, that are depleted by their own scents and forms. I'm going to pay for my coffee and head home. Sit down at the long table, and write about what Ana de Peñalosa became.

... in A., ever stable, I sense a mutation: he is giving himself over to a kind of suffering, opening up. Which is abandonment, and a waypoint. Confirmation that scarcely anything is revealed to us. I take a walk with Jade, we always go on the same walk, and this town, almost a village, seems as though it is my natural birthplace. Where do we all go? At night, I burn fragrant herbs and eucalyptus. My text has been somewhat abandoned, and Augusto's as well.

Textual is Prunus Triloba, which will bloom. I often listen to this shrub, which stands upright halfway along the front of the house. It is autumn, my first autumn in a house of my own with a garden. The still-young branch of Prunus Triloba spreads concepts through the air, in accordance with my thoughts. Spinoza declared that words have a precise meaning solely due to the habitual use we make of language. When will Prunus Triloba be strong enough to become a Habitual Use?

Since Saturday, that is to say, for three days, I have been sick in bed. I have remained in bed in a kind of dejection, and disappointment. The room is on the second floor, at the end of the hallway, and the window panes are covered with adhesive paper, which I bought in Louvain. The light is instilled through drawings that bear a striking resemblance to snow crystals. As a distraction, I said to myself: — Imagine you are nine years old, and you are playing in the garden of the Statue.

I meditated, within the confines of the house, on how I was
brought up with love. Today, I longed to sleep in the room with
the beautiful Persian meditation carpet.
To have roots here before being swept away by time. To
gaze at this window, which is the most beautiful I have ever seen
and
conceived.

Olo and Asa sleep behind the house, outside this light, but
watching over it. They are a rooster and a hen who always roam
together and to whom I have promised death by old age.

(I am typing this day up five and a half years later, on 26
June 1981. Today, I found Asa dead in the abandoned dog
shelter, only half of her body remaining. I buried her in the wild
garden in Herbais).

I never finish reading most of the books I begin. I become
despondent or paralyzed. Is it that books no longer interest me?
Yes, on the whole, books no longer _____ . I am interested in a
sentence, a fragment of text, and, very rarely, an entire book,
which I read very slowly. "No longer to write anything which
does not reduce to despair every sort of man who is 'in a hurry.'"
I come to the end of *Daybreak* and Mircea Eliade's Diary.

How pleasurable it is to write. Because of the gesture, the
concentration, the force wielded by my fingers and my wrist.
Because of the black sleeve ending in the paleness of my skin.
Because of the angle of my index finger. Because of the lower

part of my hand rubbing against the pristine place of writing. Because of my face there, unaged.

To be able to illuminate myself for people; they have illuminated themselves for me today in the context of Jodoigne and the *wonder*
of the bodies we all fear and to which we all so deeply aspire, with no return. I understand far beyond what I am capable of expressing.

Jade lives in the shadow of human beings, "our shadow is his bed."

"Are we then without pity?" asks Friedrich Nietzsche, and he suggests
"the need for little deviant acts."

My tongue is freed, even motionless. Frederick N. is close to me, without life, or death, he himself neither perishable, nor eternal. A portion of his vitality is communicated to me through music, and his text is secondary.
He says:
But I do not write what he says. The small volume of *Daybreak* is clutched in my left hand. By not writing what he says, I risk exchanging a certain thing for an uncertain one. What I feel is that *I had the feeling you wanted to talk to me, really and truly; that, in the absence of contemporary companions, you had come to my house, reflected in Prunus Triloba.*

— You were also reflected in *Daybreak*, in your thoughts on moral prejudices.

— "Hitherto, the subject reflected on least adequately has been good and evil."

— Reflected, as if your head read what you had written. At this moment, and before I have repeated it so many times, it is the word *reflected* that I feel most
with a kind of modification of the feeling of love. Creating new loves is my greatest desire,
although it may become a danger, which I will attempt to learn how to subdue with you.

How late is it? Nearly midnight.
Christmas Day has ended, the following day begins.
Augusto and I spent the day in the dining room, which has a lace coverlet in the window serving as a curtain, and which, through its transparency, instills within us the movements of Prunus Triloba; the time elapsed reading a book, or one another, or the music, or the height of the reality this environment induces; 363, 364, 365, 366 are the numbers of the aphorisms in *Daybreak* that I roam, and I dwell at length on 240, *On the morality of the stage.* Prunus Triloba is still a small tree.
"Which is why we need first to adjust and justify the goal of a Shakespearean drama, that is to say, not to understand it."

It is in this room that the objects I prefer accumulate. I think, "And when will they have to be dispersed once more?" I suffer in anticipation of their dispersal, and feel guilty for having gathered them for myself: they represent
power
prestige
money
luxury
savings
epiphanies of beautifully designed

pieces by artisans. An energy, made beauty, of security and exploration.

Objects, many of which belonged to my family, form a series of the dead, take the place of the dead, and suddenly transcend my present reflections, and the false conclusions I have drawn from usefulness. How is it possible to explain the origin of these conjectures, in the book I am writing, *The Remaining Life*? Those I care for have been defeated and are dispersed.

Frederick N., you sing the praises of the Princes, but not these, for they are not the ones who safeguard the greatest vitality of life. I look at you in the inherited objects and I understand you when you understand that, in the forces that struggle within them, the human species has been left waiting for affirmation, consumed by guilt. But not even you knew how to prolong Hadewijch's love. When she picked up these objects, you spoke of another stage, calling us hypocrites for hiding our complicity in the violent death of the first Father, rather than declaring it an action _____ that how to *exist* is, for us, to lose the memory of that shameful deed, that how to live is to quietly prolong the first feeling of hatred, and you would tell her, when she refused you,
that she did not have the courage to desire, at that instant, to joyfully prolong the gesture which kills, and be the feeling of another form of life, and when she replied, asking you   what is a lover?
you retorted, asking her   are the thinker, the artist, and the lover not a single being?
always like serpents,
ensnared in the eagle's slender neck.

Serpents pique my curiosity, for they are not kind.

I feel like spending tonight in wakefulness, not sleeping, or sleeping in a different place, so that even my dreams, during the night, will follow another current. I ask life for prolongation and silence; "what one desires of life is rest and silence."

A day will come
when it will be possible to see
that I do not know,
but what I am looking for takes shape,
and perishes.

I do not yet possess the strength to interrupt this night.

"The snake that cannot slough its skin, perishes. Likewise spirits which are prevented from changing their opinions; they cease to be spirits." Nevertheless, Frederick N. declares that only men are truly creators. But I smile at his words: "This authority of morality paralyzes thinking."

I will therefore remain, indefinitely, at the beginning of this night, traveling with authors and texts, the paths that lead me to the beginning of my own narrative:

If Hadewijch comes to participate in the battle and if I, unafraid…

No, they did not know how to introduce Hadewijch into their volition. If she died, and when she died. She rarely comes to speak to us, and will end up disappearing. She was among us *love*, as others are artists, and yet others thinkers, gathered in a single being. Among the three of us, no one is eternal.

All those who made me are here today: "in bright daylight the ear is less necessary. That is how music acquired the character of an art of night and twilight."

I aged
prematurely, but always surrounded by this evidence: *the truth*

needs to be powerful.

I will let myself remain in these days as long as I can. I will feel myself to be the object of a voice that does not hesitate to tell me that "the timid man does not know what it is to be alone."

The Book of the Powers of the Book, or *The Remaining Life*:

I felt so happy, during these leisurely days, that I only longed for the possibility of settling into an attitude. Somewhere, my temporal form had died, and the peace of the house, out of sight of the city, was a peace with verbal power. I was surrounded by the trajectory of the text: *she speaks to Saint John of the Cross, the return of John as an adolescent, John's text, 1581, the year of Hadewijch, the rumor and fear of the battle.*

It is two o'clock in the afternoon, but judging by my concentration, it is already night.

All these thoughts, these notes, are my characters, my interlocutors. They challenge me, to the same extent as my daily life and, together, they form a recurrent whole. I wanted to remain for as many days as possible in this time, which drifted toward a battle, and contradicted a single dimension of life. These connected parts, always shifting, are what I call writing, even when it is not remembered by signs. With this material, I was preparing *The Remaining Life*, not only the book of this name, but the perpetual lapse into which I had let myself fall.

Empty time, receptive to time / and friends — objects, cats, Jade, plants, Prunus Triloba, fabrics, sounds, smells, children, poor men and creative men, "the arrow, a beautiful pen for writing." Once again, I spend this wakeful night in a different place from where I usually sleep, so that even my dreams, during the night, will follow this current. "You have, four or five miles from here, a corral for your domesticated animals. These animals need to be taken care of. Will you allow me to live there with them?"

I would like to have, around my neck, a drop of water as a locket.

There is a specific reason why we are not going back to Portugal for Christmas this year either. We do not want to ever repeat the experience we had last year. On Christmas Eve, we went from one house to the next, visiting the dispersed fragments of two families, which we were unable to bring together for a Christmas Eve dinner.

We were not witnessing the necessary division between humans, but rather volitions which, separate, imagined themselves as one. That night, the future of the world belonged entirely to one side.

I do not know how to say what a human being is.

If we have acquiesced to living surrounded by animals, it is not because we are disillusioned with humans.

But because, spending time together, animals, plants, and humans, we would like to learn from one another how to live without a hierarchy of the living. We suspect there is a secret in language, *the enigma of Babel*, not so much in what it says, but in what it constantly longs to say. (It is true that we do not want to be involved in ceaseless human conflicts, nor to exist with people indifferent to its use.)

It pains me to see schoolchildren at the height of their potentialities become, twenty years later, ordinary beings, intelligent rather than vibrant, tenacious rather than creative, loving and deceived.

But even this imagining I must cast aside. The moment has passed when the future belonged to us, for everything is trapped in this present. But I know that if this future is solely human, people and time will separate. The spider that caught a few dried hydrangea petals in its web, produced on its own, and

74

through the attention with which I observed it,
an instant
which will surely have its own place in the future,
in the unveiling of the secret of language.   .

It is the beginning of the year, the first day. *The peasants lay still, with seers' eyes, and dead eyes.* On plays the tune, practiced and intimate: *and they hope for another kind of life that will remove them from the rule of the Lords; but they will be crushed by the excesses that they, in turn, will not fail to indulge.* I hesitate, as if I had lost my certainty, and looking out the window at the courtyard, I observe that the fog is hanging over heads, even those of the trees. Very often, there is a reason that comes to mind: *removed from the Power of the State.* There is no question I am fascinated by the balance of Power, and the human contradictions expressed in the idea of the battle; many of my forces are negative, but they are part of an endeavor that is woven conceptually, a weft of vibrations and complementary energies. There are thus three books, that of the Landscape, that of the microcosm of man, and that of the polymorphous woman.

From here, from afar, I prepare, at this year-end, the path of my return, cautiously, and with no illusions. It may be part of the Power I want to use, to instill in these books: A battle is being waged between anonymous writing and writing at the margins of the human, and I know the culprit is my ashes, and my way of being decapitated.

Lisbon thickens over the courtyard, and above it a layer with a series of episodes spanning Europe; the fog is like snow, but more persistent in concealing forms; in the fog, the horizon becomes more penetrating than bathed in sunlight; but it is true we are atmospheric phenomena: hovering clouds of sound.

JODOIGNE, 2 JANUARY 1976

Christine spent Christmas at her new house in Antwerp,
with her husband and children. She left with pages from the
Fragments..., annotated by me: Kierkegaard's confrontation
with Socrates, his kinship with Hamann; what we know of his
father and Regina Olsen; the feeling of guilt, taken to the
extreme, in Lutheranism. Perhaps Kierkegaard suspected,
without ever saying, that this, being what it is, was confirmed in
the unfortunate and dramatic victories at Frankenhausen and
Münster: as if it were necessary to destroy utopian hope, the
excess of possibles, for possible thinking to persist.

She mailed us a letter, which had preceded her:
"To hate hope, for the sake of thinking, or hate thinking,
for the sake of hope? Everyone appears in history wearing
masks and brings, in the new events, remnants of what they
have stolen from the dead.
    Everyone, even the poor. And us?
    If they did not disguise themselves with one another's
usual mode of dress, it would be easy to recognize them,
but perhaps, if that were so, time would
not exist;
    (news about the children follows)
    Love"

From Saint John of the Cross's room to
the light seeping out from under the door of Kierkegaard's room
stretches a rope,
on which, all throughout the night,
I never stopped balancing myself

77

on the *images* of our own future.

Christine asks me   will we know in fifty years (but by then, who will know anything of us?) whether we will have ceased to live with Nietzsche, Müntzer, Eckhart, Al-Hallaj, or Kierkegaard?

She speaks to me, and I know she is living, at this very instant, in a great whirlwind of contradictory feelings.
I hear her,
but not in that place. I listen to her, with my intense longing for the mutual
to always
return, with
more vitality.

I enjoy the night so deeply, no?

JODOIGNE, 2 JANUARY 1976
(continued)

(I enjoy the night so deeply, no?) All the moments of the
night seem to be
lost moments,
moments I have lost,
the utterly lost.

In what ways will we be similar,
similar to ourselves? I see that *they* and *we*, in the place of time,
are pursuing the identical:
How to assure the return of the mutual,
how to love in order to think it. We are always the same, and

——————— .

We do not speak about the meaning of life, of death, nor do
we experiment with materials that we manipulate,
outside ourselves. We try on our own clothing; we risk fate in
the folds that sharpen silence; the environments and
geographies we create are our exposed inmost self; we remain
sitting, observed from that inmost self by the utterance that
awaits our own created heart.

Later on, Hadewijch entertains us:

— I'm going to tell you about a king who fell in love with a
poor young woman. We cannot know what he thought of her,
but I do know that he quickly made the decision to marry her.
The king's heart was not sullied by caution; he was oblivious to
the difficulties which reason discovers to keep the heart captive
and barren, and produce those impotent situations the poets so
cherish, rendering necessary their magic formulas.

And so it was that their union was a great event.

79

Love proclaims victory, when it joins two equals. But it proclaimed a far greater victory that day when it made equal what, at the outset, was unequal. It was then that an insidious worry and a sense of anguish arose in the king's soul. One of those questions, with no origin, that ensnare every thought: Was his new wife truly happy? Did she have a sound and honest enough disposition to never remember what he had so longed to forget, that he was a king and she had been a young woman of low birth? For if that happened, if that memory awakened in her, pulling her thoughts away from the king, if he drew her into the hermeticism of a secret sorrow, what would become of the splendor of love which had brought them together?

— The poets were spared — said the Master of Guilt — from singing the insistent hesitations of the king's heart, but will now be needed to sing his insidious doubt.

— And so it goes — continued Hadewijch. — Would she have been happier, the king wondered, living according to her birth, the wife of a man of her own station, still poor, but simple and joyful in her love?

A great anguish was gathering in the king's heart, for he would rather lose his beloved than be seen by her as a benefactor. What if she did not understand him?

— It is a king's anguish — said the Master of Guilt. — And there is no name for that pain in human languages. And all languages are selfish when it comes to expressing a pain they do not even suspect.

— But if there is no word that can express it, what will be the fate of this love between unequals? — asked Hadewijch.

— And, if this love has no future, God and man cannot ever love one another. Even in paradise, there is not only joy, but also sorrow.

— Yes — agrees the Master of Guilt. — But let us return to the story, to the moment, the instant when the affections of the king and the young woman converge, when, for the first time, the love of one is exchanged for the love of the other. It is, at that instant that _____ .

Later still.

Hadewijch says	it was at that instant that the king became a beggar
Kierkegaard says	this is why he must suffer everything endure everything surrender himself to death as the last of men.
Kierkegaard says	do you see? his entire life is a passion and it is love that suffers love that gives everything until it becomes a beggar.
Hadewijch says	love does not change the beloved, it transforms itself.
Kierkegaard says	what are you looking for, Hadewijch? — love. and when you find it, what will you do with it? — love it all alone, in a hermitage.

Much like last night, tonight was devoted to the figures, which I see as a kingdom. Müntzer, the founder of the Community in Zwickau, a community without a priest, almost without a liturgy. The weavers of Zwickau, who yearned for God's kingdom to immediately be established on earth. In June 1524, the Countess of Stühlingen, which is close to Schaffhausen, forced her servants, in the middle of the harvest season, to leave their fields to pick blackberries and gather snails. Under threat of having their eyes plucked out if they killed a piece of game.

I wonder, then, about the place of others. Alone? Or with them? They, who are they going to be? What I feel cannot be shared, it seems, except for following a prolonged contact that takes place through writing. I think about the source of fear. An abrupt language, bodies and gestures that do not concede multiform expression. Eckhart says: "He who does not desire, desires nothing." When autumn comes, the time of dehiscence… Abandonment. Provenance. The gift spreads serenity (Eckhart). Blue, white. War and Peace.

I'm going to start learning how to make bread. But I keep thinking about *The Mysterious Island*, the sixteenth century, and animal architecture.

Pleasure of the animal kingdom, pleasure of writing with a nib that traces the words like the movements of insects.

What Kierkegaard did not say to Regina Olsen, but what
the Master of Guilt might have said to Hadewijch to lure her
into Nietzsche's seduction:

Will I tell her?
But what if, confronted by what I want, she departs, leaving
me all alone?
If she is who I think she is, she will take my free spirit, my
creation of the world,
my body,
and will see, in what I want to tell her,
the instant and the simple.

I would tell her
See as I see. I do not want to live with you, nor with
anyone. I want to be a nomad or a hermit. To travel or to
exist, alone. To spend my time observing what I see, and
feel, and imagine.

To create a world in my thinking, enact the paradox.
To absurdly tend my garden, clean the threshold of my
door.
To give form. To learn the language of birds.

From time to time, come to see you, human.
Perform the tea ceremony, the delight of your dwelling, the
brightness of your spirit,
the pleasure of the body.

You, who do not need me. Who will not cry, if I do not
return. Who, in my absence, are not absent from your own
life. Who does not gain prestige from our secret meeting,
who are yourself with yourself and
take pleasure in the spirit, the wealth, and the rites,
and you come and find me, and I will find with you a form
of the world that is brave, because it is stabilized in the
instant.

To be able to be with you, as I am with myself, observing.
We imagine and speak the language between humans,
moved by the world, and by Grace.

I will teach you to speak to the birds,
keep watch over the landscape in silence,
extricate thinking from thinking, you will tell me about the
life after this one, the surprising form that always casts us
further,
better
outside ourselves. To be smiling at such a chimera and see
between the open edges of your blouse
the silky and appealing roundness of your breasts
which from your body emerge in mine, and to notice that my
phallus
is inserted in your half-open lips.

You, who do not need me
never asked me what name I had,
why I dressed carelessly,
nor what I was guilty of————————————— ;
no, don't say ————— you are close to the truth.

at the kindhearted and feminine pastry shop:

We are sitting at our table, near the window, the astral twins which are Augusto and myself; all of this is, after all, an adventure of the Will to Vitality, but I do not know whether it will further anything in the universe; I have learned that sex is a motor if it concerns the libido, an obstacle if it concerns possession; intimacy brims over from there, is eventually everywhere because, like nature, "it is not the field of a single scholar."

And if we were to fragment?

A new person had joined them.

Today, Kierkegaard sent Regina Olsen an embroidered
handkerchief as a farewell.

I pack it up in the box with shallow breaths. It is the
handkerchief of sighs. I close the box, and Kierkegaard tells me
it is the handkerchief of love between him and Regina Olsen.
The box is not a box of handkerchiefs, but a small music box.
Hadewijch puts it on the chimney, at this instant, the music box
is on the chimney
        and the same box is in paradise, *at the moment when
she*, Hadewijch, begins to play the harpsichord, when the
pianissimo ends. The handkerchief smells of jasmine.
    Kierkegaard halts the intense recollection out of caution,
and turns my face away from his shoulder. Only then do I
understand that Kierkegaard is the final critic of the book I am
writing, in which — *The Remaining Life* — he will never appear,
for
we all have our remnants at hand,
and I want to see the true handkerchief over which she, Regina
Olsen, wept her breakdown. I open the box with unconscious
percussions of my own desire to understand.

Lucernarium

V. confided in me today. When the restaurant had emptied and her shift was over, she sat down beside me, offering me tea and cake.

I could sense she was sad, but not unhappy. She is an intelligent woman, with a lovely figure, and she seems to run her business very well. She tells me what I already knew — that apart from her husband, she has another. A lover, one might say, with her husband's passive acquiescence.

I was not surprised by the fact that this is becoming commonplace, but rather by the intensity of the romantic relationship, which is, if I have understood correctly, one of strict submission. Surrendered to her love, V. is not unhappy, but sad. And it was sorrow I saw shining in her gaze, when what we hope to see in that gleam is the contained ecstasy of joy.

I sat there gazing at a light irradiating the blackness of alchemy.

V. is naked and sad. I have the feeling there is a sensuality in her, perhaps because she is the center of a sensual vortex. She has agreed to satisfy the desires of the Master, her other husband, who requests and demands her availability. Naked or clothed, nothing in her should hinder, even in the slightest, his access to her openings. Exactly as in *Story of O*.

She tells me that yes, she agreed to it and, even at work, the dresses she wears comply with the conditions of that pact. She cannot explain how the Master was able to convince her to give him, once and for all, what a woman normally negotiates as something rare:
her sex.

V.'s sensual sorrow, throughout her submissive sexual body, is the demonstration that there is a methodical longing in her Master. They mutually saturate the relationship, in openings, in frequency, in methodical efforts. A transcending of limits, steadily escalating pressure, obsessive concentration, carnal ardor. There is a will wielded unendingly, to one and the same end.

"My body is wholly surrounded." And when she can do no more, when it seems everything has been given, fatigue is the precious beginning, in the Master's eyes, of the new direction that must be taken, in this never-ending process. Where harm is done, more harm can be done. Where there is tension, the provoking of more tension. Where there is more repulsion, the introduction of a more intense repulsion.

Submissive sex, however, does not encapsulate the entirety of this woman's being. V. adapts to the situation. Her pleasure is not in sex, but in letting everything be done, at the time and pace required, to satisfy her Master, whose presence and penis are a mixture of a repellent, torturous, ravenous, and spirited object. This penis, which periodically becomes erect, which systematically tortures, which ends up disgusting her, is, nevertheless, an undeniable sign that he finds a private pleasure in her.

Only yesterday I wrote the opposite in *The Remaining Life*:
Most remarkable were the wrinkles she smoothed, elucidating the cloth as if it no longer thought; then the conceptions, the preconceptions,
and the transitory mental representations came undone. Neither Nietzsche […] were present but they could not be distinguished from celebrated words and real tenderness. Those who passed from

one room to another and sought to confirm the direction of their face *knew that good/evil had been broken and that pervasive loves covered everything.*

I did see, today, in V.'s face, a great intensity. But I did not see the *intensity of the mutual.* I know that good/evil has been broken, that the judgement is, once and for all, suspended between the human. But I also know that the struggle has intensified. Good and Evil hid the true division between humans, concerning Life. They divide us into Sorrow and Joy.

Hadewijch herself:

I am, with time, what I am outside it, here given over to the
pleasure of the beloved
in loving himself. His passion and my place, I live
so that He may know my existence adds nothing to his own
    other than knowing that is the nothing I am offering him.
In my body, you can be Human.
He places his hand on the pain, on this wound that has opened
up in Him,
which summons *me*   and which I leave in life.   I thus see
that love
    is the cause that ex-stasies all things, and to be another who
I am
remaining the same, in myself whom I do not see, but sees
me
metamorphosed from I Iim in this, this in me is *myself* offering
Him purpose and time. I am the one who offers nothing, to me
who was not this, before the experience of this One. A love so
perceptive, so needful of gazing at body or cause, shows the
Lover in the stark light of the beloved.

And I see that love is not idle; so active it is confused with
action, so anonymous it is treated as if it were poor,
so splendid I am deemed a courtesan: this is how love wanted
to be seen, as it sees itself.
And why is that? When we parted from one another, weary of
being the only one who was, longing for the distinct and the
least of us, the being? Had we not begun searching for our
encounter, as soon as we had ceased to be one?

If my story has Your meaning,
give me the most sensuality of the concept, that I might
recognize the stranger who is gazing at me
who is myself,
and I, alive,
complete Your unfinished purpose.

When I write in French, I move beyond grammar, guided by ear and voice, by listening to the voices I have heard during these ten years. Voices of children, books, my conversations with Augusto when we felt the need to let our usual language lie fallow and begin to speak from within the pilgrimage.

Yesterday, I was looking at photographs — an entire series of movements from the past. I too am now living the experience of the abolition of time. I believe I can grasp everything where it is, and every single thing (which I am able to name before it has faintly passed). It is a new state that I had not been able to envision in the old state.

"He would feel so distinctly the soul of his mistress rising to the surface of her face that he could not refrain from touching it with his lips."

Peer Gynt at its saddest moment, as with Ferme Jacobs.

Maria Ledent says: — When it is time for me to leave the Ferme, I would like to play this song. — It is the morning of anticipated melancholy. I am sitting on the floor, in the middle of the large expanse of carpet. The house at the Ferme had never been coherently organized around a nucleus of meaning; I do not believe receptivity reigns everywhere, or that it is now here.

The desire to read, rather than write. The desire to disperse, rather than gather together. Moving away from writing, the read text, in a spiral, is the small room — the final room in the House, the piece which holds the verb steady. I have no truth about anything, I have incandescent intuitions that leave me bereft of expression. The sun has come through the door, the tulips are beginning to appear in front of the wide kitchen window,
and I think about the
before,
and the after
of the house.

I fear I will lose several texts which I inanely call *tulip texts for the month of March.* "The union of close blood-relatives, says the book, is yet the prerogative of kings and gods."

I express, in an ideogram, that reality means royalty and truth. I long to read for hours on end (which is also in the ideogram), to read for hours and hours without getting up. Surrounded by books, all I have to do is hold out a hand or, even more simply, lower my eyes. I read a few pages and feel as though what I am reading affects me so directly and intimately that it is being written at that very moment, compelling me to offer a response; the room is full of the reading and writing that has taken place; I then ask myself,
seeing gnomes carrying sticks and leaves, as that was the room of Christine's little boy,
if writing has a past.
Halfway through my reading, I am thirsty, and I want to do one of the many daily tasks; eventually, I want to add an

embellishment, or a detail, to the already enormous journey of the house; a need to complete, after having sought to lessen the chaotic, the non-meaningful.

I conclude that I will pay what I owe
for reading.

Often, as an impetus, this expression   sowing; that
which is ending erupts quickly and violently, and I find that this
is the title I wanted to give to a book. But I must abandon that
plan, for I am not meant to make books, but rather to put in
writing what constituted an experience; in any case, today I feel
as though I am meditating on death — the serene and delicate
objectives of death.

A desire to do what I cannot do, to be what lingers, fearless,
to throw open the doors to prisons. I dreamed I was lying on
the ground, and attempting to turn my frail hand into a
powerful wing. Finally, I took flight, and soared for a long time.
I eventually crashed into a house and the stove exploded. It was
wartime, and Augusto, also my enemy, eventually left. I got into
the back of a vehicle driven by a stranger. Before leaving the
house, I looked for a handkerchief in a drawer, and it had the
shape of a circular movement.

I also said to myself: there is no way out, humans are
everywhere; they accompany death, and lend it their vulgarity.

The more beautiful the house in Jodoigne is _____ the
more I recall that, as a child, I would play by running and
dancing; before I knew I wouldn't be able to dance (be a
ballerina), I did not begin writing. Running down the hallway
was my greatest game, a kind of channel. But dancers need
teachers, a rigorous training, and language was learned on its
own, it did not create dependencies, and even when I remained
motionless, it provoked a delicious disruption.

I recognize that the house in Jodoigne is authentic — a spontaneous combustion of my substance. Learning with no outside interference shone like gold; the inertia of my masters was fictitious — they all expected me to study them, and offer a welcome that would awaken them:

>tell me,

>do you want to retrace

>the eternal cycle with us?

In the courtyard, where I do all kinds of exercises, the snow has finally melted; I long to sit down on the soil, to fashion, in text, a tall writing desk beside the light; I would like to speak of another to someone from yet another; we all meet, as equals, in *The Remaining Life*.

After thinking it, I sit quietly at home, by the lamp, embroidery and reading at my side; I am a being of the female gender, I am a being perpetually intent on *looking closely*. My normality is its own, as is everyone else's. I have not even made the next point, and a new insight comes to me. What weighty utensils hands are.
I place
the fabric on the paper
and see, in the smallest gap between one and the other, that another interval is challenging me; and so accumulate the days, in the din of companionship with Augusto, which has not cut me in half.
And the music?
(Living) people visit us only by chance, and very rarely; today, there were many figures present from books yet unopened,
eager to incite; I still haven't eaten dinner, music all afternoon, exceptionally and alongside the reading, and the fabric;
very often, the days fulfill me and I bring to a close   thusly
_____ my forty-five calendar years.

What captivates me about the house in Jodoigne is the active vastness of the space; it is the house that will take precedence over all others, where I feel like a minuscule point; not a composer, but a minuscule element of the composition for contemplation.

In my work, I must be flexible, bending, as I do now, over the immensity in which I sew; this house is at the far end of the garden, and is unfamiliar with the absence of compassion; it is located below, and behind the hustle and bustle of Jodoigne and, if it expresses activity, it is in a vague and general way; it has no end, nor limits, and is truly our dwelling; it will never be so old that it disappears from memory.

I am using this new notebook for the first time today.

Those who feel so enfolded by the experience of language, how could they not be when they are reading Rilke's correspondence? This will be one of the books I place on our Christmas table, among those that hold (I was going to write held, but I must write *hold*) the thread.

"I could tell you so much that is fine about it. Sometimes it seems to me I could die when it is done: so to the very end do all difficulty and sweetness come together in these pages, so finally does it all stand there and yet so boundlessly capable of the transformations inherent in it that I have the feeling of transmitting myself with this book, far and surely, beyond all danger of death. [...] And if I think so calmly of no longer existing after this work, it is because I do not yet dare at all to promise myself the fullness I am gradually achieving with it: for now I am training for myself [...] a massive, enduring prose, with which it will be possible to make absolutely everything. It would be glorious after that to continue or daily to begin anew with life's whole boundless task..."

An excessive text, still full of the *hubris* of everything, upon which it rests, but with such enormous vitality that it shows Life how to breach the earth and the air _____ .

As I had to interrupt what I was writing, I am awaiting successive experiences of language. It has been a long time since I last went to the bookshops in Louvain, where the law of quantity, the manner of display, and a certain relentlessness of Universality had begun to irritate me. Today, I was able to see libraries and bookshops again, as I saw my father's bookshelves, on Rua Domingos Sequeira. They are, indeed, magnetic places, and when I step into their field, I step into the fields of the true imagination of my future books. What shocks me is the vastness of the texts that will not endure, and which today, in the closed space of the bookshop, produce a deafening "chatter" that has nearly drowned out the dialogue between the books that speak and carry on, among themselves, the art of endless conversation about the *entresser*, about the interbeing.

There is, pages earlier, a striking example in Rilke's correspondence.

Rilke speaks with Rodin, who is lost "sadly and bewilderingly" and to a-firm him, make him firm, he reads him an excerpt from a letter by Beethoven to Bettina: "No friend have I, I must live with myself alone; but I know well that God is closer to me than to others in my art, I go about with him without fear, I have always recognized and understood him; I am also not at all afraid for my music, that can have no ill fate; he to whom it makes itself intelligible must become free of all the misery with which others are encumbered."

Three eras, counting my own. Humans who speak and correspond, attempting to hold the thread of interbeing between them, in the text _____ "that can have *no ill fate.*"
Day and night,
without rest but deliberately,
she awaited Al-Hallaj's revelation. She had been told that the first shoot emerging from her body would lead her to the peaceful place where Al-Hallaj bloomed faceless as Müntzer had bloomed headless. What happened filled her with understanding, she had put aside all her work *except the sewing*, lest the *Poet and Thief* moving past surprise her unawares.

"If one *single* truth like the sun prevails, it is *day*. If you behold, instead of this one truth, as many as the sands of the seashore, and then behold a little light which excels in brightness a whole host of suns, it is a *night* beloved of poets and thieves... The *poet* at the beginning of days is the same as the *thief* at the end of days" — Hamann says to me, which is all the Master of Guilt has left me.

A group meeting at Ferme Jacobs. Atrocious, particularly
several hours later, when the anesthesia of extroversion wanes.
I wrap myself up
for warmth,
in textual and animal blankets:
Jade, Herman Hesse, Rilke, Proust, the books from this year-
end; I lie down on the bed in the room I do not share with
Augusto; I put Maria Olhuda, the rag doll I bought in Louvain,
when I still lived in the mansard on Rue de Tirlemont, by my
side. I watch the dying sun sink toward the earth, creating
fugitive figures with the paper which covers the walls of my
room. I shouldn't say I came to this room as a fugitive; but I
should say I came to this room so that I could flee and refashion
myself as a fleeting cloud of sound: the thunder of Daybreak.

After these kinds of meetings, I witness my own
fragmentation; in my body, nothing remains. I would like to
exchange the Ferme for a silent way of life, where the
meditation of writing would be possible. To draw closer *together*
with books and animals. I would like speaking to be an
experience of language.

An act of horror
summons horror, not because there is a store of horror
accumulated, but because the Body takes on a faint or striking
imprint, a hint or hill of constrained evil.

An act of love
summons love, not because there is a store of love available, but
because the body takes on a faint or striking imprint, a hint or
slope of communicative kindness.

I would like to smile from one and the other,

even if it is not indifferent to my body,
even if it is indifferent to the mutual,
to traverse the hill of horror or the slope of love.

The home of humans is unfortunately still the Being. The weft.

Don't you know — I ask myself — that to set off for movement is to accede to the desert? That great and primal engine, which holds love and horror together, and moves them in a deadly struggle, to the point of complete coalescence, on the edge of itself — a barren desert?

It is cold. I put Rilke on my lap to be able to listen to him.

Do you know what a lover's whisper is, in your lulled ear, left resting there,
when the body knows it is accompanied, and the thinking mind feels all alone?

Do you know that only this whisper gives you the beginning of the world?

Do you know that *someone* is lying beside you, lover of this complaint of almost nothing, a gratuitous drop
which is born in it and falls on you?

Do you know that you are a body oblivious to such unexpected luck?

Do you know that the lover has a fate contrary to the designs of love?

Later on, during the night:
My perceptive body gradually synchronizes with the body that, in truth and in vitality, fulfills in a single *mutual instant* all active potentialities. I want my perceptive body to rest, for I am not ready today for the Lover, of which Rilke speaks to me, of

which Hadewijch speaks to me so often. That lover who carries, in one hand, Birth, and in the other hand, Death. I *know* the Lover is someone; not a person, but a penetrating, conscious, unwieldy, and fulfilling presence. Today, I cannot indicate the deft way of acting to that *Form in Power*.

Rilke insists: _____

beyond the lover, love waits for all the images to collapse, weaker than they were, or filigrees of nothing; love is waiting for you all alone.

I am back at home. It was the first day I felt winter — the
water frozen, the snow invariably hanging overhead. The veil. As
Saint John of the Cross would say, "Tear the delicate fabric of
this life." At Ferme Jacobs, our lives, in a river, run less
ponderously, a period of greater peace has begun since the
meeting on Sunday, despite Tuesday evening, when almost
everyone was leaving for their homes, and a confusion of
murmurs and shadows made the end of the day unexpected.
Parents put their children in their cars, and the children escaped
to find their small joys again — a push, a scream, a
disappearance inside the house, in short, the forbidden. — It's
inhuman — Catarina said. — When we get home, I'm going to
lock you in your room.

Jacqueline, and her husband, drove us to Jodoigne. Jade,
ever restless today, on my knees. This afternoon, just before our
departure, he hurled himself, for no apparent reason, on top of
gentle Bernardette. I run my hands over his body to calm him. I
want, or do not want, to go to the Christmas party on Sunday,
which will be a party with multiple characters. At this moment,
I confuse them with the landscape, what I see is a house in the
cold, where, surrounding a departure, a movement of minor
emigration, there is an undone coherence.

Later, during the party, we walk to the edge of the garden,
always inevitably poorly tended, we find our way back, the
children are the first to sit down at the table. There are only
candles, brightness, significant gaps which, paradoxically, light
up. This party is an illuminated spin in the dark, a sketch of the
dream we will dream when we are all alone

because
time passes swiftly,
as I read Rilke swiftly; my time has been focused on reading his
long, twenty-six-year diary; it is not because we rebel, it is
because we want to wisely use the time of our lives, which have
been given to us in an absurd context. Use. I think, with
immense tenderness, about a qualitative change in time. Today
is Wednesday. Saturday, Sunday, when I am ensnared.
Tomorrow is Thursday, Friday, Monday, Tuesday, when I am
not entirely ensnared, lost in work. I return to the
correspondence of Rilke, that man who, like Proust, became
intimately attuned to solitude. I, being with them, have followed
another path. At the Ferme, I sometimes feel destroyed, in my
fate, by the ferocious elements of a social reality to which, deep
inside, I never belonged.

While I have a coffee at the bar-restaurant Al Parma, where
Augusto and I now spend a great deal of time, I write the text
that ends *but others were already coming, who I recognized from
many years of travel.* The series of texts to which this text belongs
had its origin in sight, rather than the envisioning ear, as is usual
for me. I have called it *Following the Gaze.* In this series, I have
rarely followed the reflection that enables me to write, when I
listen to it. I write listening, in the faultless illusion, to my own
voice

I begin to meditate and I conclude that my life's work
encompasses all manner of preparatory tasks,
including
to reconvert myself to an originality,
to steer myself to the same place.

Rilke: "I live to create my own soul." To feel I am a
contemporary of those who lived at the peak of these
vibrations, of which posterity received the effects, but did not
receive the name.

As I read Rilke, I constantly think of water.
Who is Angela of Foligno, so often quoted by Rilke?

Winter solstice.

I live and anticipate what I will have to live, now at the age of 45.

The day, which is now evening, was incomparable. I wrote the text for *The Remaining Life* that begins: "She is somewhere, and night falls ..." and ends "birds as agile as they are migratory."

In the early hours, I had a nightmare, which invokes the following dream: *Connected to love, I thought of my children, who were neither of my own blood, nor adopted. Then why were they my children? I had an intense desire to take possession of the doll I saw a month ago at Domus, in Louvain;* I will take possession of a written figure (where?), which in the image of Picasso's *Child with a Dove* — a painting that has been with me for so many years — will prefigure (what?) _____ .

I feel as though a knot is being undone, in the violent discomfort that the dream and the text of *The Remaining Life* had caused me. Both compulsive and both mysterious.

I am sitting in the rocking chair in the tiled room, looking at *Child with a Dove*. Why do I call him *Child with a Dove* when he is wearing a long dress, down to his feet. I gather myself in the greenish-grey tones in the background of the composition, and my gaze slides to the vivid colors of the ball, which move outside the frame. Fokouli is playing with a potted plant on the window ledge, which before long will be irretrievably fallen to the ground. I scold him, for he is not yet one of those figures who *gradually entered a realm where plants and animals spoke without a sharp voice or accusing silence.* He eventually comes down from the windowsill and lies down on my lap, asking me, purring, for peace. And we all stayed silent, with the silent night alongside us. I have no way of knowing how long we stayed like that until Augusto found us, marveled that we were in the darkness, and turned on the low light on top of the table. I remember that, when there was light, I looked at the intensity with which the Child so carefully held the Dove in both his hands. Augusto sat down and I gave him the text I had written, which had not yet been filed away beside the typewriter. He read it attentively and, when he looked at me, I told him about the dream I had had and the intense desire I felt to buy the doll. I felt as though he was casting off his own world, in order to give his full attention to my own. In the imperceptible gestures he makes, shifting his feet, in the way he runs his fingers around his nose and mustache, in the smile that begins in his eyes and moves down to the corners of his mouth, I know he is going to offer me something to drink.

"Would you like some tea?" I nod yes, and he leaves me alone to go and prepare it.

We stayed up late last night, talking. Not rationalizing, but putting our thoughts together, as if stitching together memories of objective facts and personal events.

My text and my dream reminded Augusto of Master Eckhart's vision of the child who came to release God from his unhappy solitude. "It is because of that vision and several others, like Ibn 'Arabi's, that I know *The One* who goes by the name of man is not yet, but surely will be."

The child that is born, in the text, is the same one desired in the dream, whose parentage is not, however, evident. The son who is to come will not be of my blood, will not be of my biological line. Nor will he belong to my symbolic line, for he will not even be my adopted son. How will this *child who has no face* be mine?

Augusto rereads the final part of the text

> *From that face, in the cradle,*
> *appears a furtive bird,*
> *enveloping her in a heavy*
> *green light — the black light is torn apart, and an*
> *orchard can be seen full of fruit,*
> *and birds as agile as they are migratory.*

That rupture between the *heavy green light* and *the black light, which is torn apart,* indicates the path toward an archaic kind of God, one who is unhappy and alone. (He walks imprisoned, in the dust, passing through moments of unbearable sorrow). The God who was the object of Faith, narrated in the Old Testament, and whose forms of violence created reverence and awe has

dissolved, as *the one who will be man* seeks, *deftly*, to take hold of
his own fate.

It is thought that there are only three positions toward God:
the religious, the mystic, and the agnostic. The texts show there
is yet another: there is a new libidinal practice as a collective,
which you call *creative gestalt*, embodied in women, men,
animals, plants, and landscape,
which seeks to effectuate the good news proclaimed to nature
and humans.

That people / or form
whose origin is the text of Job
are those who truly desire and long for *the eternal return of the
mutual*,
taking responsibility for what, in the Judeo-Christian branch of
our civilization, was called the plan for creation.

In that plan, there was always a cosmogony.

The foundational cosmogony of Western man, which begins
with a fearsome God and ends (?) with the child who releases
the nostalgic God from his incomprehension of his own work.
And in your short text, almost all the characters of that
cosmogony are present.

The first is God, who appears at the end. God, with his most
archaic face, who was never a person, a mixture of a gray,
threatening cloud, the bearer of the scorching wind, and the
green plants, a garden or orchard full of fruit. It is this mixture
that, from the cosmic, Adamic soup, formed man.

The others are the woman who gives birth, and the child
who has no face, who is neither her biological, nor symbolic son,
but her ontological son. They, too, together — the figure and her

son — form a mixture, heralding another space and another time. They are not, together, another new branch of men, but the beginning of other men (hence, their ontological relationship) from whose face will appear furtive birds, birds as agile as they are migratory.

And the fourth character in that cosmogony appears, more precisely, the bird, which coming from the powerful mind of the chimera-child, because it has no face and no name, severs the unity of the primitive God (*the black light is torn apart*). Is it the dove that Tradition identifies with the Holy Spirit, and that the Church says is a Person, never saying it is a Divine Animal?

The story of this cosmogony is the narrative of a grand plan, which incorporates, in its drama, the foundational atmospheric elements, plants, animals, man and woman, and the garden-landscape. An odd and discordant story, until Man, as Nietzsche might imagine, encapsulating everything, becomes a child who has no face and no fear.

Your text is the narrative of the *lost battle*, but also one of hope (a profound hope of recapturing time, in every sense), that this child who has no face will defeat that first cosmogonic figure, without destroying it or undermining its potentiality. It gives the impression that you are anchoring the text in a powerful aesthetics, rather than in reason, which would be rare; but all kinds of texts have their figural foundation in Genesis, for in Eden, everything was told yes (there is not a single denial in that Genesian narrative), everything was called beautiful.

And, as almost always happens, your text begins silently: *She is somewhere, and night falls, almost no light is reflected in the window curtain. What is she doing? Who is she speaking to? She isn't saying anything?*

Augusto stood up and went to put a piece by Honneger on the record player, one I enjoy a great deal. Absorbed in what he had said, it was only halfway through the record that I realized I was listening to music.

I remembered a text I had written several days earlier, which for some reason unknown to me (is it because I struggle against metaphor?) will not be part of *The Remaining Life*. I think it's because I do not value texts that stray from themselves, and are "Bibleized" into different issues. That if they act, they do so "against my will." I cannot bear the idea that there is anything prophetic, or exemplary, in what I write, except for its incandescent beauty. And I say this to Augusto, who, as expected, does not react. What is this man doing, by my side? Why does he use his immense culture to look, as if he had not looked, or had already seen? Why do I love him? It is true that if I ask him nothing, he will say nothing. But why is it that as soon as I decide to ask, he immediately offers a blunt response about what he sees and is thinking? There he is, irritating creature, in front of me, silent, having spoken to me, as he did, about my text and about the dream I recounted to him, as if we were talking about any work day, or the most banal reality. And the worst part is that I know, for him, the plan for creation, if it exists, is being banally carried out at this instant. In this, he is right. There is no extraordinary, it is the banal that is paramount in our gaze. Why am I irritated, and why don't I want to show it to him? Because I know he would leave the room and, full of remorse, I would find him in his room, reading or preparing for some activity, as if it were nothing. And yet, I know that if I were happy and deeply open to what he told me, we would make love right there, listening to Honneger's music.

That thought calmed me and made me aware that the text had been written by me rather than him, that I had dreamed the dream rather than him. It is because I sense from his face that he is telling me nothing is serious, that after texts other texts will come, and that the best chance for work (as he usually expresses it) is to leave nothing of ourselves out of our acts, even the most incomprehensible ones.

I reread the text:
"The female doves soar over the landscape, hermits, flying in a flock.
But why glacial doves? Why do you stir up the fight between God and the child?
At a distance, one against the other, do you antagonize them with your lofty laughing eyes?
Your response leaves me incomplete.
You grossly embed the joyful pearls of your flight in the crown of nostalgia of the solitary God, and he becomes jealous of the still unborn child. Child and God, flayed alive, you abandon them."

Where different figures appeared: the dove-birds, the God of formlessness and emptiness, the chimera-child. Familiar figures with other names, but whose languages remain indecipherable to me. In the same way there are others in my text who I do not even suspect, so too in these do I persist in writing what is mine. And through this opening, I return to the living, which I do not look at from a vitalist angle, but in its own language, which I cannot identify.
Fokouli is, of course, a cat, a "tomcat." But what is a cat? What is an animal? I have witnessed discussions between

Augusto and Georges Thinès, a professor of animal psychology, in which Thinès demonstrates experimental certainty about what it is like to be an animal, which Augusto refutes by saying that all of this knowledge is prejudiced. It is not that the experiments are falsified, they are simply *fabricated* by the idea of man's superiority. Thinès has never spoken as a guinea pig, because he cannot conceive it would lead to any meaningful communication. But he concedes that the correct handling of the guinea pig is essential to the experiment. And listening to him, I think about how everything depends on how we handle ourselves, for it is in that handling that we touch, that we weave the fold, *or the mutual*. Everything that is, exists in a fold or folded: in being and because it is?

Isn't it true that all living beings strive to remain anchored in certainties about the face of reality, knowing that its reverse, even though it exists, is particularly inaccessible to them? To live in safety and hope that from the fold, their own mutual, no surprises will come to them, encapsulates the mode of existence of the living being.

Yet I believe that these are more than my contemporaries acknowledge, or imagine.

Everything I feel, all around me, becomes synonymous with being alive. In every form, there is life and movement, understanding and planning, perception and sensitivity. This stone I placed at the center of our Christmas table, which I brought back from Portugal, worn smooth by the winds, *knows* that reality has a reverse and a face. But I *do not know* how it knows the reverse is not entirely inaccessible.

Before the humans we have become surfaced in the current of beings, I imagine that all of them, in unison, imagined him, longed for him, and generated him, with the *intention* of giving birth to a living form, *the living form most capable* of penetrating the secret of the inaccessibility of *why it exists*. But it seems to me that this stone, that geranium on the windowsill, Prunus Triloba Plena in the garden, and the stream running under this house, did not fully calculate the consequences of their plan. They never understood a time would eventually arrive when humans would exclude them from the sole species of the living, making the common reality even more opaque. I hear Hamann asking me insistently *how it was possible for the language of Nature to become dead*. Did that language die because we no longer spoke to It, or was it that Nature itself abstained from speaking? When did humans, the most capable form, deem themselves to be the exclusive and *sole form*?

It was a fatal moment, for in the fold lies not only the secret of our fate, of the forces that reduce us to dust without our consent; therein also lies the secret of our origin, of the forces that set us in motion, and prepared us for action. Humans were fashioned to dream that fate, and to continue the dream of the living species. But it so happened that the Son of Man did not fully believe in his dream. He proved himself incapable of embodying it to the extent that he could also *physically* incorporate the living species.

The project remains unfinished — suggests the dove to the child.
The fold is still strong and mysterious. To physically dream the new variety of beings, to long for it intensely, to learn to give it the form of a child, and to finally discover what fate has befallen life _____ . I hear Hamann, faintly:

It is a strange night, one I wouldn't describe as:
the spirit   breaches
its shroud and moves forward limpidly toward you.
It is a young woman, dressed in red, who takes the shortcut,
summoning the unicorn, lying in the sun, in the meadow.
A Christ shorn of his iconographic cross, with flowers in place
of stigmata,
comes to offer a golden wedding ring to the mute Buddha
gazing at the ground.
Such a definitive speechlessness sits on the blue back of the
unicorn and engulfs the sea.
The flowers of the New Christ adorn the winged hair of the
young woman, born out of nothingness or dead leaves.
The cycle of Adam ends here. The tree of Everything and
Nothing has withered.
We can return to paradise: the cherubs are blind.

Yesterday, 21 December, Christine's son was born

I felt as though I knew it, but not from a letter, a phone call, or someone else.

I still feel caught between yesterday and today, for it is morning, and the night was the longest of the year. I have the impression I have traveled far. We slept at Ferme Jacobs, in the windowed room where tree branches beat, our room for the night. At around eight o'clock, it was dark, and it was also, because of the slumber we were in, a kind of dawn. Augusto had already gotten up to start making bread at the bakery. In that drowsiness, I dreamed I was celebrating Michel François' birthday at my house, and Geertrui and Anneke had come:
— "Has your brother been born yet?"
— "No. Christine is still lying down." — On Anneke's face, her features seem to have spread. Risen into a landscape. Or aged. Or grown younger. It is the face Christine has today. The soul of that child has been born, I knew upon waking.

Over the course of the afternoon, I set our Christmas table. Mine, Augusto's, Jade's, Fokouli's, and that of others we think about, and who certainly think about us. With recollections, beings, and future beings, this table is of great importance.

At night, I suddenly write on the table prepared for the party: *When one is born, there is as yet no traveler… scattered lights await the only pauses permitted… the living kingdom, lowered into the crematory fire of the wombs, aspires to the new form.* As I have said, this is one of the texts that does not allow me to reflect on writing when I also see it by listening.

I also wrote the text that ends *suspended between the moment of birth and the next mortal instant.*

Later that night:

the house in Jodoigne is an example of a mother and resembles a boat: it protects, it nurtures, it navigates.

It can be alone without being afraid.

"Full of sympathetic old things..." (Rilke)

I listened to music all day long, which is not my habit; but the work came to me in the music.

"A spirit so immeasurably spirit that it can absorb everything without excluding anything."

"If there is a proximity independent of the visible..."

We ate dinner as I had once described: *my invisible guests had come, from the infallible dog to the snake.*

The day was complete because, as I had so desired, I went to Louvain to buy the doll Florbela; she was no longer in the display window, but inside the store, sitting on a chair. The day passed swiftly, there was no weariness. There was a long stretch of night.

When I am lying down, thoughts come to me. First, that of the inner seasons, the mutations of the soul which unfurl in an inner painting of nature; these seasons are even less distinct, the changes are infinitesimal experiences, and require a meticulous attention. Yet those details are the cornerstone of change, and are enormously important in a kind of heightened significance. It is summer, it is winter, it is return, it is autumn, it is ash. Very often, the landscape stays the same; only the place where the image is captured has changed. For I am certain I have been writing with a different lens over the last few days. I describe a glimpse that appears bright before me, within me eluding me at eye level.

I could give as an example:

First there is a tree in the foreground, and behind it a section of mountain, a mountain that is an animal, a sperm whale, or some ferocious sea monster; it is not yet daylight, nor an intensely illuminated place. The tree is as small as a trading card, the monster is black, immense, but a familial monster, in a domestic pose. There is a green throbbing, bereft of references, it is the birth of the green before it is known. The green is not yet upon the earth, and halts within itself, brings the tree. The light I saw, and the volume that was there, become de-situated.

Yet they move in a perfect imbalance of forces. "A spirit so immeasurably spirit that it can absorb everything, without excluding anything…"

When the light goes out, I will continue to feel, and think. But I will not be able to write, I will forget forever. But nothing is lost, everything ascends to the hovering cloud of sound.

One o'clock in the morning.

An unusual day among the days. I am already in bed, light off, drawn to the window by the air I take in; I have just finished reading Hamann; I feel my childhood body, intact, within my present body; I see it sleeping peacefully, embracing its sensations, and its own hunger for form; the form was finding its language in the air, recognizing it, and then unconsciously rendering it fate within me; I remember the light of two lanterns at Al Parma tonight, and that was the picture which flowed over the being, and set it on its path.

I am not tired, I am not aroused, I am lucid remembering the cool water which pours into a vase and makes it sweet and stimulating when you put your hand on it, or your face against it.

I read Hamann — nature is a prophetic text, he says.

The purpose of reading is not to commit to memory. I forget what I read but find myself, at nightfall, with it. The foundation of my reading is the following question:

"How *long* do you read an extensive short period?"

For a second, a minute, a year, this entire night, or this entire life? Reading stretches across time and wants the space of everyday life to cast its shadow. Reading stretches across unknown reaches, and I read little, but infinitely. From these precious metals, I choose one metal, and make it my star in its entirety.

I am not tired, nor am I aroused. I walk with my pulse. I make circles with my heart, which I see vibrating geometrically within me.

Bach had an organ that was made of books. Stripped of their binding, embodiment, and pages, only harmonic possibilities for reading. It reverberated with such mystery that his students would read for him the unawareness of the following day. He knew that he would always know how to read, and that this stringed door was his passageway over prophecy and eternity.

I am not tired, nor am I aroused. I am calm, like a burning candle. I am at peace with myself. I do not know what will be played next, I only know that in the silence, the din of the child within my body dominates; to sleep well is to clothe it in blue — the dress with the white collar it was wearing

Bach soared naked, and saw that he had arms. Those who soar toward themselves will find, at the bottom of the ogive, an open door. To soar toward yourself is to disappear into the brightness of your own experience.

What else do I want to see,
if I read?

Nothing is greater than stopping here.

A page which you have lowered into my soul, do not return from whence you came without another page.

We change days; I have the sensation of slowly proceeding with a work. I am referring to my book about Ferme Jacobs (Jacob's farmstead, an illusory name), which gradually, as it is becoming organized, seems very banal to me. Less banal, I suppose, is the reality it depicts. Does the reality of a group ultimately have a singular meaning? Only if we were not a simultaneity, but rather a succession, an order. If we were connected by a coherence, rather than by an identity. But I mustn't live in that illusion.

I woke up in a house at the back of a garden, nearly blocked by snow; I still haven't gone to the window, but the brightness is high and white, elevated and enlightened brightness of snow; behind the house stretches the land where the animals that surround us come from, although they are not always in the garden. Our white cat, with yellow eyes, slept with us and comes to the door as if he were the bearer of transparency.

On the panes of glass, the frost is thick, and it enfolds me in the desire to play, to continue writing what I am writing. I fasten one of the old Christmas birds I bought at Monika's Antique Shop to the window.

The only truly important thing, on a day like this, is to await the night.

Because at night, I am in bed and I read, I write at the same time, I think about book after book. This afternoon, beginning at four o'clock, when I returned from Al Parma, where I wrote a letter to my mother, the usual Sunday letter, I mopped the floor of the house. This house, since it is large, has a large floor I like to travel across on my knees, observing the furniture and the objects from another perspective. The cloth heavy with water is a bearer of radiance and brightness; it leaves behind it the horizon of a passing hand. The landscape of the house, which is a passageway, is inscribed on the floor. I move through a closed realm where I collect the dust I put in the bucket. The water becomes dirty, heavy, and dark. An evident metamorphosis which leaves me perplexed because it is evident. Beside me, Al-Hallaj recites:

"O point of view, from which my gaze begins; O place of insertion (in me) of my inspiration.

O whole of the whole, of which the whole is dearer to me than all or part of myself.

One would like you to sympathize with the one whose heart is seized by the two talons of the bird; in love, distraught, distressed, he flees from one desert to another; he wanders without knowing where, and his ideas wander like the traced glimmer of a flash of lightning, or like the brief conjecture, tenuous, that one casts in the shadow of the future [...]"

In the early hours of the morning, I dreamed of a house and a distant thickness where my mother had died. When I arrived, there was nothing left of her physical presence, there was everything left of her constant remembrance. She had opened the armoire and chosen the most beautiful dress made of a brocade fabric. Black and shining. She had lain alone in bed and, although I had gone to that house solely to find her, I never saw her again.

I am still working on the beginning of the sort-of book *Namur Street School — Ferme Jacobs*. I had the same dream several times: I had written a terrible book, without knowing how and when I had written it; the book had been published and had disappeared, it was a book without an author, lost. I think that book might turn out to be *Namur Street School — Ferme Jacobs*, if I persist in continuing to write it. Why? The answer is so obvious that I cannot give it an intelligible form.

Tomorrow, I'm going to interrupt my vacation for a day to make bread. Lou says to Rilke, "We must all seek our own combination, our own personal balance point between art's life and life's art." But my entire life refuses the institutional relationship.

For tomorrow morning:
It snows, and through the faculty of knowing, I walk inside and outside the house. I pass between the living room door and the garden gate.

I write a letter to Lurdes in an adolescent tone: "I wish that, among us, there was always a constant speculation: How? After the after? Where? In what other way? Or?" Lurdes consistently doesn't answer my letters.

I dream that, in a room which alludes to nothing, a bird is perched on a divan; a black dog comes in, imposing, its muzzle wrinkled, like Jade's nose when he expresses a feeling; when I look at the coverlet again, the bird has disappeared. I conclude it has been eaten by the dog, and I lament that someone opened the door of the cage, which is empty, hanging from the wall.

"The bird is undoubtedly Rilke," it occurred to me after lunch, in the small café. — "Why do you think the dog ate the bird?" — Augusto asks me. I remember that, at that moment, I associated intelligence with the contents of the cup. — "Why don't you think the bird turned into a molossus?" — In any event, Rilke must have been the bird: eaten by the molossus, or transformed into it.

On the 29th, it was the half-centenary of Rilke's death (29 December 1926); it was Rilke, the feathers attest.

If I were to stay here, writing unendingly, I would be transformed into a threadbare piece of cloth; undone when someone or something touched me, I would leave behind only dust with the gleam of words and beings.

Today, I had the impulse to place a twenty-franc coin, with a sheaf, on top of my desk; then, in the dictionary, I come across the word *bezant*, an ancient Byzantine coin, and I composed the text about Juan's birth, about his parents who, having moved through the luminous scenes, caused him to roll out of their mouths, like a wheel similar to that coin.

The life of writing has no similar.
It is the life of events that might come to be related.
Its understanding sweeps past, ever beyond, the fold of the veil: and I see that transparencies do not exist,
and that I myself,
in the midst of the Voice,
am the place of the soul.

To plunge cloth into soapy water, cloth that covers and
protects different parts of the body, or are an accompaniment to
windows, and furniture;
to behold dirt floating on the surface of the water, amidst soap
scented and softened by glycerin;
to reflect, with perplexity, on glass and on wax, when my hand
passes slowly and leaves a gleam on the planks;
to sweep the floor, which is the path connecting the different
sections of the house, those of day and those of night;
to close my eyes to the noises, scents, and lamps, each with its
own fate;
to remain within the vibrations of this receptive space, waiting
for someone to enter, and be the expected visitor: Rilke,
Müntzer, the Poor, Ana de Peñalosa, or a soul, or a similar
being.

Once the door has been closed (what door?), I lose my
singularity; the density of my spirit eases. I furl outward like the
feathers of a bird, I utter empty words. I am led by the hand of
someone who does not entirely ignore me, but who does not
read or write with me.
I go back inside, following my gaze toward the candle.
There is always a subterranean space, an utterance which
scrutinizes its own open mouth; all these returns have, in my
language, their own name; overlapping words from multiple
languages return to oneness: it is the explosion of the birth of
time; beyond a confused meditation, its description becomes
unthinkable.

As it is a vision of intense delight, threads of water run through the fire.

When my companions come for me, I greet them at the door and, believing I am the servant, they let themselves be led by me to the room inside the house where they find me writing them "an utterance which scrutinizes its own open mouth _____ ."

Today, as yesterday, I am accompanied by what pleases this house and those who live in it; I did not think the territories of my life were such a vast expanse of realms; everything forms a luminous rotation.

I start reading *White Fang* by Jack London. I mentioned this book to Claire during my walk with her through hills and valleys. Upon our return, we began the second part of the thick notebook which Claire calls *The Mortal Life of Animals*. Her greatest desire is to assemble a thick volume. At the end of the second part, we will make an index.

With Annick, the starting point will be Lou Andreas-Salomé's childhood.

Why did I push Claire to be the author of *The Mortal Life of Animals*?

It was no accident that I made this decision: Annick refuses to wear skirts, speaks of herself in the masculine; there is no identification as a woman that is useful to her, so far; there is, one might say, a concealment of her own unconscious. She is intelligent, preparing herself to dominate, and lacking caution, though with many glimpses of kindness. I should try to introduce between us, two women, figures with a greatness who have not been lost in either the obligatoriness of their lives, or in the presence of what belongs to them.

I feel ill, but did the usual treatment. No improvement. I started thinking about clay, silica and alumina poultices, and yesterday, Saturday, the part of the week when time in the house begins to belong to me, I applied the earth. In the morning, I was in less pain, I sat down easily on the stack of pillows. Water, clay, in short, mud. I saw my hands vibrating over the bowl that contained it, as in moments of writing; I do not know why, but my grandmothers were so near; perhaps one, my father's mother, because she truly loved me, and the other because she was someone who often wanted to be healed, and to heal. I feel a deep longing to plunge into the mud. Later, in a book I read, by Marie Noel, was written:

"The woman taught him to wash and to heal diseases."

In the meantime, the book about Ferme Jacobs awaits. This time is a time of fragments, of impulses whose meaning, as the days go by, will perhaps eventually be able to be glimpsed.

The mud was deposited in a place covered in dust.

I descend the stairs with a longing for eternal life. Perhaps because of the enormous contrast between yesterday, when I had to shield the roosters from death, and today, so simple, I become certain that I have always lived; my mother writes to me, lamenting her old age and loneliness. I write to her in my mind, wanting to tell her that I will endeavor, with my life, to extricate her from her old age, and loneliness; a string of eternal lives, seeking their eternity in one another.

I write the text: *always writing, always walking and wandering, someone is about to enter.*

In the early hours of 18 January, Christine's son is born. Almost a month after our dreams; twenty-nine days before birth is the moment those in the East say is the insufflation of the soul.

In the end, my life is a spiritual investigation.

How fleeting the time in Jodoigne; although, on the whole, the time spent at Ferme Jacobs is not an inimical time. Occasionally, the children turn the house into a den: they pile up debris, drag behind them a space of detritus, real and imaginary; but the house is not earth, it is not organic matter that decomposes and, in the spring, is arranged in the impassivity of its cycle.

Today, I recognize that dream. It was a dream I had one night in early March. A lake — while I was sleeping on my left side — was beside me; it was immense, although bounded by the edges of the lake, mirrored, it seemed to want to watch me sleeping calmly.

Today, the 23rd, I woke up susceptible, mutable, dispersed in the concentration of connecting different images. Tears, always before my eyes. I knew — because the vigil of the lake came to mind — this simple thing about death. I was once, in truth, lake — its shore of earth — the body of those reminiscences is within me; rotting is the way to return to the earth, to the water of the lake, to bring them and take them with you. Death is the dark night of this passageway, the only way to sublimate the captive stone.

My father was a lake bordered by the meanders of my mother; if he had been the dark lake, the mountains that surrounded it, he looked down on them from above toward the lacustrine image at the bottom. I was brought up to know that when you look deeply, depth is surface.

It does not have to be done. It does not have to be done. It
isn't necessarily needful to act. My two books rest,
let them rest,
I lie down with my mortifications in the bright sun of the
greenhouse, among the plants that depend on me, but which
love me. I am not the center of action in this house, nor *of this
doing.* My body in its spirit is also a work, I let myself be set in
motion by the sun and the distant music. Why should this be
done, and that, and that? What would cause its being to grow
more, what would add more to its being by destroying mine?
Nowhere is a geography needful, if it is not jubilant.

I wanted to express my fear.
The fear of confusion, the confusion of being fearful, the
rocky, dark caves: "When he explains to Amanda, using a
knotted silk handkerchief, that the process of liberation is
nothing more than untying the knots of our own being, knots
that we have formed ourselves and that have made us the slave of
our confused illusions _____."
"When all the knots of the heart come undone, then right
here, in this human birth, the mortal becomes immortal."

Advice: never miss an hour of sun; never miss an hour of
snow; write the texts of your own meditation: *Mesus,* that which
is secret, grows.
_____ she spent an hour, standing, beside the gate, without
daring to move away; she spent the night and some hours of the
day, until she fell back onto the path of dawn, which was her
thinking moment before being decisive.

A deep melancholy following M.'s visit. It is cold, but I walk down Le Ry Saint-Jean, weep, go up to my room, lie down, and read *The Great Captains*, by Jorge de Sena, which my mother sent me today; Aunt Alice had also written me this morning. *Great Captains*, Aunt Alice (past), Ferme Jacobs, create a strain of melancholy I can hardly bear.

Maredret Abbey,
Dear Sister Agnès,

I did not write you earlier because, in the end, silence was the most compelling; reality gradually appeared in a thousand ways, I followed it, but without changing a single aspect of my primary inspiration, which leads me in the direction of a hidden meaning, the opposite of the obscure. The work at Ferme Jacobs continues, we face our future with an ever-greater frugality of resources _____ in the sense of a harmony and building of reciprocal bonds between human beings, plants, animals, and all that I, in short, do not know how to say. I am uncertain whether there is, in this endeavor, any possibility.

Alongside all this, but brushing up against it, we continue to write, to express ourselves, only longing to make our perceptions gleam and to discover which target they are hurling us toward. Evolving is perhaps the ultimate limit — movement takes a multiplicity of directions — do not be saddened by our inability to live closer to the abbey.

That is perhaps all I wanted to say to you, this post-Easter week.

My post-Easter verb:

Augusto believes I have a love of the sumptuous, that I harbor a nostalgia for wealth; there is no doubt I harbor many nostalgias for the intensities of shadows,

as evidenced by my sorrow today.

The desire to assemble *the notebook of animals and plants* was not born today but on Saturday, the sixteenth.

A day devoid of intelligence, when the buds of the trees were as indifferent to me as numbness. The clean feeling of being nothing. A night when Chez Maurice killed the pigs at two o'clock in the morning.

Beginning in September, I have decided to work only (still) three days a week; I wanted to leave behind, more than the work at the Ferme, its human relationships; I feel overwhelmed by them — sex, power, envy, confrontation, feelings which pushed to the paroxysm of a ceaseless movement, I am not prepared to inhabit. If only I could convert them into ether, or take the nauseating breath from their mouths.

Only Jade feels like a beaten dog for not having gone to the Ferme. I gradually approach the beginnings of Peace. Tenuous. I do not know whether I will read, or sleep. I go over my budget again.

I began to observe: behind the honeysuckle, the ants took advantage of a crack in the surface of the wall to enter the kitchen. A ludicrously tiny hole. I had seen them before — burin marks on the windowsill — but I wasn't sure where they had gotten in. They crawled up the stem of the hyacinth and, with their arrival, made even larger the kitchen that is, and always will be, among all the kitchens I will ever have, my preferred kitchen. It is a leather satchel, with a large shiny opening where it is smoothed, worn out, produced, imitated. On the balustrade framing the enormous façade of the house, there are furled plants I recognize from being with me. Carried by the breeze, a delicious smell, which I also observe.

I am not writing these notes for anyone, I am writing them for the plants themselves, the names of which I do not know, so that they can take advantage of the fact I know how to write.

I see one that is unanimously called a weed, and must deter other plants from thriving, and living. It is a dandelion. Dandelion, dandelion, which punctures carpets of grass, and asserts itself as an enemy in the fields; its calyxes are transformed into soaring feathers, plumes, pennants, which place all of nature within our grasp.

I abate in the ovary of this plant; in this kitchen, and garden two steps away, I feel as though I am a convalescent who is consoled. In front of me, another's book on my knees:
      At that moment when day and night mingle their light _____ I felt the same emotions I was later to feel as an adult, both deepest despair because I was excluded from life as a man, and marvelous beatitude because I was spared from it.
      "He" is Dominique Fernandez. *Porporino, or The Secrets of Naples.*

Beneath the colorful liquid of the morning, I have to note
down what I read about Orpheus:
but because his ambiguous nature encapsulates the desire of an
era where the division of the sexes had not become the
foundation of social life _____
_____ but all things mingled, eternally one and
limitless _____

A veil descended before my eyes, such that it was neither day nor
night, it was a long misty beach with "all things mingled, eternally
one and limitless"; it was a perpetual state of subdued light,
where the leaves of the trees plunged into an ambiguous state
between writing paper and nature's paper, similar to that of
Orpheus.

I had the impression I was someone else, and lived
immersed in another era, even in the simple environment of a
house and a garden; at my side was what I needed — the
blurred image of a woman who had also lived in another era.
The difference was that I was inside the house, leaning on a
small silken cylindrical shaft around which this text was
spinning — and she was in the garden. Are humans body/
spirit, and universal, through mental projections of
themselves?

Then the standing scene played out, wherein I, with my
desire and intelligence open over the cylinder, having just
arrived in the room of the unclothed, felt a sorrow on the
horizon, without being able to specify that it was a sorrow

alongside the visionary narrative.

When I saw the encounter of the alone with the alone, I wasn't sure where to situate myself; I had longed, all afternoon, to experience the pleasure, the dilation of seeing, but nothing was forthcoming. So, I decided to briefly recount that experience of emptiness, seeing the sun in the distance, and having with me, on top of my knees and on the table beside me, the book by Ibn 'Arabi.

The land in life.
Inheriting the land.
Rosemary and sage.

I was drawn to fear in its jungle of space, reading him led me to become lost and to hope. Sage, rosemary, this book, they are my companions. From one to the other, there is a morning slope leading here. The final image I have of the creative imagination is that of upright sexes as voices:

When I began to understand that I was poor, and that I would remain in this state in the future, I also began to look with clarity at the objects I possessed, which were either to be kept, or left behind.

The perishable objects (the robes, the clothes, the household linen), becoming more and more worn, made me feel as though I was carrying them in a kind of leap, or step, toward an eternal stage _____ and presupposes an ability to experience events which are enacted in a reality other than the physical reality of daily life, events which spontaneously transmute themselves into symbols. _____
it was the "Angel" who guided him along the spiritual path.

After I get up, wash in the bathroom at the end of the hallway, I finally take possession of my true figure, and the compositions of images and ideas that had been formed during the night are remade in that instant:

I am downstairs, in the wide, white kitchen, preparing a meal, turned toward the round table, with my back to the cupboard against the wall. The kitchen is plunged into a light that comes from the luminous brightness. The window, which has a coverlet from the islands as a curtain, is, alluringly, a source. I sense someone behind me, a young, blond, almost beardless man.

— Are you alone?

— Augusto is in the living room, making collages.

I wake up to a thirsty morning: I want to write, bathe in a lake, knit the additional length to my worn blue skirt, go out, clean the house, rid it of stains, take the bus to Louvain, go to the supermarket, think about what to make for lunch.

When I was a serving maid, I watched my mistress's gestures, not knowing whether she had already served me, or whether she had yet to take my place. At the time, I was called *Candida*, the form taken by beings that should be inclined to movement, and evolving. But soon, taking another step, I became aware that, in another monad, Ana de Peñalosa existed. I remember perfectly how easily her affection for the maids developed, and they returned it. Together they climbed the steps of experience. Ana de Peñalosa, appearing from the hallway which runs lengthwise along the second floor, could either enter the meditation room — and be the Lady — or go to the kitchen, where I was, and be the servant.

She was divided by a line separating the waters — and on this side she was illiterate — and on the other side of that shadow she was the perfect image of Ana de Peñalosa.

— You can use this house — said Ibn 'Arabi — as an open world.

I felt as though she was either moving toward her ends, or returning to her origins.

— Are you alone? — asked the man. What to say with my voice?

I replied that I was not alone, but that I was handing him the key to one of the doors, and the time for listening I had the following day.

Morning.

I lean back against Ibn 'Arabi, absorbed in his magnification of the feminine.
I see him enter the room,
so dimly lit by the daylight that he becomes sensitized to shadows and
colors on the verge of death.

In the middle of the bed, She was sleeping. The room was warm and she was covered only by a white cloth protecting her belly.
Silently, after having hesitated over whether to stay, Ibn 'Arabi fetches a chair and sits down near the bed, gazing at her. He is a young man, still beardless. Image: _____ She displaying her back to the shadows _____ which gradually became deeper in his gaze.
It is not a vision, nor is his demeanor grasping.
Agile concentration in the incipient brightness which, moment by moment, forms around the nearly naked white female body, lying there asleep. With a lingering precaution _____ in no way desiring to awaken the sovereign landscape _____ he begins to pull away the edge of the fabric covering her, with the intention of completing her nakedness.

And I read to him   ruins
                          nomadic journeys of mages
                          in gardens, meadows, and houses.

And he says
to the nakedness   flowers, clouds,
                        thunder, and zephyrs,
                        hills, woods, rural paths.

And I suggest
he say to her   women who rise like suns.
                        Wallah.

He had come to read with Nizam, Ana de Peñalosa's name
when she was young, "God is a beautiful being, who loves
beauty" _____ but never before had he noticed her, her
nakedness. He gazed at her now, the majestic and gustatory
strength of her body reposing in the loveliness of her
appearance. Left to herself, her nudity was a body creating a
light of its own, spreading in the shadowed tones of the room
and in his gaze. He looks and receives the joy of an image in
nostalgic numbness, where the splendor of the beauty that
unfurls toward its source of irradiation is forever fixed.

Nizam gives him nothing,
hides nothing from him.
She is growing for herself.

In that movement, she turns in slow distensions of the
body, seeking propitious and breezy places. Strong shoulders
form, a serene face reclines, deft hands trace her breasts, her legs
open slightly, in a steady rhythm of breathing he walks toward
the growing brightness.

Ibn ʿArabi puts down the book he had brought. I see him

approach the bed and sit down on the floor, at the level of
Nizam's belly. And facing the scarcely glimpsed vagina, I hear
him murmur   is this a real woman, is this you, Nizam? Is it
Him I see in your image?

And thus began the moment for which he had not come.
Always in repose, Nizam lowered her left hand to her belly
_____ to gather the greatest brightness there, and extend
it to somewhere Ibn 'Arabi does not know, but which cannot be
found in that body.

Faint contortions of the kidneys, in a sure and slightly
accelerated rhythm. Legs that spread and arch, allowing a more
exact fit of the hand and those lips of a dark red, which is the
color heralding mystery.

"I have never seen a woman with such a beautiful appearance."
Fingers that move away from the hand and assay quick
incursions into the pubic hair, the tumescent clitoris and vagina.
And a new form emerged, one of growing luminosity, of
sovereign pleasure on her face, of a dance surrendered to its
own aims, which enfold Ibn 'Arabi and draw his gaze and his
volition indelibly:

Nizam creates for herself.

Captivated by the living image of the fire that is reborn, he
moves his right hand toward the burning bush, as if it were
_____ and it was _____ imperative to burn: "May I
be bewitched by your beauty and lured by your deepest fire
_____ may the incandescence of this pure love penetrate
me and transmute me into unadulterated crystal" _____ a
hand asking for Nizam to welcome it into the transparency of
her concept and take it further, to the depths of her fire
_____ causing it to follow the rhythm that flourishes in

her incandescence, and teaches him the pleasure of that woman who is also called Wisdom. Even if he wanted to, Ibn 'Arabi could never release the hand he had given. It will be consumed to the last.

I looked away so that my attention would not wane and I could continue to hear him as no one else ever had: "How beautiful you are, O Lord, glorious and sleeping. I will not look for you in myself, nor outside myself. I will not refrain from seeking you, for I would be wretched. I leave my right hand with you."

I go to meet Ibn 'Arabi, sitting in the garden, near the cherry trees. He holds his book in his left hand, his right hand hidden in his white djellaba. He does not see that I am passing by, and I stand slightly behind him. Only after a long silence does Prunus Triloba signal to me that someone was standing next to Ibn 'Arabi. I looked in the direction indicated and saw Nizam sitting at his feet. Dressed in green, confused with the vegetation.

They were speaking tenderly to one another.

Nizam says   the Ephemeral is not gathered.

Ibn 'Arabi says   it gazes when the evanescent gives a sign
                    of itself
                    Still the pleasure echoes, and now the
                    perplexed gaze wonders why the Image
                    fades.

Nizam says   it wonders whether the ephemerals
                    remain in this place, if they are constant,
                    in and of themselves

Ibn 'Arabi recalls where you slept, your evanescent image
                    opened the door of the *sacrum convivium*
                    for me. The conjunction of the Sun and
                    Moon was ephemeral, but so intense that
                    the Beginning and the End, ever
                    separated, rejoiced.

Nizam says   in your hidden right hand

Ibn 'Arabi continues   which I cast into the furnace, in the
paroxysm of the fire
and which broke the five sensations out
of their usual routine and, in the
abandoned confines, she saw what Love
sees when it gazes.

Nizam says   that hand was where the ephemerals
remain throbbing when they fade away,
where the rest of your body does not
know
keep it as a guide and a sign.

Ibn 'Arabi meditates   you gave me what you did not think to
give me. Your entire body now knows
what my hand knows and what you
wholly ignore.
To know, you slept.

Nizam replies   you came in like a thief, and like a thief
you left, robed as a poet
and your desire forever desires to entice
you into the company of the constant
ephemerals. Not eternity, to which the
rest of your body is not suited.

Ibn 'Arabi requests   a kind of enduring mortal, a ductile
metal in keeping with my manner of
always passing by.

A series of dreams
Two years ago, I had a dream in which I, and Sister Agnès, were
given a half hour to live.

On the 27th, I have this dream: In Portugal, and nowhere
because there are no road signs, I find a refreshing place, with a
vast landscape. I am in a discontinuous house, where multiple
generations live together peacefully; I and Augusto, my mother,
my grandmother mother of my mother, are sitting at a round
table which brings us together around the wonders it has at its
center. Augusto and I crouch on the floor. We are two
companion plants, and our curved backs concentrate the
sheltering power that enfolds us; we would say that we are
parent and child or, more explicitly
    the way we coincide determines the color of these bodies.
    One of the pieces on the table is a round clock, an alarm
clock that awakens by violence. My grandmother remains
seated on the side, the composition of her face has been altered
by an element of stillness, and faded away. She is, at the same
time, ancestor and sorceress. The clock strikes twenty-eight,
four hours beyond the day.

Today, I dream again. There is a black light and a pink
magma that interpenetrate, that exchange with one another
what is uncovered.
    In the black, no sorrow, nor catastrophe. I finish nothing I
write. A movement has taken shape which is so powerful and
yet so gentle
that I am left, while I wash and dress,

to analyze the countenance of the unasked question.

A few days ago, in *The Remaining Life*, I gave creation to the figure of the Black King (which C. feared, and which was a figure from her nightmares, Augusto told me).

The Black King experiments with the viability of his sentences in Hadewijch's body. There are tiny sentences, and distant sentences; there is hair of a washed-out blonde, and stiff wigs; there are flowers which, rubbing against her skin, leave her entirely white. In this intense duality, Hadewijch became aware of Ibn 'Arabi.

He was a consoling figure leaning against the standing people, the statues on the fountain; not being equal to any of them, he seemed to be embedded in the melodic ensemble of the water;
his eyes were inspired by blue, without being blue, and his feet, which Hadewijch dipped in the basin of the fountain, were close to those who speak. Poor, his entire contemplative attitude covered Hadewijch with a thick veil. She began to walk through the fog he opened up for her _____ on one side the Black King, and on the other the desire of Ibn 'Arabi.

We have moved on to another phase of our love; the orchard knows only its green; there, Ibn 'Arabi teaches every day; I do not know where he sleeps, nor where he eats, even without anyone present, *he teaches*; he takes long walks through the trees, long in sequence, and in time

> he does not demand silence, wherever he goes,
> silence exists;

I come across him, and I am surprised;
he is called Hadewijch and Ana de Peñalosa,
he is called Hadewijch or Ana de Peñalosa,
I have been called John, Rilke, or Müntzer.

Only Ibn 'Arabi does not give me any name; when he sees
me in the orchard, I have the feeling he sees me as green; I am
yet another green which, with the passing of the light, changes;
we do not direct our gazes at one another and, on the flat
ground at the top of the hill, we bend down over the water of
the well, we pass through. A space of blue in our arms and the
stellar scent of hours.

The sky has turned gray and dull; the rain has not yet begun
to fall but is already everywhere; in the middle of the orchard,
Ibn 'Arabi has nowhere to shelter, or perhaps he will not get
wet, nor will this depiction of the day pour down upon him. He
came from Andalusia to Silves, in Portugal, as to any other place
of learning.

While I was writing the previous text, over these last few
days, I read:
"But in the presence of such complexity, of a Figure that
discloses so many associations and undergoes so many
metamorphoses   we must lay bare the implicit intentions of
the mystic consciousness,
discern what it
shows itself
of itself."

All my senses awakened with such an intimate freshness, that mature age was an adolescent state. "This mantle is for us indeed a symbol of confraternity, a sign that we share in the same spiritual geography."

A cloth
a veil
are the words of the day. How do they awaken the senses? Mine,
through halting words.

In the center of the courtyard, a patch of clover persisted,
and the cherry tree leaned, facing the wind; at dusk, the present
invaded the courtyard in a great brightness of light. "...That the
Form under which each of the Spirituals knows God is also the
form under which God knows him, because it is the form under
which God reveals Himself to Himself in that man."

I speak with Augusto about the Lover and it seems to us
that the Lover cannot be a person, that is to say, a mask that
portrays itself as a living agent or character of its own fate. The
Lover cannot be someone. If he were, seeking him would cause
the seeker to be dependent on the symbolic relations which
govern the game of love and beloved.

Augusto tells me that no one *will ever have* the Lover. And I
agree his emergence is unpredictable, as is his evanescence,
which Ibn 'Arabi tells me about. Not because he wants us to run
after him unendingly, as we read in the *Song of Songs,* but
because he changes form.
Not being, however, a form.
The intention of his movement is to compel the beloved to
forego the form of love and beauty.
Cruel words only the volition is able to hear, as a sentinel at the
extreme limit, when even the Name itself is an enigma. When it
is accomplished, the beloved usually looks for the Face that, in

accordance with his taste, comes closest to the ideal Face to which he aspires. But even this will always and only be a Face, whose majesty and strength will be fatally inferior to the impulse that led the Beloved to seek it.
To love is deceptive.

The Enigmatic Name thus has a specific movement: to expel the Face, in the gradual hearing of the enigma. To hear the Name, without connecting it to a Face, to a sex, to a particular form. To accept it as a simple sound, timbre, and cadence which eliminates, in its gradual utterance, the vocalic and musical form.

But what then *is* the Lover, I ask. Your sex journeying beyond repulsion.

I sat down on a jetty, on the side of a road. I picked up the book and began to read it, as I became more and more overwhelmed by the unusualness of my situation _____ finding myself in a strange land, far from my house, sitting on the side of a road whose name I do not know, at 11:30 on a radiant sunny morning.

I was alone.

And only then did the lapping of the water make itself heard as a distinct movement. A gradual tension was created between me and the water, and I knew I was with the Lover. I was also a lapping, but not of water. I observed that it was a verbal and sonorous infinity which did not abolish, animate, or sublimate the aquatic form of the movement.

A naked form in an intense consonance with another naked form

gave reality to the space of the Lover. Beyond fear, I accepted that on the margins of my usual world, other created realities would come to reveal themselves.

And I take a path from the jetty and followed the current.

Now I was the non-water in motion, conscious of my lapping.

I walk a little further and observe another form tentatively emerging, the chirping of birds in the treetops. Quick, sharp chirps which, even this time, indicate to me that I chirp in my lapping, without being a bird, or liquid.

The Lover emerges once more, in the space of this similarity and this difference, simultaneous. Chirping and not being a bird, any bird can say the same of the wanderer I am: "I wander and am not a wanderer." I travel further along the path, which takes me to a clearing, where I arrive, always accompanied by this intuition of the unsentimental presence of the Lover.

What was He, present there, witnessing me?
Not-water, like me, but lapping like us, I and the water.
Not bird, but chirping.
Not wanderer, but moving.
Not-person, but an active presence, revealing itself through repeated, ephemeral acts of tension.

I sit down on a log at the edge of the clearing, closing my eyes fixed on its center, letting everything flow, even in its stillness. And I notice a breeze moving through the trees in the clearing, like a murmur, which evokes the word *murmuring*. The *murmuring* of the treetops, as I say *the murmuring that I am*. And I bring the kinesthesia to an end.

I could, in reality, say that trees are birds, but if I did, language would lose its discriminating power. It would be a pleasant poetics, whose most visible effect would be to identify the different agents of the same manifestation. For everything to remain, I would eliminate what occurs, enliven the trees that do not fly, sublimate the rootlessness that I am, without being able to fly, nor run away. And the Lover would become lost in language.

I did not take this movement as a discovery of nature.

It is a simple landscape, precious, because it is slow and silent. So alone. Such a vast manifestation of life for a tiny fraction of consciousness. And in this disproportion dwells the Lover, an evanescent form, which drew me to this clearing, in a

strange land. Constructing and abandoning forms, until one
loves what pleasure does not envision, and then ceases to love,
in the body of the path,
not by ex-altation,
but by in-altation. And I return.

Returning from shopping, I arrived in front of the gate. For me, this time is the time of Ibn 'Arabi. He was certain that to imagine was to access self-revelation, and that beings approached the act of creating by baring themselves in solitude. That, to the initial creator's act of imagining the world, the creature responded by imagining its world. At that moment, I imagined that behind the gate there was a round medallion, and a horse nearby,
and within the medallion was depicted
in miniature,
yet without smaller proportions,
the surrounding outside world.

When he left for Brazil, Paulo gave us an iron chest which I
thought contained sheets; I covered it with a cloth, without
opening it. But on a dull day — which causes me to avidly
observe the usual things I have at hand to see if I can discover
uncommon details that stimulate me — I looked, with growing
curiosity, at the chest. I lifted the lid, thinking I would find
dampness to remedy, or create a mystery that would only be
within me. There were no sheets, there was a vague dampness,
but there was, more importantly and almost entirely, twenty
volumes of the Encyclopædia Universalis _____ .
In the middle of the dawn, on the side of night,
knowledge was
alight.

_____ the plants, particularly the cactus with two red
flowers opening at the tip of one stem, which called out to me,
based on the sudden inclination I had to water it,   absorb
water.

I am correcting the proofs of *The Book of Communities*; it
isn't a book like the others, it is a sourcebook; its beginning
brings me to a nocturnal landscape where the water is a
brightness that is dawn; end of the closing? A night has fallen
which loses its usual meaning.

The book I wrote causes me to write; I gather it up like an
unfettered dream
alive; different texts on the table   on my knees   in my
eyes   in my hand;
on the ground, I also discover a text which I gather without yet
being able to read it
The Book of Communities:
how beautiful this book is; I reread it as I corrected the final
proofs; someone wrote it who is not only me; if that is true, I
have become dear friends with them; their name has an S
— *Sun at night*; I hiss; but I only encounter the air shed by them
circulating in the house,
scriptor.

As for *The Book of Communities*   *she envisioned a
living writing she could take for an encounter.*

I tended the garden in the morning and all afternoon. I still feel as though I am in the garden, amidst the brightness and a perpetual green.

Augusto hurt his foot. Not seriously. There is an atmosphere of peaceful convalescence pervading the house. In a corner of the courtyard, behind the herbs, I found a brown cat calmly waiting for death. He lifted his head and drank the milk I brought him. The cats come to die here, outdoors, and are born in the cellar. I look out over the plot of land, protected by old bulwarks — laurel, lettuce, thyme, lemon balm, mint, cactus, geranium — and other unending names; it has been almost three years since herbicides were sprayed *against* the plants in this courtyard where horses were dismounted; and the herbs, and other species irreconcilable with the orderly and methodical arrangement of the gardener, grow with all their wont; a cat takes a circuitous route along the roof, through the errant twilight. I remember that Docinha and Doucette are behind the house, hatching eggs that have not yet cracked open. All these animals write tenaciously, with the plants and against the plants. Cars pass by on Avenue des Combattants, behind the fence. Why are they passing by?

Everything became even more peaceful with the night. I myself. I sit on luminous dust, slightly tired. Today I have become a companion of the color green. It is my writing oil.

I am now almost fifty years old, and what I write is
somewhat hidden. I like to bake bread, that is, earn a living, but
not always, not that often. And I do not enjoy, or can hardly
bear, the other distractions — the Wednesday workshop at my
house, for example, which turns out to be nothing more than an
alibi to keep me, on those days, away from the Ferme. What I
wanted was to be able to write, to read, to understand
boundlessly. Words, means of expression, seem short and
insufficient; this slow decline in the second half of my life
begins to make every moment a precious entity, which I wanted
to handle only with joy; rising from sleep, like today,
thinking about all the housework I have to traverse, as if passing
through a wall, knowing that perhaps I can find,
in my visions   humans, beings, in the tension of evolving
without becoming completed; I go now to a supermarket like
someone walking on the surface of water, among lights and
voices which appear to me with no transition to the future other
than through myself, who vaguely sustains them.

My impression is that nothing was, everything is being;
now alive, I can look from above, or from outside; I wake up
and find that a hundred years have passed in a single day, and I
go down an octave, or several, in the key I use to describe it. A
summer day, so bright. Neither snow, nor cold, nor opaque
brightness. I would prefer a day more centered on the house,
the courtyard, the movement I now sense on the avenue
beyond the gate, which is my lover (Augusto crosses it when he
arrives, or leaves).

Yes, things are a vehicle of knowledge, the way they are
arranged experiments with our thinking and challenges our way

of acting; I arrange them in a certain way and other perceptions begin to emerge, I change their place, I establish other reciprocal relationships between them, and new beings are present and begin to express themselves (to me), so that I do not abandon them, describe them, maintain them, reinforce them in their nascent reality; when everything is abandoned by me (I am thinking about death), there will be objects which, in other houses that inherit them, will summon someone to their fate.

The narrative which underlies these pages will not, in the end, require fiction. It will be a posthumous book, or an ancient book, and it will be called, referring to a woman, *Biography*. Not because I am a writer, or a woman who bears witness; but because I was born a living being; I speak without enigmas, with the clarity and sincerity that ease spirits.

HOUSE IN JODOIGNE, 3 JULY 1977
Thirty degrees Celsius, at five o'clock in the afternoon.

Living here in Brabant, I am not accustomed to
a day
with so much sun, and my bestiary,
constituted through limited and unlimited duration
rises
and occupies every corner of this house and its furniture.
One day I will awaken,
and I will live
my entire life;
not my life of my name,
although that too
with my entire life.

JODOIGNE, 19 JULY 1977

Mother says Aunt Alice wants to pay for my trip to
Portugal, that she is still hiding the sale in Alpedrinha from her.
She speaks only of a hypothetical purchase, not of a sale that
has already taken place. She fears my judgment.

I feel nothing toward Aunt Alice. I feel as though I am the
heir to a family wealth which, including them, goes far beyond
money, furniture, and the objects resting on it.

In whatever form possessions come to me, they are neither
owed to me nor not owed to me. A number of founts have
converged in me, that of Father, Grandmother Isabel, cousin
Álvaro, Grandmother Isabel's adoptive father ("the good
stepfather"), who was a bookbinder, and others with no visible
water of writing.

I am necessarily the heir, I have brought together many of
the lost perceptions of these beings, and related them. I no
longer haughtily make, as I did when I was young, a distinction
between what is owed to me and what is given to me out of
another's supposed generosity. I am a family, I will receive much
more than the balance between ought and shall.

I suppose that if I had had children, all this intensity of a
final convergence would have been lost, or would only survive,
in identical circumstances, later on. I am grateful it happened in
a girl.

I had invited them to come, but wasn't sure whether they would accept; the house was majestic, poor, and secluded, at the same time; I knew what word to have for each of them, and even where to take them on their first walk; I no longer considered myself young but, moving alongside them, I steadily moderated my pace. They had overcome their fear and scruples about leaving the country just to see me; we happened to have been born in the same place, and I from one of them; another, I had hated, the way those who are about to free themselves hate the nearest branch which restrains them; another, I had wanted to see from a certain distance, because she was too similar to me; the fourth, who, out of a habit of respect, I followed slightly behind, had been the first of my imaginary life, or understanding. I knew what I could say to them, but I could only hear them talking in their profuse joy at being with me. They seemed close, they, who sometimes quarreled, and did not always look kindly on one another. It was late afternoon, and I had not noticed they were already very old, as my cosmogony was different; we took a short walk through the fields and returned to the house, sorting out the rooms for the night. I had put up a small sign for each of them. On a chimney, the portrait of my grandmother Isabel; on the nightstand, a gift for Alice; on the bed, for Elvira, the portrait of me writing; to Maria Amélia, I gave my own room, which the others found natural in this environment of the house.

But, when I noticed she had found it difficult to climb the stairs and, at the top, had stopped gasping for breath, I thought of giving her the room next to the greenhouse for the night, since the heat during this month of July has been intense, and the sun was watching over us.

To Alice I would like to offer the chance to participate in the dazzle, and to Marguerite, the supreme degree to which I feel myself to be in love.

JODOIGNE, 6 AUGUST 1977,
The day I finished writing *The Remaining Life*

'74, the year of Portugal's political liberation, was spent in
Louvain. We only left for Jodoigne in April '75, although we had
already gotten the house ready during the entire month of
March. The house seemed large to me, the garden a vacant plot
in the middle of well-considered and weathered walls; at that
time, the gate was not yet a key in space, although I had the
prescience that coming to this house would give me a more
assured writing, made of the experience of the silenced and
other realities habitually abandoned, or unpenetrated. I do not
remember the first summer, it must have been an in-between
summer, although I had already planted Spirea and Prunus
Triloba, for my own peace of mind. I went to find them in
Flemish territory, in Tienen, and they grew with bursts of
tenderness and strength; with visionary intelligence my days
would lengthen, in dark nights and fruitful, almost endless
hours, hourless. But I am moving ahead of myself in time, which
has granted us the privilege of almost becoming eternity.

I search the memory of those summers to find an old book.
What book is it? One of the last, one of the first? The summer
stretches out in walks around the town, and does not rest in the
garden that is growing. The summer I came from Portugal was
an empty summer, not even one of expectation, or of the
slightest encounter. The house still belonged to its uninhabited
era, one might say. But then, the summer of '76 was one of
radiant heat, possessed by a dryness which vibrated in figures,
in my imaginary understanding. The floors became crowded,
shadows and beings descended to the gift they would give me

during a definitive portentous period. '77 was a year of only two months, those of the House of July and August. Not the house reduced to those two times thirty days, but the duration of those periods extended to the transcendence of time throughout the entire house.

Yesterday, Augusto came to my bedside and told me,
not knowing it would prolong this impulse
that I would eventually write about us,
that is to say, also with you,
and since our birth
in your time.

II.

A Falcon in My Wrist

Just as I am accompanied by lakes — natural and abiding dormant waters — so too should this diary be part of the shadow,
which moves with me,
inscribing the days stretched out over a long period of time.

The notion of night — a week, a month, a year of nights — should immediately be imposed upon its calendar. Without the calendar, the flow of time should seem immeasurable to it, and become an obstacle to the clear separation between the figures, who return at regular periods (perils), at the same point in the domed vault. While the months generally begin with the new moon, it will span eras in which there is no dream other than that of knowing, and all the books, boundaries, and indications of everyday life will seem to it small microcosms juxtaposed with the same end, or the same origin. That is why it is particularly important to have a calendar that steadies the environment, and gives protection to the House, which, with an abyssal meaning, could become the universe, and disappear.

The unrelenting phase of wanting nothing more than to look carefully, and read, spend day after day interrogating books, *The Poor in the Middle Ages, The Spanish Man*, in short, to make those who are less mute speak with time, and accomplish something which is desired. I beg them in the name of a power of language, knowing that this life, in which there are no minor days, is an art of narration _____ for the possible death of Jorge Anés at the stake is a thread that has a brilliant and serene hue, and unhurriedly sharpens my language.

I am confronting these days with the final period of my adolescence, when I was troubled by a mild fatigue disorder. Coming home from school, or on vacation, I had only enough strength left to read, motionless, adding to it the illicit pleasure of my own body. Under the sign of scarcity, I took pleasure and read and, becoming agitated, without violence, in this contradiction, I lay the foundations of writing.

The birth of Jorge Anés and Luis Comuns, from the doves taking flight in Praça Luis de Camões. The freedom to be able to *write* and *imprint* myself. Is writing not a protest of innocence?

Bend your language, articulate.

Bend your language, articulate.

JODOIGNE, 10 MAY 1979

It is my own house, but I feel as though I've come to pay a visit to someone.

It is hot, like summer in Portugal, but there are already shadows, and in the late afternoon the electricity builds up, like summer in Brabant; I relieve myself of literature, and move to the margin of language; I believe that Portugal is a land of travel, stellated, or with the arrangement of the stars, due to the itineraries of the Portuguese, fugitives, Jews, merchants, emigrants, or navigators; such is the family tree traced on the margins of Portuguese literature. The themes, circumscribed to the country bereft of its travel routes, are carceral themes, which reveal the mediocrity of societal relations, in general, and the normative development of a literature; or, it is the interrupted line of continuity of memories, interred in the sands of a celestial map; nearly hidden from the dominant literature, it fears the emergence of a field inundated with language, in which knowing oneself through language is a part of intimate loves.

Thunder; this is Brabant; I read, to console myself for having to pursue this path, several paragraphs from *In the House of July and August*, and I have the feeling that someone has made a work which has its foundation in itself, whose echo is only a new sequence of work; and so, knowing how the trees protect us, I live to write and listen and, today, I was one of the first readers of *In the House of July and August*; I was struck so deeply by the text that, having forgotten what I was going to say, that is, write next, I sat down on the green bench in the garden, next to Prunus Triloba, reflecting that I must stray from literature in order to narrate how I traversed language, longing to save myself through it.

Later on, night fell, and with it a concentration in an intensity that I never translated as darkness; the effects of the night are the House, the animals, Augusto, a bright and imagined understanding with them, unaltered. If it were day, I wouldn't be so happy

I am alive,

nor would I turn with equal acuity to the pendent work which is to follow.

I lay in bed for hours and hours, as though dead, but did not sleep, I saw myself as the outstretched space; from a distance came the memory of myself, in relation to the space, sitting on the stool I keep next to the kitchen table, tending to the eyes of Marfolho, a two-month-old cat. "Do you think he'll go blind? Or perhaps not?" was the question the space was asking me. But the only expanse from which some light still came to me was my field of work, with the gesture of dipping the cotton in the macela solution; I squeezed gently, watched the fragrant liquid drip off, and cautiously dabbed a few drops into the eyes of Marfolho, who didn't want to stay still for so long a time; the time I spent with the blue cloth, the macela used to make medicinal infusions, the white flowers, the glass cup, the beings in mortal peril.

The keenest feeling I have ever experienced, and one that often still strikes me,   is having nowhere to go, having been besieged by the desire to move unendingly; I remember that when I was growing up (1935–1940), confounded by the familial convention of childhood, I called myself "the captive doe"; here is the true nature of my spirit. I am a vast weight for those who are kind enough to keep me company and, if I have acquired and retained a knowledge of the art of writing, it was out of necessity, having discovered that writing and fear are incompatible.

I go on walks in the infinite vastness of the gardens (Loving
Cause, or The Birth of Ana de Peñalosa,
first title).

At night:
I think about Giordano Bruno, about who his mother might
have been. Where are you living now, Giordano, on what day?
Who was your mother? If she came to take refuge among us, we
wouldn't leave her on her own. We would play a kind of game
with her, but she would never suspect how you were killed. I
wanted to sing your praises, for I saw you approaching the
threshold of the world; who placed you on the threshold of the
flame, plumb in the flame, a man entire? She was always a thrice
radiant woman.

An exhibition of furniture made by Augusto, in the oblong room in the greenhouse, which was our first bedroom in Jodoigne. The room, with the window at the end, the black and white tiles, the furniture, their reciprocal relationship, were beautiful and enduring. Behind, in the uncultivated land, I did not forget the presence of the hens, the roosters, and the half-wild cats. It was a haphazard week, one of crisis, dispersion, replenishment, although I had no time to sort out my impressions, reflect, and write.

On the 10th, Sunday, I began to feel apprehensive that I hadn't yet received my mother's weekly letter; as I understand her, she would also have accepted motherhood for a cat, a horse, a swallow, but not an eagle, or another animal of prey. How will Marfolho's eye problem progress? The desire to possess the absolute power to make him live, to have his sight restored; he cannot see, his eyelids are stuck together, Laura, who gave birth to him, has no milk, and he was left alone and, even worse, alone and dependent; but I have become familiar with some of the signs of his species; Augusto tells me not to interfere, to be willing to let him pursue his fate: his abandonment.

While we were preparing the furniture exhibition, the garden emerged from its untamed disarray (came out of its liquid environment), without becoming a manifestation of the House; I myself had introduced a slightly dispersive inclination to it and, moving through it, you might say that all the plants, which were growing there, were free to roam to different parts; but, at present, it is possible to make out, in the white clover covering the center of the courtyard, the comings and goings of visitors.

Being a prisoner of a day of extreme brightness (Loving Cause, or *The Birth of Ana de Peñalosa*).

Seen over time, Lisbon is like no other; it is itself, without any obviousness; the Tagus River has died any number of times, and the city is powerless to restrain it; rivers sweep along with them the shape of the cities they span. It was in the unfurling of these tracings that the servant Engrácia appeared to me, waking up with a chill and closing the window to warm herself in the half-light. It is the introduction of Engrácia who, seeing me working with the needle, *immediately understands that transformations are the daily bread we lack, and that she is going to read what is written on the table, and revealed by the lamp we will put out, the vegetables she will bring from the garden, and prepare for lunch, with her, in the end, setting the right tone for the narrative sequence, and I going to the kitchen to take her light. I decide, at that Christmastime, to remove the g from god, and use od to refer to whatever difference robs him of his volition.*

She tells me, from the living room, that she would like to write in order to propel what I live; I reply, from the kitchen, that I have the desire to live in order to continue what she is writing. When I become aware of this loving relationship, I notice that a child, neither her own, nor my daughter, has joined us; she draws a bow and, according to Engrácia's narrative sequence, spurs her to write like this: the days of the night, and the days of the night. The three of us clearly conceive the days with the night, and the days with their night. Mindful of the reason, we share what has been brought to us: Engrácia remains with the writing, the child with   od, and I remain here.

185

What we experience, we put it into the dreams we make. I slept a single slumber, and had a dream:

I am in an electric streetcar, in Lisbon, and I gradually recognize the man sitting beside me; but his presence seems dead, or distant. In time, without any events that can be described, I, the man, and his wife, have become friends. I am glad I overcame my reluctance to form relationships, and to enjoy that conviviality. Also at the house on Rua Domingos Sequeira, they notice I often go out.

Then I am lying in bed, between the man and the woman; the man touches me, and the woman startles. I lean back against her, and ask her if she has children.

— I have three.

From the involuntary representation of the dream, I pass to *The Birth of Ana de Peñalosa*. That is, I plunge into a nebula compelled by an intention to decipher: "If I find a suitable optical instrument, I will eventually discover the composition of the nebula."

In my later dreams, there is a clearing, in Lisbon, the tutelary clearing; this circle, where a lamp is planted, or a tree, or a thunderbolt, witnesses the dream. Augusto and I always walk around that sign, understanding that the fog which surrounds us is the navigation of River-Tagus. No longer, for us, will it have a winding shape, typical of a river. It has become a potential narration of the world.

As in a waking dream, I feel as though the meaning of the first dream is revealed to me:

I am between life and death, in what Augusto calls the *entresser*, the *interbeing*. The wife is my protective figure, and the husband represents death. They feel the time has come to continue to keep me alive, with a living voice. Behind us, in the center of us, is inscribed the deep dilation of the book, in which we are three, Augusto, me, and the book itself, which Tagus-River shepherds, or guides.

This book for me is a plummet, a source of light situated above; wherever I am, whatever I do, I always see myself falling, ebbing, pages closed and open.

We were the same age, and I often looked at her from my seat during class. She had a kind of factotum, named Amália; today, it makes me think about the origin, and the nature of affections, and I envision, whether they are appropriate for us or not, the definitions offered by Spinoza.

She made me feel astonishment, joy, envy, sorrow, and, finally, pride, which is "for love's sake, rating ourselves too highly."

She was a knowing-girl. Even her face, and her silhouette, knew what beauty was; she could hear herself read, she bent the Portuguese language with the knowledge of another language, she drew with the precision of those who write. I had, more than anything, an ill-fated desire to possess such an understanding of the sciences, or a memory of events. But writing, or reflecting on what I had read, was insipid.

When I looked at my fellow student, I was forcibly aware of my ambiguous relationship to knowledge, and my avarice for writing.

If the spirit was the body where it was ...

I need an eye operation. The windows are behind me, and I am seated; the doctor is a tall old man; thin; wearing glasses; he explains how he is going to proceed to a person who has just come in. I stop him from continuing the explanation: — I am not an object.

The ophthalmologist's nurse is a child of about ten. She places two cotton pads over my eyes, and I know the operation is about to commence. I feel no distress. I am not worried. When the operation is underway, a woman who could be the one from yesterday's dream comes in and, bending over me, begins to read a text. I wake up seeing, in the tutelary clearing; I tell Augusto, who is scattered everywhere, that I was put to sleep and awakened with no difficulty.

Will this dream respond to the question
"Will I achieve eternal life?" I would rather, to draw my interlocutor (?) closer, say, "Will we achieve eternal life?"

How these words seduce me
backstreets, eaves, copses, foyers, alleyways, staircases, levels,
easements, courtyards; a single Rossio — the Chafariz de Dentro; a
single avenue — Remédios; a single monument — the Torre de São
Pedro; shutters, corners, edges, gravestones, acronyms, railings,
forgotten portals.

This could have been one of the beginnings of *From Hedge
to Being*

but

I do not know a word, spitfire, and I am left to conjecture about
its meaning; these are the atoms of the text, and I am in concert
with them.

In this atmosphere emerges Lisbon, the companion, riven
by other possibilities of existence. Atmosphere is the weight of
a cylindrical column of mercury.

This time, the river closely studies the city, divides it into more
terms, and segments _____ sturdy stone benches, records of
tiles, loose stones, remnants of walls, and a writer who eventually
wanders away. His voluble figure is burdened with the obscurity of
language, and the woman he lost by becoming great; Marguerite's
volition climbs the mast of a ship moored in the river,
and the other caravels, which surrounded him, turn back, to their
place of origin. Marguerite, ever ascending in sacrifice, finally
presents her son, Lord Luis M., to the stars. The stars, turned toward
the polychrome hills and taverns of the city, tell her, in the hollow of
a staircase, that he is kin to the sea. — No, he is kin to the text —
corrects Marguerite, crucified on the highest mast of the ship, which
soon trimmed its sails, and entered a garden as a port. Surrounding

that garden was a squalid townhouse, which now replaced the old palace which had stood there, and had been the university attended by Luis M. His mother, Marguerite, knew how he had been bound by the first word he had ever uttered — detritus — and to which she had added, in the days when she had still taught him — detritus of writing. He liked to utter detritus of shutters, detritus of corners, detritus of eaves, detritus of gravestones, detritus of acronyms, detritus of railings, detritus of forgotten portals, detritus of all variable terms. At this School, which was not secret, and was only open during the day, Luis M. had imperceptibly become the wielder of his mother's text, and the wanderer who passed through the narrow streets of the city of Lisbon. Having known that good and evil had moved away from one another until they had abandoned the struggle, he and his mother began to try to teach heaven to bring down from the bells of the Sé Cathedral and São Vicente a city without its weight and decay. A city Luis M. carried on the tip of his tongue, and jealously guarded under his cloak, for fear it would be ruined by someone less generous than he. He macerated the acronyms in a liquid — water from the Tagus, or the Meuse, or the Euphrates, and formed curves over the wall with his loose abbreviations, rather than going around it. He wanted to surpass his mother, and his mother wanted to surpass him. From certain heights of the city, they both sought stratagems, but with scruples. What did they talk about? Where did their family relations, corrupted by rivalry, founder? And had the umbilical cord that united them ever existed?

How many times?

Under what sign?

Expressed in which human route?

They often spat on the ground on the night they parted, but the spit did not metamorphose into loud, ringing voices. Luis M.

climbed the staircases, and fell asleep for a moment upon the reflections of the river, convinced it was necessary to be orphaned in order to savor life. His mother, who was in exile, would throw pebbles of experience at him from the top of the masts, so that he would leave for the inmost part of the city, and exalt it. The city, however, had no inmost part, except for a few doors, and a river. Luis M. covered himself in ink. In his dreams, Alfama was teeming with people, and the Beco da Mosca runs through a boundary in his spirit. He thought of Spinoza, and of the reverberations of his own city, particularly the aspects of the primitive part. He tallied up the number of his contemplations, and found himself at the beginning of the same dream, in which his mother was already traveling. He sensed his writerly figure, and did not know what it was, and why such sinister thoughts would not leave him alone. They were the thoughts of a child, not a man. And his mother was already gone. He must not turn back. Not even to the shadow. Marguerite was leaving at the mast of the caravel, and a coin was rolling toward him, or else a whirlwind of gold. It was not the coin of the city, it was his mother's final coin coming to him. He crossed the amphitheater, and traveled through Lisbon until several troublemakers, who had dragged him into a fight, stabbed him in the morning.

They had stabbed him without grave injury, in the place where the coin protected him. The mark stamped on the alloy made it unmistakable, and Luis M. decided he would never trade it. It was a bezant, a heavy Byzantine coin, minted at the height of the empire. After he had pressed it against his wound to prevent his blood from flowing freely, he saw that the waist-deep river was a desert and that a breeze was indicating the place where he should go. The coin had stuck to his chest, and he felt unsettled by the sudden existence of two hearts that would always have the other's cadence. The bleeding had stopped, but his lower lip was also bruised. After the moment when he knew where to go, he felt unsettled by the vastness of the city, which was a sign of weakness. But on closer inspection, the city was not vast, it was unknown, and that was not the Tagus River, it was another river flowing through another river city, in which every reference was absent. A thought came to him following a different thought, and it was cold, when the season in the city that had been transformed was summer. Between summer and winter was the lacuna of autumn, and he began to run through the array of autumnal words, light, swift, joyful. Which swiftly led him to the idea of death, which lay hidden, fearful, behind that constant progression of thinking which had cleansed the city of its persistent foul taste.

Yesterday, I was truly unsettled by the Brontës' secret society. The nursemaid, the dog Keeper, the hermitage, the game of writings that belonged to the environment and, from a distance, the perspective of my gaze, examining them with admiration and compassion; the hermitage is a painting consonant with certain natures, and there is in it a practice of a conscious non-distinction of worlds; I wanted to begin speaking of the poor, and I will eventually find an apt portrayal of them beyond;

for now, an immense thickness intercepts my view; I only sense Emily Dickinson has just arrived, without being an intruder, at the Brontës' hermitage; yet another enigmatic face which has chosen me, and the frame of the new painting forms around us, like a hedge in a garden. Outside. Or within. The poor. In Europe, there were places without inhabitants, but,

as long as, in one of those places, there was a single being with a ritual of life and thought,   a hermitage,   it became especially perilous for civilizations.

This text could continue like this:

I mentioned the Brontës to Juan, and he was seduced; in that secret society, Juan found a seducer, and now, during our journey, not only by sea, he is incessantly asking me questions; I, not being Psalmody, the oracle, do not want to deprive him of one of the most familiar episodes of our journey, and I promised to transcribe, only for him, my own personal use of the world.

Juan loves me, and I draw his attention to those beings, those women he can only attract through other avenues of sensuality; Juan,

like Doctor Faustus, and if he believed in the two distinct persons
within man,
Body,
Soul,
for that knowledge, he would be willing to exchange
the latter.

    Inside her house, her orchard, we see Emily
Dickinson,   who will be someone here,   in an only
apparent stillness; she crafts one verse, then another.

              The Soul selects her own Society _____
              Then _____ shuts the Door _____

    She sits down, stands up, an idea gleams before her, behind us,
and so she ties her apron and, climbing up a ladder, picks the fruit of
the orchard, which, if only one more day were to pass, would fall
tomorrow in the shade of the tree; for her, the brightness is slow, and
the house analogous to the hermitage.

    Her body is empty of pleasure: pleasure enfolds her; when she
plies poetry, there is a kind of nimbus around her; meters and meters
of unwritten cloth separate her from Juan,
which I soon tell him.

    At this moment, we leave her behind,
without losing sight of her in the far reaches of Connecticut; the
woman who is sitting in front of her, her head yet covered, is
Marguerite.

I have continued this text with the feeling of the profuse posterity of the beguines.

Her arrival was no accident; she received a letter from Anne, from Emily, from Charlotte, from Branwell, asking her to confirm them in the Bestiary; even today, there is a constellation in which the different layers of the presbytery have become luminous expression,
through writing; she went in, uncertain whether the children would know any more than she did, and found, in the place in the house that was the most difficult to access,
authors, printers, publishers, and even a counter where books were sold; there were, for each of these occupations, separate spaces, and Charlotte was rhythmically intoning the episodes that Branwell would conceive in writing; Marguerite saw, occupying the entire floor of the room, the painting with Branwell's portrait of the four, still lacking any sign, which she would later recognize, of having been folded like a single sheet of paper;
she devoted herself, with them, to the composition of the miniature novel: the copy in legible handwriting, the cutting of the pages, the stitching on the spine;
never,
at the Plantin-Moretus printing house, had she felt an emotion similar to being there with those children, who were not precocious, but sudden.
When she looked at them, she looked at herself, until she was run through by Ursula, Ana de Peñalosa, and all the vivid reflections the afternoon brought; in the printing house, meaning was constructed with signs of flowers, leaves, stones, threads, and the stroke of the pen, beyond, covered Branwell's voice,
with the rite of writing; on either side of Charlotte, who was

printing, Emily and Anne held a candle in their hands, and counted the drops of wax that fell on the floor.

I prepared this text with them at my house in Jodoigne, and gave Branwell a drink when he fell silent; when his voice fell silent in fragments of silence,
Emily,
if she so desired,
could put out one of the candles; I had never seen anything like it, I felt my chest constrict as if I lacked air, or a shawl to cover me; they resurrected the dead and, having attained the form of expression proper to a being,
played a game involving who each of them was, including Keeper, whom I call Jade;
surely, these children had been born dead, or immortal.

They already knew almost nothing remained of the writings mentioned by Emily and Anne in their diaries; this ritual of the room where no one else could go, except Keeper, is *the luminous scene*, or the ring, which remained of them; I concluded,   but dared not tell them, that it was necessary to find a common exorcism for the truth of the imagination;

when the time came, on one of the following days, for me to express myself in front of all of them, I did not find, in the end, my own words, but those of a litany by Buddha:

"Even if I wanted
— O monks —
to explain to you,
in different ways
the subject of animality,

197

I could not
express, with words
— O monks —
the depth
of our suffering, and that of the animals."

I then turned to Emily Dickinson — speaking is not
inevitable; she worked without speaking and, by the end of the
day, they had almost forgotten she existed; all that could be
seen, without any roots, was the outcome of her work.

He felt the breeze was guiding him outside the walls, but after a few wanderings, he was surprised by the symmetry of an even gentler breeze, blowing from an ashlar; on that stone, which went halfway up the wall of a building, the day had begun to dawn and, among the decorative tracings, it was written that the records of noluble families were kept in that chest; because it was morning, or for some other reason, there was, for the time being, no living soul, and all the details, in those circumstances, depicted those absent from the city; perhaps because of the weakness caused by the blow, however slight, or because he felt a sense of delight, walking along a deserted sidewalk;

he felt the need to calm himself and reflect near a well, and dip his handkerchief in the water to wash his bezant, his hair, his skin, and his wound. He then had a city to observe, which at that moment, was deserted, with human traces whose footprints he was loath to follow. Beyond a full-length doorway leading to a carriage yard, with galleries supporting the second floor, he began to recognize, in the warmth of the night that had fallen unexpectedly, such a covert coolness that he told himself he would be willing to wander through uneven terrain and narrow paths if, as he suspected, there was a well there; indeed, sheltered by a vaulted dome, there was a wide-mouthed well, which had once publicly supplied the city with water, with the sign of worn-out ropes, and from which evaporated, cooling the air, the dampness that had drawn him.

Without knowing whether the water from the well was drinkable, or whether he had any way to reach it, he let himself be carried away by the delight of,
on his own,
being able to irrigate his thinking and the vegetation which covered

the place where Lisbon had once been.

The water, which he had grown accustomed to hearing murmur, indicated that a band of the poor would, at the height of the heat, sweep through the city from one end to the other, removing the coats of arms, causing the genealogy books to disappear, destroying the evidence of the granting of tenures, pensions, and positions in front of the Paço Real.

    — A dream, a dream — replied Luis M. — And if I had a fever, not the one caused by my injury, but the one I developed as a result of what I was intended to do. — The well was causing him to lose his strength, with its deep, damp breath; he leaned over it, as if to suck the water from its mouth.

    I interrupt the text here because it is sliding into metaphor. I wanted to unravel the knot in Portuguese literature that binds water and its greatest texts. But that knot is very strong, a paradigm which cannot be assailed directly.

Surrounded by hedgerows, and a fence, there is a plot of
land in front of the House, onto which the outbuildings open,
where animals, including horses, once lived. In one of the
corners, there is still a muzzle — esparto woven to prevent
feeding, or suckling. I spent many moments between the inside
and the outside, and when June arrived, submerged in that
place, which showed me a corner of nature regenerating in the
midst of the city, I kept, to myself, the certainty that the green
which involves, or enfolds, all the green, cannot be named. That
part was a part where I rarely went, and I sometimes used to
speculate that on the other side of the fence, there was also
someone with similar inclinations. Small domestic animals were
raised there, and only died natural deaths, without ever
experiencing the slightest violence. Only the thistles were
uprooted, as their seeds would proliferate in the neighboring
crops. The nettles remained, and I gathered them to make soup,
with the sensation that my garden was spontaneously tending
me. I remember one day, with a light rare in Belgium, I sat down
on the floor to pretend to sew, facing the open stable doors. As I
didn't have a wristwatch, and needed to know what time it was
in order to return to the front of the House, where I lived, I had
brought an alarm clock with me. To stop myself from hearing it,
I covered it with my clothes, while it marked the time of my
insistent desire to observe, and to meditate. I myself scarcely
moved, so that the animals who were sheltering here would
deem my body to be as absent of danger as possible; I simply
put the sewing box away, out of sheer pleasure, and slowly
recalled all the details I saw.

(On the way to Portugal)

If I had to return from voluntary exile, writes the girl who
feared the imposture of language, *to live outside these nocturnal
wanderings, these inventions suspected of truth, the surprising
friendship of Engrácia, the dictionaries of John of the Cross,
which he shares with me,
I would again step through the fence,
enclosing the small houses,
where, with strength greater than themselves, and longing to enter
the first ascesis, my sisters live.*
    *Yet I always hear their voices; when I lie in bed, the night
speaks to me sincerely, as if arriving effortlessly from the other shore;
I imagine that, in some and other rooms with closed doors, living
alongside expectation takes on the image of dust, or keen forms of
study. We yearned to, in the worst of circumstances, be possessed
anew by our families, our homes with no way out. To give each other
courage, we confess, in a loud voice heard from room to room, that
we are afraid of time, of having to pass through it in its everyday
retreats. Blanche tells all of them that when she reaches old age, she
will no longer want to travel to her country, for fear of the shock of
her mother's physical decay. We began, on those nights I describe, to
have the same kind of dream,
in which John of the Cross says
that the propitiatory texts
we write
give us light.   If only Luis M., or John of the Cross, could also
shoulder their shadow,
without ancestors,
or descendants.*

In truth, they lived off a milk that was too acidic. Off animal humanities. Off movements of species. Off anxieties that left them perplexed. Off staircases constructed through the centuries. Off everything they made life and their instruments of work. It is these sources which define them as authors — those who were always placed at the beginning. There must have been days when they were only pessimism, sluggishness, an absence of volition.

It is painful on the ebb of the cycle, when we long to go out, to travel by train, boat, or car, not to coalesce with beings, even in a gold alloy. As my sister says, our mother vanishes in a distance of connections; the joy that once uplifted us fades away; I am indecisive, and observe that today I am working with emotions, but do not become emotional.

I am reading an author, I reflect on the opulence of his compulsive language. Language, in him, is not an instrument of work, it is the work fatally undertaken, circumscribed to the language that possesses him. As such, in the areas of his books, the more he narrows the thematic scope, the greater, and thicker, is their development. I feel as though I have meticulous diaries in front of me, which someone has written in the third person, for others. And I wonder how certain human groupings, in their manor houses, farmhouses, and fields, would have existed with any significance if there had not been those ways of saying, of naming. I thus reflect, for my own purposes, that those who write have different areas of language, with openings that enable their reciprocal interpenetration. Otherwise, there would be nothing more than the reenactment, insignificant, of an old age. To write is to magnify, by degrees.

I have returned to the desire for stillness, for not taking part in anything that jeopardizes the body; when I think of Portugal, as I do now, a veil of words is immediately formed, from which is born the southern coast, the undulating space of *The Birth of Ana de Peñalosa*, with its mysteries and realisms as yet undescribed, which protect me from incompleteness; with it, I contemplate the done and the as yet undone; I attempt to grasp faces, attitudes, places of intimacy — their presence pervaded by John of the Cross's conversation. It is in the differences, and in the similarities, in the experience which also causes me to suffer, that I seek counsel for establishing a narrative which is a struggle.

I often think: "And if Vasco da Gama had not returned…"

I write a text which I am not going to use:

I receive a request from my father. Sealed. Although he has been careful to include a sender, I find he is always out of my reach, for his addresses are multiple. It leaves me perplexed, as if I were the daughter of several men who will never decide to make themselves known. In one corner of the letter was written: Come and see me. In one corner of the letter was also signed your threefold father who beseeches you.

Herbais: the island for which we were bound had been
stricken from the map; unless the place where we found
ourselves, unfurling from the steady meadows, led us to it.

The days are not what they were; we had never imagined it
would be necessary to rely so heavily on writing:

> "If you push far enough in language, you find
> yourself caught in the embrace of thought."

The loss of the sea for the sand is inevitable; from the
candle that burns to the page that breathes, her face always
remained latent; and any object was always being surrounded
by her.

Augusto and I sit down on the plank bench in the Garden; this is the moment when The One appears in the book. We speak about the geometric modes of intelligence which are produced in this place cultivated by me, and on which I collaborate with the untamed nature. We speak about the conceptual penchant of certain trees, for we believe there are trees that act mentally. Thought is not reasoning, it is a clutch of reflections, feelings, visions, which intertwine and open up a path to this place.

— Is there anyone who doesn't like this garden?
— Anyone who doesn't have this thought.

The garden in Herbais causes my back to ache. After only a few hours of work, I can barely move. But plants are just as necessary to me as empty spaces. Empty spaces are also plants. The part of understanding that remains unknown?

A day of crisis is a day when I lose the memory of our
cosmogony; crisis is the peak of a mountain, in a period of
unyielding cloudiness,
because there is not even a division of days; it is almost always
the prelude to a great serenity, the word-garden, and an ending.

Today I began a work of syncretism with *The Lusiads*; there
is a shoal — so many years as a commonplace of collective
admiration; I spoke with Augusto and, as ever, he tries to help
me reach the serene part of the crisis, and suggests a plan for
gathering my intuitions from *The Lusiads*.

Last night, always captive to this distant village of Herbais,
where the initiative to live must belong to us entirely, I turned
to the light of *The Book of Communities*. It was a book which,
written by me, soon revealed that it was now my reading. It is
now a published book which I myself could read in book form.
This certainty is enough to be able to reach the slope of danger
called serenity; immediately, as yet unpublished books
stretched out all around,
like the finite remains of my life and symptoms of its meaning.
All this is FACT,   and I myself was left perplexed by the
fight waged between the known and the unknown.

This early morning dream performs an abstraction, even of a line. I dream that I am in my parents' house, my grandparents' house, my great-grandparents' house, and that Grandmother Maria has become tiny and shriveled, as if she had been drained of all her water, and has died. I must return to Alpedrinha, which is next to Herbais. So that I do not make the train journey on my own, my mothers, in a single cloud, accompany me. It is the cloud that purchases the train ticket, and handles all the problems along the way. We arrive in Alpedrinha in cloudy weather, inside the house, which is a single room, there is the same fog, and the living calm of the outdoors. I pick up the telephone and, on the other end of the line, there is a female voice which has always been well informed about what was happening in my family. I tell her Grandmother Maria has died. The cloud and I leave for the countryside, and I never stop looking up at the Gardunha Mountains, which have no end. It is not through any of my senses that I know that, from the top to the bottom of its flow, water is bubbling.

Since we have no personal means of transport, and a bus only passes by once a week, Herbais is, most of all and secretly, a source of autonomy. Seen from the outside, our life may appear monotonous, but in this place, and amidst the parameters of time, and the pastures, with the woods in the distance, volition, cultivated by reflection and imagination, has become more capable of opening up other perspectives. Yesterday, at dusk, we went out to the edge of a wheat field, up a hill, and the eight cats who live with us came along. They chase after us as soon as we open the gate, we have, all of us, relationships on this outing, and during this time of the afternoon.

Today, I am sad because hours of fleeting sorrow are inseparable from Herbais. I waxed the floor of Augusto's room, made the bed, left the window open, and sat down at the head of one of my work tables. The summer, which is so dreary here, leaves me nearly inert, and I suppose I should express my unceasing desire by embracing the reopening of the world, which is now underway.

My body flees from us, and it seems as though, alone, I am traveling down a river, and making a careful examination of its bed. This was not, however, the faithful beginning of my thoughts today. I should also have said that my body flees from me, and that, one or the other, they slip, unprotected, into a work; no one can interfere; I should also have said   that I am undergoing the test of a cosmogony, and that I read, passionately, texts from the medieval world. At the same time, I converge on Spinoza.

Middle Ages:
When to read a text was to comment on it... the idea that a text is meant to be put to good use causes me to evoke my own body, and the sensuality of understanding. Abelard offered the following advice: "Learn for a long time, teach later on, and only what you deem worthwhile. As for writing, do not hasten."
Am I at the point when I stray in order to delve further into the confusion of an experience, of carnal pleasure? I do not realize that, like the *lectio*, I am a free being, loosed in dependence, and in obscurity.

I rose before the light (early),
enfolded by the question   how to be among the people of
my blood. I place no importance on the fact that I once lived
with other people, in the same house, that I once lived familially
with someone. It is nine o'clock in the morning, but I still feel
the effects of the early hours. I pulled away from the movement
of Augusto, my mother, my sister, who are awaking and,
drinking coffee and eating slices of buttered bread at the kitchen
table, I attempt to grasp my feelings and ideas, to discern their
hidden place in the invocation of the labyrinth. The crowing of
the rooster, Jade's urine on the wall, the cats of different ages
around the plate, and the jackal that sets me spinning, deep
inside myself, and howls at my serenity. I do not recognize
myself solely as a woman, but as a ring, with several wounds.
Basking in the light that rises in the kitchen, and falls,
thickening, from the multicolored flag on the front door, I turn
to Spinoza, to subdue my jackal with his geometry; another
passion, another moment of hate, another hesitation, another
insight which turns into a subtle thread of power, another
instant of fear, behold the day. And the sign the dawn is fading,
shattering into its elements, and vestiges. However dreary the
days may be, the company of Spinoza never lets me linger too
long without earth, air, and fire.
Trawler.
First light.
Insufflator.

The first light which appears at the top of the door with the
other words belongs to my genesis, and thrust me out of the

country with a single language; it is necessary to give different understandings to the language gathered in a whole, which has but one corolla.

My country is not my language, but I will take it with me to the one I encounter.

Today, after the sun rose, I continued the day with the dreariest part of me; my memories, present, past, and future, were unloosed upon me, and I could not find a clear path between them.

It is not only important to write *successively*, but to know who will succeed me in a constellation of meanings.

What are descendants?

The sap rises and falls in a tree, spreads through the branches, and is regulated by the seasons, the tree and I are prepared for one another, in a place as yet unnamed. This place has no dictionary meaning, it has not transmigrated into any book.

Now the sun, the soil, in a single voice, bind me in words. As the sun rose, I moved closer to the certainty that the text was a being.

This month of August is causing me to remember, now in the past, *In the House of July and August*. Yesterday, we went to Brussels, on an outing, and the understanding with my mother and sister proceeded unhindered.

In the early hours, I was attempting to determine the extent to which female restlessness, which pulsates with trivialities and details, constitutes a potential faculty of the spirit. A kind of consuming of reality which could conceivably precede the use of reason and desire. The use of desire seems preferable to the use of power. If I desire to write, it is to seize the signs of life as it metamorphoses into power; to reinforce existence with the landscape of its disappearance, to turn it into a book awaiting another freedom, or simply, a desirous reading.

Just under a year ago, following my return from Portugal, one snowy winter day in Belgium, I was reading Virginia Woolf — *A Room of One's Own*. Through the snow and, without knowing why, beyond it, I also felt like a wolf. All the cubs of a wolf that was following me had perished, some from violent death, others from abandonment. The rush across the landscape was far too swift for them.

A very painful end of the month. Always the same nostalgia and the feeling of things already seen. The Convento dos Capuchos, a beach, Lisbon, should be *next to Herbais*.

In September, prior to my departure for Portugal, a splendorous string of days, in which I let myself indulge in sewing, the text, the animals, the garden.

I am in the garden of Prunus Triloba, in the heart of its own land, and because I am thinking, I run my eyes over the herbs, the garden opposite, that is to say, the garden of *The One*, which he is cultivating in front of me. When the *old man* gave me an armful of plants yesterday to put in my garden, I suddenly became aware he was *The One* from the book, in short, the only *The One*. I say the Old Man as the prophetess would say the king, or the wretch.

Of late, the idea of the poor has taken hold of me. Working on my Diary, there are times when an extensive series of journeys *From Hedge to Being* seeps into it, or emerges from it; these journeys are made by bands of poor men, mobs, by groups of people who do not cultivate any preconceived idea of themselves, or do not use any perfectible or wandering idea to disguise who they are. They roam the streets, or certain places, to maintain the order, scarcely known, of the journey; and I feel as though the very point of being a human is called into question.

The garden of *The One* is a better tended garden than my own, an expression of a certain human civilization, in which everything is part of the need for a framework, even an alternative framework for wealth, or poverty. *The One* tends this garden, but he always comes up to its edges, where he gazes at my own. How *The One* became the owner and gardener of such a restrictive garden is an enigma. He lives with two women, his wife and his sister, who care for the contents of the house, the kitchen, and the affective life. Several times, over the past few days, I have attempted to identify the geometric figures of my garden through the colors, the arrangements of plants, the shadows, and the shifting brightnesses. During this month of September, Herbais has become truly summery, a displaced Lusitanian region. I do not regard Portugal as the absolute country of the Portuguese, nor do I want this garden to be solely the realm of the word. It is the realm of everything, it became warmer today than I expected.

Errant intimacy with the day.   I spend it in the
garden of Prunus Triloba, in the shade of the central shrub,
which is the most mature. The plant, at its base, has become
strong, and I grasp on to that woody part. I observe the square
of the future trees, and the others, smaller in size than the trees;
in front of me, in the garden of *The One*, a knot of walnut trees
makes the view, which is of hills, and the straight line of the
plain, less stark; I reflect that, today, I am supposed to go to
Portugal, that I will return at the end of the month, and that,
not long after, winter will come, passing quickly through
autumn. I think about *From Hedge to Being* and, living with this
book, about my *Diary*.

I observe that, in the distance, the tree is a book which has
arranged its leaves on the branches in such a way that none can
evade the Sun; there is such an incandescence in the sun that
lowers, and is hidden, that I can scarcely concentrate always on
the same green place. The distance is my journey, and in the
vastness of the sky, I fear I will find no sea voyage to guide me.

There was a dead animal at the edge of a ravine, which I mistook for a mound of earth. But a trickle of blood, and the stiff form of a quadruped, undeceived me. From death to life passed a malleable form, a gleaming fur, and a dense gaze, and I stopped, hesitating as to whether it was my young cat, *Melodia*, or rather the unknown cat, a universal shadow of a cat. As burying it would be offering the refuge of unknowingness to ephemeral shadows, I moved it to a better place, and dug a grave: if it were my cat, Melodia, I would not hear her again. Although I knew the passage, in that *luminous scene*, was from life to death, rather than the other way around, I began to gather pebbles in my hands, lending them the significance of loving memories. I rose to follow my description of the journey with two images: that of an animal returning to me, and that

of a thing,

derisory

form

shaped

by

an outline

of a living

being,

or with the distant appearance of a living being, as it had moved away from life to an uncertain part.

This is why the dead, for us, are vagabonds, and with this form we associate with them, hoping they will pass far from our door.

Literature does not exist. When you are writing, all you need to know is which reality you are entering, and whether or not there is a technique that can open up a path for others.

Today I dreamed that, on the windows of the remembered house in Jodoigne, flyers had been posted with news of a revolt that would resurrect the city. At the entrance to the gate were hanged men, and they were unable to explain the chaos. I do not lock myself inside the house, and go down to the street that is nearly deserted. During the night, I was not aware, but only learned later, that a band of women and widows, prisoners and soldiers, passed through the city, and is preparing to return for some nights yet. The hanged men they left in different places are not members of the clergy, and monks, they are their own selves. And they are pseudo-hanged men because, in truth, they were already dead and, if they put them in that position, it is out of one of those gestures of madness which the sedentary usually ascribe to pilgrims.

I do not know whether to bury the dead, or leave them as proof of rights. But if they were already dead in and of themselves, what slumbering sign do they represent in the city?

There is one I recognize.

If only I were able to reflect with absolute honesty, I would be able to guess the purpose for which this poor man had been hung. There had been a wedding and we, carrying his plate, watched patiently as he was given food, seated, with others, on the floor. He had been as lonely because of his meekness, in the midst of the throng, as I was when the truth departed.

Ana de Peñalosa
    says
she is leaving this house behind
for the strongbox of "needfuls,"
the name of these men on the road,
in her mouth. Who is a pauper? No one should consider
themselves
obliged to pray for her soul,
for a soul
she does not have,
nor do they know where to imagine it.

I long to return to the abiding shore of the sea.

When I was five years old, I used to instantly fixate on certain melodies. One of them, from a collection of texts for the first years of secondary school (1936), which my sister read aloud to me, said: "Once upon a time, there was a Moorish king / lord of a boundless land / whose greatest treasure / was a beautiful princess. / The princess was from the North / from the land of frozen earth / and was on the verge of death / simply because she could not see the snow. / The king came to save her / crossing entire lands / and decided to plant / a field of almond trees. / What a beautiful flower, and so delicate / the entire earth opens into bloom. / Then the princess exclaims: / — Snow, sweet miracle of love."

But, from the anguish of tonight, which ushers in another day of rain, there was only one account and final product: *a narrative — Tales of Wandering Evil.*

They live in Sintra, in a house by the side of the road, and the town is close. When she walks alone, or with Copernicus   on the road, there may be moments when she stands between the house, protected from behind by a thick wall, and a dense tree, with open branches, which nearly grazes the ground and casts a shadow on my dwelling, without ever touching it. This dwelling is hers, for after spending eighteen years learning a strange language, she abandoned the royalty into which she had been born, and settled there with the bezant, who made the walls, created space around the house, and protected an infinite number of cacti and trees.

Because, in reality, nothing disappointed me, but in the impasses of my powerlessness, I spent, more than anything, too much time.

It is early in the morning, which is why I am writing. *Having encountered so many beings, she was now yearning to choose her own, on the way back from her pilgrimage to this house.* What I have learned is that there are no absolute beings, and that the world is bounded by the walls that await us.

The desire was so overwhelming that I accepted her as a figure. Her name is Isabel, and her husband's name is Dinis. I live with her at a distance, and we never wander together, but at different times of the day. We do not strengthen our friendship, so as not to disrupt her nascent relationship with Copernicus. My first happiness here was thus to share my mansion (which is enormous), with someone who has always inhabited it.

Musil just passed by on one of the three streets in Herbais; his face is not very clear, it wavers between the only two portraits I have seen of him — one from when he was very young, the other from much later.

Musil's presence in Herbais, a place that is not the center of any culturally created world, and which in the learned eyes of many people must be considered a non-place, is one of the compensations I have received for the death of my cat Blanche, who was also not an animal who would allow herself to be tamed by the images of knowledge which run through natural history.

So Musil is in Herbais, and Blanche has disappeared in my Garden, in plain sight. It is morning, and it is simple modifications of this kind that embolden the desire to write. Musil and I are interested in the thinking that unfolds and is arrested in writing; we have abandoned literature as commerce, at this intersection of meadows where we encountered one another by a fortuitous circumstance — the death of Blanche.

I show Musil the stretch of land where She rests, a no man's land between my garden and the nearby meadow. It is a paradoxical joy, for as we move toward the key points of our encounter, my nostalgia for the absent figure grows, and howls interrupt the silence we were using to keep us from being alone; Musil's keen gaze does not know Blanche, but he believes my face; he now leads the way, and someone else who did not have his measure would think I am leading him on a journey far too long for such a small garden. Everything there was recently planted, and our shadows are the tallest, against the meadows and the path that surround us. We are bound by the acquiescence that striving to write is not the same as squandering words in a void. I do not know whether my house, with my marks, pleases my guest, and I show him the spaces I prefer, to keep him from treading on them. Yet we should not mutually dread the vertigos of resonance. As a result of this alliance, Herbais will always remain oblivious to the calculations which govern the known world.

— Why not compare yourself to a piece of cloth? — said Musil. — Sometimes I am a thick piece of cloth, other times a medium-thick one, and there is no end to the nuances of thickness. Today, having come here, I am a diaphanous piece of cloth.

At this moment, I venture to abruptly tell him:

— In the early hours of the 6th, I struggled, swallowed up by a desire for absolute death. And either I sensed the death of Blanche the following morning, or she hid my own death within herself.

What more is there to say, for today?

541.   The bands of the poor, their journey as yet unbounded, are the raw material for the development of *From Hedge to Being*; I do not know, following my return from Portugal, whether I no longer possess the book, or whether the revelation of the being is in other hands.

Today, I have decided to divide this Diary not by years and days, but also by numbers; it is not the first time my own life has struck me as strange, or belonging to the outside world: a diary can be more objective than a personal life. An adjective which makes me think of Pessoa, and of a morning when I was searching the Imprensa Nacional bookshops for his photobiography, which would only be on sale during the month of October; I was not looking for Pessoa for any personal reason, it was for a reason that appeared independently of myself, and which made me endeavor to find images of his body, and the atmosphere of the time that had feared him. It was necessary to prove, first, that he had been expendable; second, that he had existed. But not having glimpsed it anywhere, and continuing to feel as though the same urge was present, without, however, being part of me, I opened *The Keeper of Sheep* and was all the more alone, for I could not follow him, neither in that city, nor in the light of the public seduction which had taken hold of him. I then withdrew to a corner where there was a row of thick volumes, published by the Institute for High Culture, and picked up two of them: *Poverty and the Care of the Poor on the Iberian Peninsula during the Middle Ages, First Luso-Hispanic Conference on Medieval History*. I brought them back to Herbais, and during the first few days, when I could so easily remember certain places, particularly Sintra, I read a paper (a short commentary) on Queen Isabel and poverty, and began a text, which I thought was going to become autonomous: The Name.

They live in Sintra, in a house by the side of the road, and the town is close; this dwelling is mine, as after spending eighteen years as an itinerant, learning the shadow of a language, I abandoned the band that brought me; behind it, almost amidst the clouds, is the Castelo dos Mouros, but I have entered a phase of my life in which I prefer to look at it from here, rather than climb up to it.

After that, a more fervent inclination to write the text about the figures, which I usually divide into books, and to write the Diary, with the desire that, between the two, there would be only a single step. Then the idea to name a book *Tales*, which would only capture a second meaning of tales, however clear. Wandering Tales in my Language became, as the substrate of my affections, *Tales of Wandering Evil*. I was with Spinoza when he said that sorrow is the passage from a greater to a less perfection.

Very often in Herbais, the weather, absent any light, becomes green;

He (Musil) says: — The gift of enfolding reality in a suggestive atmosphere (the poet).

I say: — The gift of enfolding a suggestive atmosphere in reality (which I strive to develop by degrees, and which I call writing, whether or not it is expressed verbally and embodied, by signs, on paper).

I know I must struggle against the taciturn aspect of things, and the constant mental wavering that my own questions compel me to accept.

542.   The garden, which is now beginning to rouse, has moments when it lies at the bottom of the valley, or else it is propelled toward the edge; the earth moving in this way causes us to stand resolutely on our unsteadiness. Copernicus says that, in this region, the days slip away without leaving behind a single needless gleam.

543.   Sometimes, like today, I begin the day by convulsing my face — one face upon another face causes both faces to tremble; my thoughts then run over my features, and I feel as though my entire organism is rebalancing itself because I did it out of irony.

544.   To arrange her succession in a last will and testament, Isabôl asked for Hadewijch's cloak; that cloak   had the scent of another body, a glimpse she had never had.

The wind encounters no obstacle in the meadow. The green veil envelops Blanche. The colt runs — how I loathe what they call a dream, which is a way to render a new horizon insignificant; that dream is an invention — the relationship between a person's knowledge and their body.

Ever since we put in the stove, and I shielded the window with a pair of curtains, I have had a certain preference for this room; arranged for silence and the work that provides our daily bread, it is the final stop before the door to the street.

The street is a courtyard with all too evident vestiges of the same work, and a path along which roll trucks, and farm machinery.

The attraction of the animals to this part of the house, where they sleep on wicker chairs, on either side of the fire, or lie atop bills and papers, causes me to think that the time of stark distinctions has become less sharp here. We ourselves sometimes write, and unfurl dreamless heat and light, and sometimes dirty our fingernails in our labor. We endeavor to read as one who becomes a descendant of the text's author, and if at times there are contradictions between myself and Augusto, I wonder whether they are not the gradual path of our encounter.

When, during this November of a single tone, I am only able to write in the Diary, I feel as though it is because the pursuit of the specific man who underlies the figure is now seeping in; when I reread what I had written down during those days in Jodoigne, I became aware that, today, there was a vast difference at the level of the scene in which we lived. What is happening is happening in a garden, or in a house, or in a room, or on a street, or next to a tree, that is, inside, or outside. I am halfway between the inside and the outside, and what I must describe, to be comprehensible,
is how one of the hypotheses of the journey actually takes place.

The bed is warm, the night was one of nightmares woven between my room, and the room beyond the wall. I write mentally, feeling a great desire to remain still. Putting on my wristwatch helps me to lift myself up ever so slightly. On the one hand, time is slipping away; on the other, I know I am only writing because my experience is mortal (it ends with death). Had I not written it, I would have preferred _____

a less ardent happiness,
a lesser complexity.

My life has changed, and so too the equidistant text. I
believe I will continue to write unabated, but from the point of
view of Herbais. There is a second, a third, a fourth, a fifth world
that many an experienced man can grasp, which translates as
the radiant world, the luminous world, the unknown world, the
tenacious world, the world that subjects one to all, from a great
distance; but what I name the struggle of Herbais has thrust me,
by degrees, out of the presence of the figures, of Müntzer
defeated and displayed in a cage, of Nietzsche gone mad, of the
scattered beguines, of Psalmody with the power she had to
predict the future for, or against, herself. In Herbais, there is
only the time of Herbais, the time is the present, and reality has
no thickness, it has been abandoned by the *luminous scenes* that
were its vastness. I am glad no one is calling me, praising me, or
compensating me for my share of labor, corresponding to the
desire for vanity with which I would have lived, identifying
myself as a bird of beautiful plumage.

I thought Herbais was a desolation and, on many days,
lacking confidence, I was nearly inert. But within the silence, I
was transforming into a figure, entering the figural order, or the
natural life of the figure.

My spotless room, the door open, gives me the impression
of a motionless, evocative space; I go, in motion, to call Augusto
for lunch, feeling, today, much more conscious of what I am
meant to do than I have been over the past few days.

After lunch, I was alone on the first floor and, although it
was a rainy day, the large room was dark inside, but illuminated
from the outside. I was going to read the first volume of Musil's

Diaries, which I always associate with the death of my cat Blanche. I pour boiling water into the coffee filter and write these lines, intrigued by what I have slowly come to understand,

that I belong to the figural order

and that I can therefore place this *Diary*, which concerns the figural order of everyday life, alongside *The Book of Communities*, *From Hedge to Being*, and *Loving Cause*.

A dense winter day, and one of anticipation. Christine has come to visit us. There is no prodigal son here; we have all of us behaved prodigally. A rainy day is a perfect day to proclaim new days, a serene and welcome darkness. Yesterday, we made a few changes to the entrance hall with wicker furniture, and when I go there, I am there to stay, as if an enormous vastness of meanings held me there, and listened to me.

I spread a crocheted coverlet, which I need to repair, over
my knees, I spread a veil, I spread a thick veil, I spread Isabôl's
last will and testament *where the cloak passes, at her bounds.*
Isabôl does not spread her final wishes, ill-suited to the movement,
real or apparent, of the band:
she spreads her life, which is still living; the coverlet, made with a
single needle, is malleable; evoked by the serpent, the boat-will-and-
testament evolves by itself, and leads to an island which stretches
north of the archipelago, and where, in a great mass of land, the
metaphors of meaning founder. Isabôl's last will and testament tests
Isabel,
and when she sets foot on the beach, she does not halt
(she continues)
her steps on the globe of figures.

At the final moment, each poor person in the band
becomes an extra-numeral, outside, or beyond, the number.

When I woke up this morning, I was troubled by the certainty of not knowing whether I had already written everything, or still very little. I was waiting for my period, which would be reflected in the coming days by a mental propensity to become entangled in problems, and would end with an eruption of sensuality. During this time, my analysis of situations does not proceed from any creational speculation, I let myself be almost determined by existing social forms. A terrible sorrow is accumulating, as if I had no access to the millennial realm of which Musil speaks. So only the text (in the work) can pull me out of the act of sleeping.

The more I write, the more difficult and fuller of obstacles I find the path of writing. In my opinion, I should not write so that others can read

first   what I have already said

second what has already been said.

I conclude from this that I do not know how to write, and that I constantly long for changes in my life: horizons, perspectives, intermittencies, periods.

I would prefer to begin either from the fore of the crisis, or from the reverse of the figural world, which is, in the final reckoning, transparency.

I must cross a street and enter another field of complexity; Herbais was Herbais; today, wherever the essences of silence accompany me, the different phases passed through by a person who has ceased to speak coalesce what remains of the usual days — "O ancient and serene night."

So different is the center of writing that in Portugal, or wherever I am asked to express myself to someone, all I do is fail. What I say when I speak is always a reflection of what they expect me to abandon, is always subjecting myself to an instruction; but writing, in the peace of not being compelled to cast it aside, has another caliber — I do not want to deceive with the reasoning that may exist in my explanations, but which has the nature of excrement.

All this occurred to me as I was taking a bath. Bezant and Cisca wait on the carpet, at the doorway, for me to finish this confession, for me to leave this peace which denies them milk, and affection; I am then certain that my text, unlike speech, concedes nothing,
circulates in order to rupture what is captive.

The sky grew dark, and it began to rain. *It is Herbais, in Belgium.* I embark on a weekday that I enjoy, with no interruptions from the outside, without the noise of farm machinery in the square, with a latent formless scene depicted in every thought, action, or what is yet unwritten. I find that I do not wait to write, nor do I stop writing to live the experience which produces writing; everything is simultaneous and has the same roots, writing is the double of living; I could say, by way of explanation, that it is similar to opening the door to the street, feeding the animals, or encountering someone who has the place of a breath in my fate.

I am grateful for the people who breathe on me in a particular way in order to set me alight, even without that awareness; I try to repay them with the feeling I possess that is furthest from hatred, which is a lingering feeling, like the one Isabôl presented to Hadewijch and Copernicus on the stairs.

When I saw them together without her, I thought first of the paper; it was dawn, and in the slant of the first falling light,
I saw my paper — the consistent, lightweight matter which holds these signs. I stepped forward toward Hadewijch and Copernicus as if they too were signs, and I merged with them, with the certainty that I was cloaking them in eternity, and that they would come to me wherever, even alone, they happened to meet.

_____ this beginning of a sequence, which can also become the hiding place of a figure who is imminent, appeared when I was thinking about a fragment of text I had read by Levinas, and about a plant called wall pepper, which a neighbor gave me yesterday during our afternoon walk. The cluster of stars, as conventional as the deep despondency in which I live, was part of the transformative role attributed to wanting, knowing, and endless waiting.

I await my book as one of those that Levinas mentions, which are neither a fundamental unit of measurement, nor belong to the person who is speaking. "It is from the reading of books — not necessarily philosophical — that these initial shocks become questions and problems, giving one to think. The role of national literatures here is perhaps very important. Not just that one learns words from it, but in it one lives 'the true life which is absent' but which is precisely no longer utopian. I think that in the great fear of bookishness, one underestimates the 'ontological' reference of the human to the book that one takes for a source of information, or for a 'tool' of learning, even though it is a modality of our being."

If I could play with the dismay that blankets Herbais, at the edge of my day, make microcosms out of it, and laughter, I would have found yet another foundation of my life, to be able to possess breath for the writing of which I speak.

A perspective so uncommon that it drives passersby away from Herbais.

Even merely the suspicion of _____ can bring

with it a constant and fearsome disturbance — the proximity of the meaning of life through the constant action of being.

Levinas emphasizes the verbal aspect of being and I, leaning against the fence, with *Tales of Wandering Evil* upon me, am moved by the acceleration of the verb that is flung; what soars beneath the vastness of the literary work is one of the possible epiphanies of Herbais: *the wall pepper that bears yellow flowers on the sharply hewn fortifications, upon which I celebrate victory and the expulsion of the tyrant, in order to continue to devote myself to Hadewijch, and Copernicus, and to flee from them.*

I do not know if this is a page for the book or, conversely, for the Diary. Two beings refuse to assume any kind of finitude — the Diary and the book; but seen from a distance, I do not know whether they amount to what was expected of me; during the time I meditated on Münster, I couldn't stop thinking about how events unfolded — as I saw them, or as I will see them. The urge to exist is a delight that determines our volition.

My greatest responsibility is to do my part in making a book into a being; at this point in time, not to make a child into a man, which I have already done.

I have come to a city where I run a great risk: Lisbon. Nowhere else is it as troubling for me to transgress any precept or rule. Even if they do not speak of me, and I have not yet been rendered into any language; yet I arrived in the city, and decided to stay because an acquaintance had sought me out far away, in Herbais, saying that he would come back to see me with an unexpected task, if I waited for him in a garden in my neighborhood. It still took me some time to finish *Tales of Wandering Evil*, but in Herbais, by that point, it was already possible to read the vast movement and restlessness of the end of a book.

There is an attic, in Campo de Ourique, where I often think I am writing; writing only fulfills part of my desire to write. Other forms of my desire to embrace are lost, for lack of opportunity, and timidity. I myself never decide who I am going to write about on my own, and it is not my ear, nor my sight, nor my voice, which participate with me in this elective friendship. I believe it is the previous text becoming a being. Its effect is to cause the memory of myself to disappear, to be detached from the life I possess.

It is through this gap that the stranger I mentioned above entered; with a way of dressing so inseparable from his body that, ad infinitum, I was afraid I could not help pulling him out of that habit.

Then, I had no more effective intentions, and approached the nascent stranger through small portraits. Depicting how he rose up from that place and, testing my keenness to follow him, returned from that path; how, having called himself Pessoa, he now encountered in that name the greatest obstacle; how he had to leave the city where he was born, in the shadow of a theater where opera was sung, and cease to be the horse, or the pair, with the double of his heteronyms, at the helm of a cart; how I — the lady from the card game — passed by him that night, and siphoned out of him all that hid his nakedness, and that it was other people who were engaged in the tempered study of language.

The tempered study of language was primarily concerned with the ears of the horse, which is my favorite animal, after cats, his dog, and chickens; his dog, now in my visionary role as to our fate, for he had never had an animal to keep him company; nor had he ever given himself to anyone with a reflected desire for love.

In the prologue of the book, I ask myself: *he is so close, and, both of them belonging to the family, how can I be the intercessor?*

In the beginning, it was necessary to burn something — make a sacrifice; the lives of the great musicians — Bach, Mozart, Beethoven, Brahms — and several others who cannot be recognized by the ideal of their name, dwell in my ear; I had to pare him down to music, alone with what can be uttered about him through this means; the changes, which occur over the course of my thoughts… but I tenuously lost what was uttered… related to opera, musicians, and horses.

As if my contact with him had been newly sealed.

I do not want to go to Lisbon for Lisbon, but for him; I also do not want to listen to music and read opera libretti for themselves; drizzle — lightly falling rain — is, for the moment, the beginning of my desire to bind him to another composition.

The activities of the cooperative began today, and I am working in my room, transformed into an apse for music _____ on a new table, which is a new function.

I recall the music I possess, and which seems rarer to me when it is writing with me; at the moment, I am listening to Liszt's Piano Concertos Nos. 1 and 2; I have come to rely more and more on certain musicians;

but I feel free with them; *the realm which is ours has no fetters, only rhythms and melodies.*

The character of the tree is what is lacking in Herbais; there is no enclosed area that is a firebreak, or a paradise of beings in isolation; the house is like a metal pole, bare and unprotected. Neither a wall at eye level, nor a wall at chest level.

The Diary of Jodoigne, *diary of the tree*, held the movement for itself. The Diary of Herbais, diary of seclusion in the meadow out of ugliness, is pervaded by a pulsating current where pupilar images — dreams — will surface.

In the end, the one who first brought my morning to a standstill was Schubert. I hear his *Impromptus & Moments musicaux*, and here, what I suppress, because I haven't yet written it, makes a strong impression on me. I / it / the Diary, can be revitalized by writing. After *Tales of Wandering Evil*, I have been circling the music of Bach, and Fernando Pessoa. Even absent trees, the mutilated isolation of Herbais is fertile. But I am also drawn to diaries, not written in the present by my own hand, but as if I were already distant, and my life purported to be in fragments, and in the form of a path turned into a book. The Diary is the cloth with which we clean the years; more real than other texts is its configuration as a currency — the price. I type without corrections; there is no manuscript of the final text.

Since my life is so isolated, let us distance it to the whiteness of these diaries; in the background, there was a figure who wrote about others, but now is going to draw her solace from them.

A bright sunny morning, in contrast to the rainy atmosphere of the past several days; wanting to keep writing *Tales of Wandering Evil* is my luminous response to the morning. Lately, I have been convinced that my body was less malleable, that where some desires were broadened, others were narrowed. But I know the body responds to the booming voice that beckons, and itself cries out; and so it too still contains carnal love, which is a good conduit for the human. Jade thought I was calling him, and quickly ran over. I felt happy on the surface of the earth we trod. The return to Augusto's body yesterday could not pass unnoticed at this hour of the Diary.

I return to the work, and the experience, not yet determined, of *Tales of Wandering Evil*: a moment of inner fear, of not knowing how to leave enough time for what I'm going to say, and that the book will mature before its own time. I will now place Hadewijch, who arranged an encounter with Isabôl, in a library in Münster. It is true she exists, as it is true that she is not the same person. Copernicus will not be there in that city of our encounter. And he too is doubly loved — in that cosmogony, and in the world of bodies.

Münster besieged, and settled in a stable form, though to be reexamined and completed — the remains of John of Leiden have vanished. I will return to it in the season preceding spring, when the fertility of the mansion, expressed in the haze, will have reached the end of its cycle; the darkness of Hadewijch's soul, by now, must have retreated, to allow some light to seep in;

Hadewijch, in winter, is less absorbed by her inner conflict; I would have liked Copernicus to be there too, for Isabôl doesn't appreciate her in the same way on her own; both have dark roots, and Isabôl's soul is not a steady force, nor Hadewijch's a surrender; what do both of them want in this enigma? I will think about the path toward Hadewijch and Copernicus, also about the context of my life; Isabôl is going to ask Hadewijch about the repulsion and attraction with which she flees from Copernicus, and tell her that, for Copernicus, she is and Hadewijch exists; only a day, a single being against another being, is what repulses her; this experience of metamorphoses is fearsome, and expresses an unending renovative action.

It is nine o'clock, and since I have already fed the animals, made the bran mixture for the chickens, and treated the new Bezant, who has conjunctivitis, I feel as though I have just finished slicing off the upper part of the morning;

moreover, I feel, keenly, a nostalgia for the streets of a city — a city in the morning; but my task for the next few hours will be to dwell on *Tales of Wandering Evil*, to cure my nostalgia by recognizing as authentic all that is useful for departure.

Bach. Pessoa: for a very long time, the text was suspended
between this evocative mass of two words. To write about
a musician demands a labor of identification in the deepest
part of his harmony; for those who have no knowledge of music
— as in my case — "outside there is a stillness as if nothing
existed,"   which was Pessoa's desire.

I was then led to understand that he should be in the
musician's house, and that a light-hearted kinship with Eckhart
should be enough to extricate him from the excessive prominence
which paralyzes him, and haunts him;

"Pass, bird, pass, and teach me how to pass," it was with this
request that he arrived at the musician's house, and saw that man
in his family, and in his time.

It all began because he willingly placed himself at his service,
as if Bach, from that moment on, would act as his counterforce;
he was dressed as a gentleman of the time, characterized by an
overwhelming capacity for an infinite renunciation of the singular
aspect of his poetry's countenance, which we all know; since they
were going to delve more deeply into one another, Bach told him,
relations between them would be discreet and, seemingly,
confined to the rendering of services. Assuming he knew what a
key was, *the name he would use for him to change keys was
Smallness.*

With her sixth sense,   Anna Magdalena could see they
had stereotyped his form and physical strength _____ rather
than the flight of the bird; creating about the creator could

fill the house with a harrowing atmosphere.

The creational night was November 1 to 2 — a bond was thus established between the living and the dead, and the living took responsibility in the realm of the dead, and the dead assumed responsibility in the realm of the living;

for me, Bach was closer, Smallness more distant, they were familiar to me in the inverse proportion of the times in which they had existed; I needed to change the order of the letters in Pessoa's name to make him involute, to pull him out of the inveterate habit I had of him; the description of his life was not the appropriate way to subtract him from Smallness.

Pessoa, read from right to left, yielded AOSSEP.

The punishment of writing is as arduous as the gift. What effect would Bach have on Aossê? That was where I began, from the fat over the thin, from the connection to others over the solitary, from the abstract space over the space of Leipzig. I only believed that the instinct of the creational species guided us; but that perpetual attitude of confrontation determined the birth of the book, which was present, but without a cause capable of making it develop page by page. Paginal   ly. Should Pessoa have his battle? Which one? A simple sentence? A rumor concerning the inmost part of the text? Would "Unseen" be a fitting impetus for him?

What if I approached the Bachs' house as well? "Unseen" had come to collect a debt; in that place, people and furniture were perpetually used by music, there was scarcely any atmosphere; Anna Magdalena opened that door, and gave an evasive answer; "Unseen" stepped forward toward a chair, and wanted to wait for the first hour when, in Bach's locked room, music was playing; it was not the collector who had spoken, and he understood that the wounded game was being caught there, and that all morning long, inmost feelings were being overheard; the intonation itself was thus determined — and he wanted to render his services to Joha. Seb. Bach.

But I was outside the Bachs' house, and was the organic propulsion of this text; in my mind, I placed the naked, unclothed, posthumous servant — solely desire to act; it was a fundamental ascesis for us to approach a stream, alone, and ask after them. — "Dust — all is dust" — he said. — He drank water from the stream. From us. Because his stereotypical figure had been ingrained in my memory, *I suddenly wake up at night*; with that absence, it is unbearable for me to remain very long, but that night repulsion and love were reversible; would I have had the courage to endure the tedium caused by the motionless figure of the poet, and attempt to look after him, on the periphery of poetry?; but what does it matter, if I felt the desire to offer him a different renown?

In Leipzig, rumors were already circulating.
I began to read the texts in which he had appeared, resulting in a great hesitation to fracture the Baixa which surrounded us.

"Herr Bach,
I have come to ask you to help me settle this debt,"
said Aossê.
Mr. Bach leaned over,

and I wasn't sure whether proceeding further
would be a true success,
or a disaster.

Despite the difficult
confrontation
between Lisbon and Leipzig
I press on.

Aossê was enlightening Bach's children through his new
work; *he could not feel the nature outside;* it rained copiously, and
the water-blinded windows formed a wall which altered his
memories, save those of the Work. But even the adolescents in
Bach's house knew that everything can be exhausted, or
depleted.

——————— then I remember what I had *written-seen*, in the early hours of 20 February 1977; two figures who impose themselves, one after the other, without my knowing who they were.

In the East, and on the wall, among the flowers on the paper,
the image of a powerful male figure, clothed in a habit, lingers before
my eyes. He does nothing, he is motionless, and yet he moves toward
me, his face hidden. I have the impression that he is merely a
vestment lacking a body. But, at last,
he shows me his body,
which is the crystalline mind that holds sounds.
*   — Nothing separates you from the others — he tells me. — I*
am made of glass, and I will fracture for all eternity. — He still
lingers in the place of my seeing. I understand he is endeavoring to
shatter, there is already a clattering of pieces preceding the
fragmentation and the fall.

It was Bach.

Another character then comes to the center of the wall, overlaps
with the first, who moves away; this second character is all white
immensity,
is nothingness,
is a deep emptiness
which takes the sharp form of a well. A well parallel to the earth,
rent in the air, with indeterminate walls, made of a material the
name of which I do not know, except that I am overcome. I attempt
to fathom it with my eyes, I know intuitively that it is long and

solitary — a perfect interrupted path.

I sleep beside him with no need for contemplation,
nor even to wait for the following moment,
for there is a coincidence that operates independently of fear.

Lying beside him, I look at his scattered body, and witness his unsutured dream.

It was Aossê.

I have nearly finished *Tales of Wandering Evil*. I have called it *Tales* not because it is a book of tales, but because, in every part of itself, it is a shrouded confidence.

I wrote it after *From Hedge to Being*, which, of course, is a book that distances itself from the life of the beguines, transformed into legends.

Tales of Wandering Evil is a distant echo of that world, made legend and, in reality, subterranean.

I feel the impulse to have them meet, and to be present; it is
the prologue, without any tedious and useless exposition about
their physical features, and garments;
    while I was in the drawing room of the house, under the
concealment that would most please them,
and which I assume is that of a pastoral force   *I never kept*
sheep   and a musical harmony,
Johanna Catharina came in wearing a blue apron and, in her
hands — and against her chest — the tin basin for ablutions
which would appear in the inventory of Joha. Seb. Bach's
possessions.

They saw each other for the first time from behind the wall,
and Johanna Catharina, who was only nine years old at the time,
emerged without delay, startled by a laughter that was shared,
and yet terribly specific to each of them; Aossê shrugged off all
his responsibility with that laughter, and the noise they both
made as they seemingly entered through the pipes of the organ
fell upon the heirs of Bach's gifts; both appeared to have a
keyboard, pipes, and a system of bellows, which filled the child
with dread;
Johann's house, barer than usual at that time in Leipzig, was
chaotic and poor, solid and neat — and gave no indication of
what was happening inside; there were objects of pewter,
copper, silver, and, from these pieces, and the atmosphere, there
was a tone of restraint. The succinct set of furniture included
chairs, beds, and tables. In the master bedroom, a single
wardrobe for the entire family.

Regina Susanna, the youngest daughter, brought a vessel to feed the pigeons, but she heard nothing other than the final vibrations; she observed, however, that the guest said in a foreign language that "it was no use"; but what she had understood was the musical translation of that language, from which there was nothing Johann Bach could extract dead, or render useless.

To extract dead, or render useless, is, nonetheless, a condition of oblivion, and oblivion is the energy of work; that din, a cornucopia of abundance, was the final volute of the first encounter; never again did any of the children, not Johann Christoph, not Johanna Catharina, not Regina Susanna, ever sense them together: they had shared the space, despite not encountering any limitations in it.

_____ I divide *The Keeper of Sheep* into passages that I focus on, and I do not attribute an author's face to them, I attribute solely existence; he who is a verb is a person; all other narrative traces of what is dead have vanished; he then performs the task of giving Johann Sebastian Bach shelter through flight, just as Johann Sebastian Bach offers him his house as a distant and auditory dwelling place.

*In the profusion of silence, Aossê hung the branches. His
nostalgia made a deep impression on his companion. They began to
speak as they walked.*

— *Nothing can be heard in this corner of the world.*

— *It is the corner where the prelude is born — replied Bach
— where the flame has not yet been born, and is imagined. — He
put his finger in front of his eyes, and his companion sighed heavily.*

— *I, however, hear the lapping of other shores, which I carry in my
ears, and I am trying to recognize the water here.*

— *Don't you hear a murmur?*

— *You should no longer recognize yourself by the murmur, but
by the possibility of reconstructing the ashes in a flame.*

— *A kind of miracle?*

— *I wouldn't say that... "Our hearts are a single Virgin."*

As I see them together, Bach is the Master.

He has mastered his instrument, his expression, the chaos
which comes to each of us in life; in his rightful place, the
Church in Leipzig brought together the songs of the peasants
killed at Frankenhausen and the formal painting of the Princes,
who defeated them in the clash; Bach appears to me as Heart of
the Bear, who, at the threshold of the Modern Age, sets down
his myths in Music, which in Bach is full of the Reason of God.
Otherwise, in the confrontation, Bach would have lost all sense,
like Hölderlin, Nietzsche, and Pessoa.

I was waiting for the final rejoinder in the dialogue between
Aossê and Bach; as the latter was the Master, the final Word
belonged to him. Christine stopped by to visit and we both read

passages from Al-Hallaj, which I don't believe have been translated into Portuguese. The text was translated for me, and I compared it to Massignon's translation, until I fell into the breath of Al-Hallaj, after he had spent a year in prayer in front of the Kaaba, in Mecca. I had just identified his soul, which, today, I would say ⸺⸺⸺.

I am overtaken by a deep nostalgia, and I tell Christine how unfortunate it is that Pessoa never encountered Al-Hallaj, but only shoddy theosophists. There is an arid truth in his virginity — so great that I ask for dew, drizzle, a fine and persistent rain,
and the hand, only the hand, no other part of the body, of a female figure running through his facies, astonished not to have encountered the crucified man of Baghdad.

Still under the influence of what I wrote in this Diary on
the 24th, and speaking with Augusto about the dialogue
between Bach and Aossê, we were talking about how European
culture, of which Portuguese culture is a part (to an extent that
the Portuguese themselves cannot imagine), was defined by
confrontational encounters that did not take place — and could
have been authentic fresh beginnings of new cycles of thinking
and ways of living.

We imagined Camões leaving Portugal to meet
Copernicus, who would show him his unpublished
calculations, as he had done with Rheticus. How different the
ending of Canto IX of *The Lusiads* would have been (the
driving force of the discoveries "demands" a heliocentric
theory, since Giordano Bruno is himself inaudible) and the
amorous encounter on the island would have reached a level
that it can never achieve, regardless of how many cabalistic
calculations are made. Passing through Krakow, where
Copernicus was a dull, sedentary, and extremely circumspect
deacon, Camões could have come into contact with groups of
the Faithful of Pure Love, which would have given his poetry
an indelible quality it fails to achieve, compared to what
survives of the Love poems. There is a Platonic undertone in
his poetry, which is a sure sign of absence and inexperience
(there is a difference between having lived and being
experienced). But the opposite is equally true. What would
Camões have given to Copernicus, what would we have gained
if his nascent science had not been an "arid knowledge"?

And Pessoa? So many words, so many images, so many masks, to say "I did not find." Ten centuries earlier, Al-Hallaj had said the same, living in a time as troubled as his own, with the entire Muslim world being reshaped. But what a difference between the two. Al-Hallaj said it. He did not find because He found Himself, and in Baghdad Square, where they were tearing him apart, knowing he was right but blasphemous, he died declaring to them, "I am the Creator."

I cannot move the stone of this tomb. It will not be Lisbon-Baghdad, but only Lisbon-Leipzig.

Always writing, always walking and wandering, Aossê knows someone is about to enter. *Full of innocence   he looks at me without seeing, and my feet are in his way. Fragile obstacles rise in the brightness of the candle, which illuminates a voice that is reciting, is at my side with reflection and fear. The one who is there is not a known being, neither man, nor animal, nor word, nor plant, nor a being which expresses itself. He is a mortal and unknown god like myself, silently asking me to join him, and keep him company in expectation and fear. But this fear is joyous and travels, surrounded by sand, encounters the desert, rushes into it, and pursues its world all the way to the water. A spiritual surface gathers the thousand sands and sings at the azimuth of the sail, where this being reclines, neither sleeping nor indolent, smiling with an abrupt and sweet love. The one he is loves me, despite being unaccustomed to human presence, save that of a man who smells like a beast in a field of snow and earth. The one he is surrenders to this painting, and passes through the space in his feathered smallness. I do not attempt to decipher him, so that he may evolve in peace, he draws nearer and leaves me on the abyss of this abyss, where the endless doors we are* opening for one another are shining. Strange spirit, thus you navigate between love and closed doors. You slowly disappear, in the wake of my eyes. You leave me unhurriedly, but you remain forever. I can almost see you, you become more and more unknown, it is snowing in the garden — there is feed for the birds on the doorstep. Your footsteps move away, you evade the house, which you cannot leave   and in the end, leave.

You are no longer my father, nor my friend, you are an absent season. My eyes follow you forever and you shine in them, I never knew that your remoteness was so sweet. And so you enter your house, chest of a bird, gleam of a star,   where they await you. Without time between us, the years irradiate an ever-present light.

Another wound, another mourning of animals, or plants,
appears on the horizon:
our newest neighbors want to purchase the detached garden,
which according to our contract, is included in the commercial
lease of the House, and outbuildings; Augusto is going to
contest it, but I believe they will win the dispute, and I see that,
in this dubious atmosphere, our departure from Herbais is
taking root, and that, in the future, I will no longer want to plant
any shrubs, or trees for myself; whenever our space, or marrow,
is threatened, or coveted, the plants, or the animals, are the
victims; I suppose a phase is coming to an end   the phase of
stillness — and that in the years to come, we will be marked by
the sign of passing through provisional places;

this morning, however, I was inconsolable at having to abandon
the shrubs to their fate, who can say they will not cut them
down, or move them, give them a secondary importance and a
fate as human playthings?; and I would be denied the sharp
horizon of that little bow-shaped piece of land; as I slept
tonight, I had conceded I was a neighbor to the compassionate
roots of Prunus Triloba, and later, explaining what came next in
Lisbonleipzig to myself, and the method I was going to follow in
that work, I had the feeling that the garden I was going to lose,
where last summer I had created geometries reflected in shrubs,
was going to be transformed into a territory, or the marrow of a
book. The marrow of a book no one can dominate or destroy, or
eliminate out of cruelty, or greed.

It is two and a half years old and immensely beautiful;
comparing it to the space, it is more space than the space; its
shrubs, and trees, are planted erratically, but they have an order;
the winter frost overtaking the growth on the ground heightens
its aerial part, which resonates behind me when I return home.

The garden thieves, what are they doing with the garden?
Does the garden remain blind to them,   or is it they who
close their eyes? The day the land is traded for greed, what will
be the purpose of pages for this book?

I go out to feed the black cat, and then I leave. I return. She
is frightened, but soon grows calm.

— It is nothing — I tell her. — It is the nothingness I am.

On those days, Lisbonleipzig was the only direction to take,
· asking Bach and Pessoa to surrender themselves to my
company; I had the oppressive feeling of being at the window
without seeing anything, and that my great struggle to find
them had ridiculous, if not counterproductive, effects; my
patience with living in Herbais was coming to an end, and my
hope of laying the foundations for a new book which would
correspond to an ambition perhaps beyond my measure was
uncertain; I felt as though I had no ears, or had my hands upon
them, to tame the voices which summoned me toward the
vastness, and toward exodus; I might collapse exhausted from
writing. If I could produce a special sound ⸻⸻⸻⸻⸻
a large number of singers or musicians affiliated with the church
service were gathered at dinner; when Aossê entered, he
remained standing, and they thought they were in the presence
of a Jew because of his light complexion, his beard, and the
striking attitude that accompanies belonging to minorities; the
pseudo-Jew was tall, and had never had the desire to learn music
from Bach. Yet he was fascinated by the idea that when Bach
died, his Organ would perish from consumption. In truth, he
had had multiple reasons for coming, all of equal value and
importance, and if he described them, he knew it would destroy
his desire to stay. Anna Magdalena set another plate, and offered
him a place at the table, but his primary intention, coming from
Lisbon, was to learn even more about the abjection he was
perpetrating on himself.

How to separate the art of accompanying and composing
from the art of disappearing? He sat down at the table under the
following impetus:

I'm guided only by reason.

Anna Magdalena, assisted by Johanna Catharina, moved and arranged the plates, and when dessert arrived, he offered the cakes he had bought at the pastry shop. Bach, at the head of the table, expressed an opinion he held close to his heart: — It must be possible to overcome that obstacle, as well. — No impossibility was ever heard there — which makes for a truly beautiful obsession — and all the musicians, seated around the Father, it seemed to Aossê, as many and numerous as they were, had one leading voice.

During the night, whenever I awoke, I heard a phrase which, at long last, clearly expressed my inner feelings: trim the sails. And asked the following question: if I am, by nature, a nomad, why do I plant trees and shrubs as soon as I arrive in a place, and later want to remove them from the garden, to take those that have roots along with me?

I am now working in a somewhat haphazard way, obeying impulses, and many ideas that are lost; today, when I heard *trim the sails* and that rousing command gave me the courage to leave, I felt that to shift from being conscious to writing requires a piece of paper always at hand, and a voluntary interruption of daily life. In the end, the text reflects, causes me to cleave to my own inmost self, and my own path.

Trim the sails was my oracle today, an instruction given to the space in which I dwell in Herbais, where I set about "creating questions." It is not a metaphor, it is truly the command to slip away from Herbais — the hermitage. The pain of leaving it, and the joy of departing, were in balance; it is a time marked by an important experience — on one side, isolation and abandonment, on the same side, rapture and conveyance. "Incarceration" has relationships with the luminous scenes, and I had no idea what the connections were.

Here we had a foretaste of what the desert was, without ourselves witnessing the sun, the arid expanse, and the sand; I let myself be moved by this unpopulated place, by these inhabitants who normally live in arid regions. Incandescence, temptation, and the usual aftermath of incommunicability. In this rhythm, I would like to lay the foundations of *Lisbonleipzig*.

What shocks me most (an offense I commit against myself), in this experience of isolation, is the abrupt explosion of hatred. It settles on almost innocent pretextual beings, who suddenly disturb me, rise up as enemies. I am tempted to become entangled in them, to turn them inside out, and drive them away toward a new burrow;

and tonight, unable to mend my fractured bone, I am on the Bachs' window ledge; the temptation to look at them in their own dining room is immense, and I struggle between the inside and the outside, I am a presence imprisoned in the glass. I feel the need to extend courtesies to Fernando Pessoa, seated at the table, and to raise him up in a transparency that runs and plays. I have   more than anything, the desire to enter the room, and open the door to the church where the organ is; I have, more than anything, the desire to pass through the preambular glass in which I find myself.

I am left, in the night that ushers in winter, and almost without feeling it, hating this persistent attempt to create without a single vibration to guide me.

The organ:

Here, the one that commands is the organ. I am a string, not an adornment, and we are all part of it. With Aossê, a certain vision of the world was introduced into the Bach household, of which I am the representative. I entered with the power to manipulate the absence of quantity, and I am present.

The organ is a devourer, and when Bach played for the first time, in front of us, with I as one of the strings, Aossê observed that his fingers were red, particularly the tips — and it was difficult to bear his air of kindness, so grateful and appreciative he had come.

Aossê was not the collective name of his four writing exercises; but he was the one who thinks when he travels, and that was why he had left, ready to enter Leipzig, and abandon Lisbon — just as it had been the moment before.

I am looking for a woman, a new female figure, for now I
see it was she that the metaphor contained. The words
forgotten, I do not want the figure to disappear, to stop seeping
into the darkness. She is a figure who sings different masses of
water, and strides forward over a forest of hair. It is night and
there is sun in the place of moon. I find what I was looking for,
always forgotten. The figure moves through her body and says
she is visiting me without any purpose, on the verge of falling
silent and expressing herself. I follow in her wake without
moving, my hand over my eyes, and my eyes over my mouth. I
look for her name in my memory,
all those I utter collapse her image, which is fleeing ahead of me.

I am clothed in white and wool, to purify myself, the lamb,
after being resurrected three times, did not die forever.

She tells me her name is Infausta,
that she is a rampart,
and I keep it in the last line of the voice.

A female figure who wants to enter,
Infausta,
a spirit of perseverance and meekness. A smiling disposition,
she knew how to sew as one who smiles. She left countless
pieces of embroidery and lacework in the library of the house.
Opening the pages of the books, she would look for ideas and
designs for her pieces of cloth and, sighing, would feel the
breath of her hands. She is a young woman who opens doors
noiselessly, and brings silence with her like a veil of ideas. She
sits with vast writings upon her knees, and dreams of the death
that will bring her here. She stares ahead gazing at the opacity,
she wanted to see me today out of an absolute necessity of the
spirit. I sit beside her almost weeping with listless joy, I ask her
to let me read her lacework, to lend me her hands where dogs,
roosters, animals, and plants take refuge between them. The
other day she found me in a dream[1], I was in a low, open room,
looking at a fox and a wolf, and when I heard her voice, I said,
"If I could, you would live here always, without encountering
violent death, or ill-treatment in the coming hour."

[1]   Dream on 17 December.

I see a girl striding forward. She is dressed in long skirts with a narrow waist. She is walking along an incorruptible road, lined with orange trees as tall as sycamores. Light shines from behind her, preceding her in her journey, leaving those who come to the gates astonished. On her face is a mask, and her hinged wooden body seems destined to be thrown into the flames.

It is summer, or a similar season, unknown to these inhabitants, but not to Infausta; and at the bend in the path, a tree has been planted. The sycamore. It falls down in a single piece, the trunk separates from the branches. The branches catch fire, the greenery gathers in the flame, and the fire has no smoke. Once the fire has been consumed, she retreats to the other side of the path, to sit down beside Aossê, with whom I leave her forever, in this language.

——————— I depart for Portugal, for an environment bereft
of joy, or even hostile; the valley of Herbais, where I intend to
deeply wield my abilities and senses, is now showing me its
greatest possibilities, and that is why I call it a valley, a
hospitable harbor, and a receptive place; I depart writing
through the Portuguese language, having consciously left the
sun and water ever latent in the terrain of Herbais; here I
imagined, in the form of Pessoa, a single cosmic river that is not
split by borders, and I saw it, with no bewilderment, emerge
into reality; on that occasion, I remember feeling the desire for
there to be no countries, which are like sentries of packs. Yet I
am departing from Herbais with the experience of a still
unwritten fate, having supplied my ship with the necessary crew,
for the time being. Everything I have said is based on
knowledge gained through practice, *realized*. It is not a mixture
of reality and the supernatural, as I read the other day.

Infausta is Aossê's female heteronym — the key to the gate;
and I have the feeling that what I write is furling out over a
density far vaster and more fearsome than my own personal self.
At the moment, I am troubled that I cannot grasp Bach's
specific art — music. I have spent my life listening to music, and
now that Aossê is silently listening to Bach, I feel as though I
have heard nothing.

I took a branch of sage from the stolen garden. I am
referring to the garden I could not keep on the lot when we
bought the house. I have already forgiven them for the
abduction. My only condition for forgiving them was that they

would let the trees and shrubs grow in peace, and would not devastate the grid of triangles and intuitions that tiled its vastness.

At the airport,
a while later:

the airport as an exercise; I depart at five o'clock, and am gazing at the twilight realm outside. I find I am less depressed because I feel as though I have the ability to wait, and to write;

my mother's illness reflects the neurosis of my entire life; seated on a horse, what could I do but keep my balance?; I never expected to use this word, but for me it has no derogatory meaning — it is one of the possible wings of my fate; without a certain number of inabilities, I would have remained without a light of my own, far from this vigil.

Yes, there is something that constantly supplies me with work; that will not let me be deluded about my strengths, nor by the assumptions I make about my life. It is a kind of consolation to know it never fails.

In the air

On the ground it was night, climbing into the sky I think about the continents in the northern hemisphere, about those who usually live in very cold places, for the immense remainder of the day was still bright, and the effects of the light we were passing through were full of gaps; celestial landforms of all kinds paraded monotonously, as though I were turning a crank organ; and because it was dangerous to be in such a distant

enfolding space, I experienced a sudden fright, certainly shared
by a great number of passengers, and I made an invocation,
surrendering myself to space, time, and movement; the flight
provoked many ideas, I soon felt as though I was poised
between hollows, shapes, and dimensions, weights and heights
of depths unknown; I had come to handle family problems,
with a great willingness to humble myself, and that panorama in
which everything can be conceived, to a greater or lesser extent,
reminded me of the study of geography applied to psychology.
Nothing would ever be the same as it had been in parental
relationships, I had exhausted the part I had to contribute to
ensure that the column of smoke remained in the hearth.

In truth, I felt protected by this entire ancient domain from
dawn to dusk; at one point, a mantle stretched out behind us,
on which seemed to be drawn the backs of sheep — it was the
last place I had ever been,   *with a first rhythm in the form*
of a dream.

Today, in Herbais, it was difficult for me to leave the
Dictionaries, the cats, the image of Jade, who was no longer
present. It is a contradiction to love Herbais, and to want to
distance myself from it, but at times, I am merely myself, civilly.

I must never mention Pessoa's name in the book; the
names that are not those of the author are determined based
on the place they occupy in the detailed description of the
house,
in the frieze, shaped like a table, above a door; in the interlight,
as if to say the interbeing;
in the silver snuffbox, with a shallow chamber;

I should travel more often, rupture portions of territory and, more than anything, feel the breeze of movement; journeys are moments open to any affective state, which, coupled with intelligence, take the structure of a book far into the distance; I remember a Paris-Brussels journey by train, when it was snowing. The snow moves me, and makes me discerning — everything seems very old to me, or only to be used later on; I was gazing through the window for no other reason than seeing; but suddenly it became an optical prism, the light polarized, and I took the steps, or necessary efforts, to be able to barely touch *From Hedge to Being*.

The heteronyms conceal Infausta and Aossê; Bach is the one who has been defined, upon whom a determination has already fallen; as well as the one who is known. Penetration, my access to his music. The art of music, what even is it?

My mother greeted us with immense joy and serenity. As old age shapes her, a new face is appearing, one of luminous kindness. Augusto took several photographs of her, as he wants to capture the image of someone who is turning toward death, without losing her footing — and who is allowing us her face.

Christine, prior to our departure, had sent us a text by Levinas, specifically about the essential emptiness of our face. I was reminded, very distantly, of another text by Borges, which today, on the whole, seems to me — only the word *bluff* is appropriate. Enclosed, alongside it, a few Persian poems and, more importantly, a poem (I think) by Al-Hallaj, which he addresses to his own consciousness and which I translated into Portuguese, instinctively rendering "O consciousness of my consciousness" as "O vastness of my sound," the continuation of which I set down here: "That you make yourself so tenuous and escape the imaginings of fear itself. And that at the same time, and hidden, you transfigure everything, at your own initiative. If I were to ask you to forgive me — you whom I touch — it would mean forgetting your ubiquity, revealing my doubts about our union to you, revealing that I am undecided, at the moment you make me your mouthpiece. You, who are the gathering of everything, are for me not another but I myself. And so how can I ask you for forgiveness?"
It is evening,
looking through the windows of my mother's house at the points of light along the Tagus (which for me will always be River-Tagus from *In the House of July and August*, when they

bury Müntzer's image in it and Alisubbo says, "This is the sea"),
Music's arrival at Bach's side came to me.

In the end, I didn't want to know what music is, I longed to
see it. To see it with Bach's eyes, as if I were sitting there like
him, looking at River-Tagus.

*Slowly, the night closes in, and falls. I intentionally sit down in
front of the window to watch it fall behind the lace curtain. They put
it up today. The candle flame divides the singing voice. The spirit of
evil passes, makes me intelligent and lucid, the spirit of evil is part of
life. So tenuous the lace, so tenuous the telluric layers through which
I travel, I arrive at the maelstrom where there was nothing. Neither
birds existed, nor had the first wing extended, Good and Evil were
growing like twins in the same force. I am in the place of the plant
within the germ, the flame illuminates the Volume, an archaic
creation, sound confronts the air, air is part of the family tree. Sitting
in this chair, I am sitting under the tree which, at that moment in
time, may have been the shrub of paradise. My image of Music is
always present in front of my mouth. Her silhouette appears in the
inmost part of the house, Jade, at my feet, is sleeping, and we gather
our spirit in what we say, and in the brief whispering
which never abandons us: — I had given you a flexible metal rod,
with an ornate tip, just like the one I have. — When I received it, I
thought you wished for my death. — Music lays her head on her
lap as if she were brushing her hair. She inherited Müntzer's gesture,
his smile. Love leaves us but returns on horseback, enters the room,
and touches its paw to the candle. I ask Music to stand up and
accompany me, for I wish to see through the torn curtain, and in the
night, the percussion of the flame. Slender and fulminant, beneath
the paw that vainly attempts to crush it, and runs through our
bodies. Music makes no movement, her head has become singular,*

more intelligent than the transparency of her dress. I leave alone with the voice behind me, and the ancient weight of the house that summons me, and reflects us always. In the beginning, what beginning?, all the beings were gathered in the same demonic vastness of the darkness. Sex and soul, hands and feet, paws and brain, ears and speechlessness were buried, without being dead as the dead are believed to be dead. They waited in the illusion of life. Music now falls asleep, terrified by the enormous shadow that evades the wall.

It is a vastness so intense that I take her hand to calm her, although I know my fear is ferrying me, and the horse is not yet love
but its fearsome manifestation.

Bach averts his gaze
and lowers it to the place where Jade was sleeping, but then it
falls on Aossê, who had seen Bach's lips moving, and heard
nothing. But Bach continues

when you are born, there is as yet no traveler. Heavy drops are the
first drops of the Spirit. For Music to descend to a lower tone,
I, too, descend to the place of births
which is an entire subterranean Cathedral. From its stained-glass
windows stream a thousand incandescent deaths, which pierce the
women lying there. Scattered lights await the only pauses permitted,
and the living kingdom, lowering down into the crematory fire of the
wombs, aspires to a new form.

I had a restless night. To calm myself, I picked up the manuscript of *Loving Cause*. Insofar as I had forgotten I had written it, I took great joy in reading it, and I imagined that the true alchemical salamander was the human species, which had already endured so many trials by fire.

I was reminded of Jorge de Sena, who is Jorge Anés, in the book. I kept thinking I had seen him as he would have wanted to have lived. There was a bullet, or a piece of shrapnel, in him from other battles (perhaps from the North African campaign — Ceuta, 1549), which no one had ever been able to remove. But it was there.

I never saw him, and I was there in the night, thinking of him.

Was there someone else, in another place and at that very moment, thinking of me?

In the afternoon, I go to the Jardim da Estrela. I sit on a bench, despite the cold, in front of the old Bandstand, and read over the notes I had written in the early hours, imagining Aossê's reaction to Bach's revelations:

Following my gaze to Bach's lips, there is always a subterranean space, an utterance which scrutinizes his open mouth.
I lower my eyes to the gleaming, enamored brightnesses, visualize a vastness that, in my language, must have a name. I then look for another vastness, for which I find no words, or surface and image: unfettered water, neither river, nor sea, nor lake, nor fog, water full of silence at the moment of fire, or perhaps a volcanic climate at the

center of the lands. Overlapping terms from multiple languages return to oneness, it is the explosion of the birth of time; it is its principle of stellar escape in the marrow of creatures; (a breeze rises, its description is unthinkable beyond a meditation of mist).

It is a vision of such intense delight that threads of water flow through the fire, which is all-encompassing and weightless. There are living beings from the dawn of the centuries to the end of mortal lifetimes and, above them, dead beings are indistinguishable from the all-consuming throb: my companions see for me, I close my eyelids to them; I awake by opening my eyes.

I left Aossê in front of the old Bandstand.
I had finally heard what Bach had heard, but in reverse.
Bach retreats. Aossê enters.

He was on his way: he would be run through by the water.
Within the water loomed the dust which had long ago become
known to him; it was an abstract dust, wholly bound to the water
that fled from him. He, in the middle, surrounded by aquatic veils,
was the statue
watching over the shape of the whirlpool.
Round and round, he penetrated further into the depths of the
water, which, having become the motionless landscape of glass,
penetrated the earth.
And on and on it went,
he reached the mouth-core of the Spirit
which was immense and unmade water,
and which could also be Music.
His head covered the water, he moved forward like a sound in
your ears.
A great reverberation of voices slowly descended to a lower tone,
and hung suspended between the moment of birth
and the following mortal instant.

It is night behind the writing.   Aossê is still writing,
although he is old, and much goes unsaid. Evening falls with no
transition,
he himself does not light the candle,
the candle lights by itself,
behind his shoulder
where the bird is perched
sleeping ceaselessly
as if eternally dead.
  "One more word and that will be the end," he murmurs to
himself without writing. A shadow looms at his side, on the opposite
side of the bird, and a drop of blood falls on the ground, which the
dog, very young, licks,
        and then rests his muzzle on the pen,
in memory of the nearly finished work.   He then enters the
field of his images, aspires to eternal life as he had aspired to
writing, and lands at the foot of a tree like the bird Lisbon.

I return to Unhappy Harbor in Belgium. Unhappy? Do not forget that Infausta is the joy of Aossê _____ I feel poor, miserably woven into the human. The light of the sorrow I left behind falls upon me, to be conveyed to the place where it could be transformed into a direction, or a new approach; Augusto, at my side, endures the drudgeries of Portugal, and surrenders to his more withdrawn side: he does not listen to me, does not hear me as he usually does. But in some way, or another, I always feel connected to him by the sense of our alliance. Yet his company cannot seep down into my bones, for a being is a being caught in the weft of being bound to themselves.

The composition of Aossê — a dramatic character and figure in Lisbonleipzig — was the composition that followed the line of a man not being a man; it was an amalgam of possibilities; my mother's ever so precarious life as late causes me to reflect on the persistence of the birthplace throughout life — the act of being born, remaining relatively detached after birth, ultimately disappearing beyond the reach of its image.

_____ today, I feel solace only in the act of writing — the thread of light through which I escape the lines woven around me.

_____ I feel like playing seriously with writing, since everyone, myself included, partly thinks of it as a game. But the writing which encompasses me is an illuminative power, and a life's purpose that strikes fear. The fear of writing. It is better not to speak of it than to speak of it. Making such an alliance with the potential horizon of nothingness creates a new tree branch on the horizon.

_____ we move toward the horizon and, as we approach it, even if we do not step across it, we fear its perspective; the horizon is a scale that measures distance and emptiness; and gives each its own weight.

This was the area where Johann Sebastian Bach's house stood, distinct in the night; only very rarely was there a dilemma between singing an aria or putting a child to sleep, between creating a score or enduring the cries of another child. Johann Sebastian Bach could concentrate in the din, and be interrupted without being pulled fully out of his work; it was this conflictual area of the house for ordinary mortals which drew Aossê _____ man or vacant place, both man and vacant place. His figure, his reason for being, was transfigured before our eyes; one might say he portrayed himself in a thousand ways, and grew through the most subtle of words.

The North as a work

This morning, despite the strangeness of being in Herbais
again, I did not delay the moment of writing any longer, for it is
to roam that I returned here. I had a feeling similar to the one
caused by gliding between two layers of clouds in an airplane.
On this most recent journey, at a certain moment, we left
behind the darkness of the night which was already upon the
earth, and entered an amphitheater of brightness that the sun
still illuminated;

the North, as a work, today seems to me to be exactly the same;
the work does not feel joy but is luminous, it reemerges today as
the threshold of what is called the end of nightfall; it is a
problem of paradoxes and contrary directions, and I do not
know which will have more weight, or will produce a greater
effect on the veil, which is, at the same time, billowing and thick.

Moving from enactment to _____ the word was
hidden.

The North, as a work, is a plangent and virile place — virile
with hope.

This writing, done in the North, makes reference to a
request that has already been made.

Then, it still had so many channels to navigate, that it had to
protect the body from a negative, or cold temperature. Having

the character that was necessary would prevent it from proceeding with.

My conscience is not at peace; I am not where they say it is essential for me to be. It cannot be otherwise, nor cease to be.
Who is speaking?
What do they say? — Go back to Portugal — they insist.

Guilt?
I would be susceptible to guilt if I were unaware there is a fate. But there was.

— Stay — Bach told me. In Leipzig, no one can take your place. Your mother's fate was to bring you into the midst of our conflicts, and it is being fulfilled.

I have come to the end of this day, and the encounter with Regina Louro gave it a truly thought-provoking inclination.

Based on my books, we roamed together through different territories of thinking, and her reader's eye seemed to reshape my own, accustomed to seeing and writing. I returned to places I had traveled alone, where it had been written I had traveled, and I felt, through the presence of another, that it was so.

I proclaim images that are not images, and hearing them spoken — not by me — lends them duration and intensity. I meditated, then, that there were not only beings with a recognized historical significance, but we were, all of us, the long-vanished beings of one moment, and the vibrant beings of another.

We touched on the following points:

Writing as the pursuit of truth:

I am not the bearer of a truth because the truth cannot be borne, but I experience the impulse to pose questions to the truth which I see as fitting. Beings have an irrefutable feeling that there is a place where they will arrive at their own coincidence.

To each their own.

To say what it is, is a pendent datum. Truth as matter is inaccessible to us, but we all stride through "form" to that compelling point. There is no one who does not amble.

Truth as matter

Truth is neither subjective nor objective, but the final and finished outline of a life; the answer given, with good intentions, to the just entreaty. To ask "who am I" is the question of a slave; to ask "who is summoning me" is the question of a free man.

Genesis and meaning of the figures

When I dared to leave behind the representational writing that made me feel so uneasy, as uneasy as I felt spending time with others, and in Lisbon, I found myself without any rules, particularly mental ones. It felt inane to give life to characters in realist writing, for that meant I also had to give them death. And so it goes. The text would fatally move toward ineffable and/or hermetic experimentalism. Under these circumstances, I gradually identified "constructive knots" of the text, which I call figures, and which, in reality, are not necessarily people, but rather modules, outlines, delineations. A person who historically existed can be a figure, in the same way as a sentence ("This is the garden that thinking allows"), an animal, or a chimera. What I later called luminous scenes. In truth, the outlines I mentioned involve a radiant core. My text does not proceed through thematic developments, nor through plot, but rather follows the thread running through the different luminous scenes. There is thus a unity, even if there is seemingly no logic, because I do not know in advance what each luminous scene contains. Its core may be an image, or a thought, or an intensely affective feeling, a dialogue.

But it turns out there is a formal identity between these cores (hence the formal importance of my texts, even at the graphic level), which I identify by the vortex they evoke in me. When a reader reacts in the same way, this vortex is corroborated, and the constructive knot deepens.

An example: the figure of the one who reads.

The audience of readers is initially multiple. At some point, I began to have a vision of a single reader, a bluish form, without any human aspect. But I knew this bluish form might later become an entreaty for a book, as it longed intensely to understand how to decipher my own signs. Which in and of itself could elicit the dynamic of a new text. Perhaps the bed of a river, mutating from reader to riverbed. It is a process very similar to that of sound composition. The figure is never inert, but an active principle, whose harmonics and trajectory will fade away if they prevent it from acting according to its own principle. With experience, and technical refinement, you learn to write in this way, as you learn to steer a glider following the winds.

In reality, we have already spoken so much, and know so little, that it is not even a risk — rather a necessity — to seek out other sources of knowledge, the origin of words, unconventional associations.

It may seem strange that this trajectory through non-human worlds leads to new human harmonics.

It is the heart that guides.

Intelligence is a leash which harmonizes the impulses of a seemingly haphazard pursuit.

The maternal space of Ana de Peñalosa

I am not Ana de Peñalosa,

but she is someone I think about, saying *beloved Ana de Peñalosa.*

I am also not her daughter, nor will she be my mother. I am convinced that the one who is summoning me is not something, but someone.

I am convinced that I will answer and will see who it is.

And so the path may be rough, but it will not be aggressive. It is not a feeling, but a companion figure: life is mysterious and bewildering, but it will not be a catastrophe that mutilates us. We will remain unscathed if we do not separate our body and soul.

Ana de Peñalosa is someone who, historically, aided John of the Cross with the goods she possessed. And so, in the human horde, there was humanity. A glimpse. And her greatness consisted in having believed in that glimpse.

Becoming as simultaneity

As a civilian, I know the present, past, and future. But as a writer, I have a gaze that primarily touches space, absent time. There is no power in it, which is always the power to choose and to arrive at death. I look with a vague gaze, as if nothing were clear, staring through a window. Everything, in its substance, is equivalent. No one point is worth more than any other. What draws my attention — gaze unfurling — is a contrast: a point speaks because the space is sound, the vastness of this space is its sonorous vastness, which in my experience as a writer, does not appear to me as a timbre, but as words. A pitcher is formed by the sound of pitcher, but I see the word pitcher, which has its swell in the *c*. All words have the same incandescence. They touch one another. Every era has its plunder of just words, and I am not surprised when I hear words from other eras in the present day. My space is an utterance, it is books, readings, restlessness, dictionaries. The first voice that gleams is the one that summons me.

Words are, like everything else, impulsive forms, teeming with a river, holding fragments of time and events, in a wholly chaotic archive. For example: Müntzer. In his Z is his inexorable beheading, but the Princes delude themselves into thinking death would follow, as the effect of the cause. He is a lasting being, harsh and enduring in his desire. In that living body, head in hand, you can hear, even now, the rare, and ever so resonant voices.

Having lived now for half a century, I do not see how narrative could compete with words, which are the most ancient and unrelenting witnesses of human becoming. Most of the internal movements of a word are silent. But some of them are sonorous, and only a minute fraction of these are voices. They are the ones I have grown accustomed to being sensitive to, trained myself to listen to, they are the ones I follow and, with that guidance, enter into. I recognize that this is the most radiant part, the lamp which should not be hidden in the chest of silent movements.

I am always surprised by the genetic and destructive potential of certain words, of certain semantic families, which form clumps in the dictionary.

The becoming of every one lies in the sound of their name.

Neither hierarchy, nor rupture between body and spirit

Thinking is compelled by the geometry of bodies.

There is one who is slumbering. If it is looked at from outside of itself, it could be said that it sleeps, that it is stagnant. But I know this body knows it is accumulating energy.

Looking at a white wall, it is very difficult for me to think. But I know the wall is guarding my gaze.

Awaking someone is awaking what? Sleeping, are they not in their full moon phase?

Is painting a white wall hiding its gaze, or allowing it to gaze at me with some of its hues?

Is it not necessary to have stamina in order to think?

What does a bad thought do to the body?

Are good intentions part of the body, or the spirit?

If thinking does not love the body, what form will thinking have?

When I give an intense written form to my suffering, am I not further burdening it, as if it had depths and a luminous escape?

When body and spirit are two experienced lovers, the hidden ratio emerges, they know how to extract the immense ardor to create from almost nothing.

Can a beautiful body and a just thinking coexist in a chaotic context?

To write in the shadows is to seek out what power? Does the visible follow the arc of the day? Will the invisible follow the inverse arc? What is this being who writes on a table where all the vegetal is absent?

The context is that of the body and the text; what is sick in man if he only looks at the body? If he only attends to the text? Is the thinking that abstracts from the context not intended to define the body?

The living body is an uninterrupted form.

To say it is matter, thinking of viscera and humors, is a form of maliciousness, or blindness.

It is matter, and only matter made of images, as when fear comes, and paralyzes it. The fear comes from it, the paralysis is its own.

I am certain that the Text has modified the body of humans.

The text, a place that travels

The text is the shortest distance between two points.

Because we speak, we think about a skein of plot, and feel a tangle in our stomach, or in our heart. The word novel is the escape from this pain. A quick sting, or a brief encounter.

Just because words are laid out in order in the dictionary does not mean we imagine the text to be flat, and without topography. We feel that words usually have the shape of a soaked sponge, or, alternatively, the topography of small rocks with jagged edges and indentations left there by erosion.

If we were to take an aerial photograph of a gigantic book, we might mistake it for the circular image of a city defending itself.

Access to the book is immediate. Only afterwards, already inside it, does the loss begin. Saint John of the Cross says it best: "We will arrive in places we do not know by paths we do not know."

How to return to a place through a universal space

I set out to find our context. And writing about alien, foreign places, I gave the impression I was not speaking about here.

But I never left here, in the sense that I never abandoned my body. My form of rebellion was merely refusing to live it mutilated. And across so many centuries, it has put down roots or left footprints in places we no longer have any memory of. We reached a state of such utter fragility and smallness that it became important to understand whether we had lived, or whether we had dreamed our past. The difference is minimal, but disenchantment can be fatal.

To seek out plenitude is to ensure the harmonic and methodical breathing of my body, born to persevere.

This morning, I transformed the courtyard into an outdoor room of light, and despite the pain in my back, I do not want to break the rule of obedience out of a lack of sensitivity.

Surrounded by vegetables, animals — the lateral part of humanity — I feel the internal secretion of this state of living, analogous to space and duration. Herbais does not obscure Portugal, and introduced a new figure to *Lisbonleipzig*, named Infausta. The description of the book is not the book, but the ideas in the interview I gave to Regina Louro caused me to plunge into an intensity of perceptions which lie beneath the page, and are the instrument for measuring the height of the text I have assembled.

Perhaps what I have written so far is a preliminary proposal, and I feel a certain dread. Am I capable of separating celebrations of thought and language, in a narrative? Do I have an embryo within me? Is my very self not part of a vaster strategy of solitary places? I would like all my work to be gestatory and this period, populated almost entirely with wildernesses, to be a chemical element, an experiment, and a study.

Impulses are not plants, such as "morning glories." I glean a creative energy from my return from Portugal, of which there is, as yet, no shadow of depression. Only the pain in my back indicates that there is a vulnerable point in this geography.

From Praça de Camões to Rua Domingos Sequeira, along the tracks of the streetcar, I recall my first geography, legs still short, not even capable of navigating that tortuous path on foot. How beautiful that modest path is today, with old-fashioned stores that still evoke rural pleasures, and village encounters. As soon as I arrive in Lisbon, in a meditative corporeal amble, I connect the two points to one another, and make the first meaningful journey. I was shaped there, and the trip I used to take with my mother to Baixa, by streetcar, almost always to go shopping for fabrics and clothes, haberdashery, buttons and threads, is my ancestral journey, the damsel from whom I broke free. In Chiado, there were shoe shops and bookstores, and returning home, clinging to the beauty and the beacon of maternal matter, which controlled my movement down to the last gesture, arm in arm, or hand in hand, voice dependent on her voice, was truly the end of a dream. I longed intensely for a map of intimate steps, far and near to her own. Because we always got off at Rua Domingos Sequeira, when the streetcar passed Largo da Estrela, the atmosphere was particularly overwhelming, the inside was outside the Basilica. There I had read aloud, for myself and my peers, the confirmation text. It is on these now somewhat calloused feet that I stand up to move, this is my primordial experience. From Estrela to Camões, I rehearsed my voyage over two countries, I began the preliminary leg of this journey. But the phantom of ambition is also an awareness of powerlessness. Someone, behind me, casts my shadow in a place that I know will always be larger, and more imprecise, than I am.

Fabric and fearfulness. I feel a growing sense of trepidation that they will speak of me when I am dead. Being dead to myself, and alive to others, what does that mean ontologically?

Is my body in disarray? Or is it disjointed? There are parts that hurt, parts that function perfectly, little watery blisters that migrate from the alveolar cavities to the lower lip, or to the finger I use to strike the typewriter, and the face is splendid.

Afternoon:
last year, I went into one of those shops where they sell tableware and knickknacks, and the conversation with the owner led to a promise to bring her a white cat from Belgium.
This year, to buy fabrics for Josée, I went into another shop on Largo do Calhariz, and had a conversation with the owner, who spoke to me in the tone of an emigrant. Since, in relationships with people, my intrinsic personality almost always bothers them, and bothers me, I pretend I am what they believe I am, and let them suppose there is a genuine identification with this superficial aspect I possess; who could I be if not my outward image?

_____ I haven't left Lisbon yet. I walk the Estrela-Camões route, I am a vehicle, I always ferry a journey that is unfeasible. I take pleasure in this votive walk, first along a slope, then climbing up to Rua Luz Soriano. It is the district of the printing houses, and I know this pleasure, achieved perhaps three times a year, is implicit in my perspective of Herbais.

I go to the Portuguese Writers' Association, registering as a member, in response to their invitation.

There is also a café/pastry shop, where I usually sit with Augusto, deep in its depths, for it is long, and in the haze of cigarettes. Here the smoke has a meaning, contrasts less with the sharp outlines, as in Herbais. But here, thinking is practiced at the very moment you are struck by it, whereas in Brabant, it is determined by a modification that bends, or curves it. I am trying to say that, in this environment, you think about thinking, and attack it from the flank; knowledge is prodded relentlessly in those green, dense, flying, aromatic, and occasionally deeply distressing wildernesses.

Dense, flying, aromatic can also be used to describe a period of life.

But I was walking up the stairs at the Writers' Association and, at a certain moment, I sensed that everything was poised on a fault — uncertain operating hours, decrepit rooms. It was in the afternoon, or around that time, and I suddenly felt very old in that occupation, and that everything around me had become respectable because of its antiquity. I was a traveler there, but I had that old piece of cloth as one of my ancestors, and at that vesperal hour, I let myself be covered with it.

Every room I passed through was a cross distanced from the next, which reminded me of the Passion of Writing, in the presence of which I would like to make a meditation.

A conversation with Lurdes, in her room bounded by shadows and windows, which always creates a special mode of space for me, so pleasant.

In response to my question, she says it would be interesting to send *The Remaining Life* and *The Book of Communities* to the Portuguese Language Society, which is organizing an exhibition of books by contemporary Portuguese women writers in June. Because, according to her, there is a female writing.

I don't believe that.

From the moment the text acquires a certain power, it is no longer specific to a man or a woman. I take Emily Brontë's *Wuthering Heights* as an example. I myself feel a neutral part in my being — the promised land of strength, and the no man's land of sex.

My body was born where it was, and yet it is far less original than that of Volondat, the twenty-year-old pianist who won this year's Queen Elisabeth Competition. My body was born where it was was the first sentence that came to me today and ushered me into the day with which I had to struggle to establish the visual field of Portugal, and the visual field of Belgium. Always Pessoa. All the more so because Volondat surprised me with his hieratic body, which seemed to have fallen unexpectedly to the ground, and was neither normal nor abnormal, simply another mechanism. The similarity between the two is so blatant that when I heard him play, I followed with my eyes what Pessoa's work would suggest to me, the work being not only the text, but the body. That is the crucial point, the orifice through which I see today, with *Lisbonleipzig* always as the backdrop. They were the common element of a composition, the mechanical place of the soul. But they also both reminded me of the fine paper used to write sacred books. When I write *Lisbonleipzig*, I become lost in the difficulty of gathering the waters scattered over the surface of the music, and of a new language which delves into the effects of Pessoa's body. It is the book that will prove to me that I can write against the current, to shape, for listening, material which is not only to my own taste, nor of my own body. It is strange, writing *Lisbonleipzig* seems to be an obligation, a trial that will anchor me in the firmament of intercession. I maturely assessed my strength, and felt I was descending perpendicularly over the distance between Lisbon-Leipzig.

How to proceed? It is a sunny day, but Portocalho cannot be seen in it. Yet this cloudy day compared to another will bring me an opportunity: it is the moment to divide the book into *the thirty final moments of Aossê, and the thirty initial moments of Bach*. And so I dissolve a preparatory work, and discover the true face of the text at this moment — one that is not solely intuitive.

How Aossê returned from within holding an apple —
his refined ear was not in harmony with the way he used his body, once Johanna Catharina Bach had returned from St. Thomas Church, and had gone to the kitchen to eat apples ripening in a basket,
he asked her for one, and carefully washed it, pouring out water from a pewter pitcher.
Infausta was behind him, wearing a dress from her own time, which Regina Susanna, one of the children in the house, coveted for a costume. Infausta confirmed she could not give her the dress, and Aossê interrupted, saying he would offer her his apple. She made a sudden movement with her arms, which opened wildly in their direction. Infausta, at her side, was watching her consciousness for her own curiosity, not to see what was happening and then recount it later.
Regina Susanna cut the apple he was offering her in two, and at that instant, music was loosed from the organ, a finely solemn breath associating certain games. The qualities and defects of that moment twinned the figures of Aossê and Infausta — the female Pessoa.

What can be expected of love with a body so dense, and one with elliptical seeds?

Johanna Catharina — the eldest daughter — was frying meat for dinner, and Regina Susanna stubbornly preferred Infausta's dress. Aossê gave her the fruit, which ended up going bad, and was all for nothing.

_____ I am in my favorite place for writing _____ place of the summer solstice. It is the entryway, between the door to the street and the flight of stairs, which clearly reveals the beginnings of the house's isolation; after the task of setting up the table, it is already late, I have only two hours remaining ahead of me. A warm light coming through the crack in the door left ajar falls on the typewriter and I have the feeling, which has seldom been the case as of late, that I am a great distance above my wilderness.

Lisbonleipzig underwent an upheaval today, moved away from the monotonous equator where it seemed to be stationed for several days and, like a hungry animal, left the place sheltered from the sun; how did that happen?

Rereading *Current Account*, by Vergílio Ferreira, I opened the book to the blank pages at the end, and read to Augusto what I had written in pencil some time ago — the period when I had written *Tales of Wandering Evil*.

That text follows:
For us, several cities changing geographical locations had settled around the place where we lived. The sun had reached that place at a point on the elliptical; there was Münster, there was Lisbon, and others remained unknown in the vast space surrounding us. There were also the ruins of Antwerp, unfathomable — while snowflakes fell in the same place, and recreated, in captive waters, an aquatic plant which is difficult to find. None of this was an illusion, but our consensus to produce a new atmosphere, in which consonant and

consoling letters were very important. Every day, I read pages from a book about the siege of Münster, and as I lean on its stone or metal pages, I recreate the city. Neither I, nor Copernicus, were idle around Hadewijch, nor were those cities idle around us, and the thousands of Converso pilgrims in the band. But if Hadewijch lived in Lisbon, it would be entirely lost to us, vulnerable to being described by a single language.

Then followed a note on The Morning Plight: the bezant, wherever it comes from, is a precursor. With it came Eckhart, via the obstructed path through the ruins of Antwerp..., and on The Clues: from the perspective of the years, We live for a short time...

Then we began to unfurl possibilities — a scene, another scene, outer walls of the embryo:

No. The bands never reached the island. They were lost. How Pessoa explained his disagreement with Infausta. Bach goes unheard in Leipzig. Pessoa goes unconsoled in India.

But the great common desire is the journey to Jerusalem.

Bach: — One more step, and you will be in Jerusalem.

Pessoa: — One more being, and I would be in Jerusalem.

Me, making mine an outburst by Pessoa: — I do not know what tomorrow will bring.

Those who think open themselves up to an infinity of realities beyond themselves.

HERBAIS, 27 JUNE 1983

_____ a twilight day, with an almost motionless breeze, in which nearly all that will be doled out for me to live on is Aossê, Bach, and the hope that I will also be a person who someone will have liked to meet.

I returned from Portugal on the 8th, Wednesday, and the ley lines of my return were drawn rapaciously: my writing is not yet fully developed and I retreat to Herbais, although unmoored from two beloved people, my mother and S.; the rebel finally revealed themselves, I hadn't been playing that it had a fate of its own and, "because she is ill," my mother cannot bear my not responding to her summons; but I must cover my ears, for there are not only mermaids in the sea, and where is there a greater seduction than within the confines of the maternal body?

The return has been a spiral around these losses, described by a point which makes a series of loops around Herbais; I do not want to lose my head at the hands of an enemy. I am comforted by the short period of time in which I open the correspondence from Portugal. Here, Lisbon has become the Indies, but I retain all lucidity.

_____ everything is fine and sharp this morning following the rain, even the absence it represents; I know nothing, no one knows where I am,   except that I am a vague example.

It is liberating to live here, but I feel the vertigo of soaring high into the air with nowhere to grasp onto tightly.

I need branches.

On the night of 26–27 August, when Bach and Aossê had a
violent conflict, to the point of exchanging blows, Bach slapped
Aossê, and I saw a homicidal gleam in the latter's eyes; it was
because Aossê was not capable of establishing a connection
with the outside, had expressed himself poorly in making a
request; he had forgotten what he was at that moment, what
language he should speak, and he felt as though all roads were
closed to him, except for that of poetry. In desperation, he threw
a chair on the floor, for *everything I do or think is always half
done.* Bach then slapped him, "a reflex," he said. Aossê shouted
that Bach's beast had broken free, that it was the hedgehog in his
body, that he wanted, whatever the price,
to be *green and natural.*

But that night, because of the extreme violence he had
given himself over to,
and because he had an unbridled hatred for Bach,
he was unable to sleep. Never again was it day, the night
unfolded into nights, and on their threshold, no incandescence
was quelled _____ nothing more inaccurate, or
distant, than the morning.

... *the text,* Aossê thinks, *is a texture that penetrates the water,*
          my death one winter is present because winter is my
resurrection. *With my head lying on the page,*   *page of*
water, page of snow, page of stone, I rest, gazing at my figures, in the
eternal resignation of the mirror. Thus written, I enter the winter
that reflects everything that is happening, covered by the water that
is liquid and frozen. Throughout the summer as well, some animals,
and All *the Peace of Nature, follow me persistently in their loyalty,*
letting fall their innumerable garments. Or it rains, and murmurs, it
is death and that great sorrow, I have the head of an animal and a
hand that is a page, I do not become lost in the labyrinth because it
is a mirror
with multiple exits.

                         I do not know. But, at this
moment, I know everything I do not know without knowing how to
name it. I gaze, with my eyes closed, without memory.
     I fell into a dazzling and aimless communication,
revealing such a deep keenness of remembrance that I have been
everywhere
with all equality.   *I have been and will be without*
living the present, which is only a journey and an illusion of time.
My anger fades into tears and a wrinkle of my mouth. Humility lifts
me up, and chooses, between beating drums and cries of war;
either Music comes with Infausta, or the seasons will blind my soul.

She was a phenomenon strictly associated with distance: she often wondered about the quality of her memory. When she thought about the place and time where she was, about the places and time she had left behind, the emotion she felt now seemed much more intense and, in certain aspects, more real and akin to reality. She remembered it as it had been, but with a certain inconsistency of energy, or a module, which gave the slightest detail a singular sharpness and amplification of meaning; the disguise fell away,   multiple recollections emerged in a light which was not that of the simplifying Final Judgment, but that of knowledge hoisting the sails.

For example:

I was in my bedroom, at my mother's house, and there was a strident ringing at the door; the maid moved down the hallway and I, lying there, knew that the glassed-in brightness of the landing was going to flood a protected angle of the runner.

If I were to go there now, the summer of 1983 and Rua Domingos Sequeira physically present, it is Rosário who is walking down the hall, and the bell seems to be ringing, with the door already open.

III.

Inquiry into
the Four Confidences

LATE JANUARY 1994

I'm going.

This *I'm going* is like the heading
of a letter.

I'm going,
my "modern" world is unsettling. I shouldn't say it until the
end of the text, but the end of the text is unpredictable — it
suddenly halts. It has been said.

I stand up, with some difficulty, feeling a piece of lacework
in my hand, heavy as a silver salver; it rained torrentially during
the night, the wind rushing, I am literally immersed in the
water, images flashing by — I reread *Loving Cause*, and marvel
at its constancy, I am grateful to it for having gotten me out of
bed, accompanying me in the bath, and having a sound that
transports me to another place. It seems to me that Herbais is
now in every part of the house, and that a deep well inhabits

Sintra. I wear short socks very often this winter. They barely cover my ankles. It is as a child on my feet that I enter my "modern" world.

The territory of this house, today, a rainy day,
trembles
like a cup in God's hand. Although it is fragile, I find it beautiful. It is part of my current existence, it is the notebook I keep, where I write my observations before going out into the street, to do the day's shopping, drink a cup of coffee from the espresso machine.

The happiness of living more permanently in a city is, indeed, crossing the street, on a rainy day, stepping into a café and hearing music from the jukebox
and hearing
another customer
say it is sensual and sublime. He is referring to the music and what he says is part of a dialogue moving back and forth across the counter — about a name, the one belonging to the person working — who I look at with a certain astonishment at encountering a woman's face which plays at innocence.

"All this is happening in the manner of Verlaine," whispers the family tree of my sensibility and tastes. Not that I hear it, amused as I sip my coffee; it is whispered by the cadenced hoofbeats of a pair of horses that abruptly halt in front of the bistro. They also tell me, covering the seductive dialogue occurring beside me, to the rhythm of a song by Elvis, "The horses' metaphors about the text are not metaphors. It is not the text which halts as we do — everything suddenly halts." Everything that exists suddenly stops. And, unceasingly, begins again.

I'm going.

I'm going to think about my life from the outside, watch it
pass by on the street as I feel the flush of morning strength.
After breakfast, I climb the stairs. Two flights. On the white tiles
in the kitchen, I see a ball of dust that has accumulated other
materials and taken on a visibly entropic consistency.
To my mind, here, the floor should be uninterrupted and
smooth,   it is, I believe, one of the mirrors of heaven
that was intended for me, where I must work. Washing it,
especially with plain water, has always been an enormous
pleasure, particularly at the house in Jodoigne, where the
expanse of the floors was immense. I capture the tiny
whirlwind, open the window, and want to throw it out onto the
lower roof, where I do my part to feed the season's birds with
rice; but the whirlwind is entangled in the breeze, and comes
back. For a moment, it stalls, and I watch it enter my house
once more, as a sentence rushes white and fast through my
mind, "Behold, this is the great event of the morning." I let it
enter and it drifts over to settle in one of the corners of my
bookshelf — the one place where, amidst tableware, objects,
and books, I am the author of the maps of all the authors. Or
the globe of the written world.
    I sit down.
    At times, I no longer see the incidental world which
determines my reality, fragilely necessary small objects slip away
to another place where I am unfamiliar with the cartography, I
do not know where I put my glasses, where my nail scissors are,
where I left my handbag. And I suddenly halt. The fragility of
beauty is a more pressing necessity than the spoon I use for
soup; I do not think I have ever written out the word *pressing*; it

offers no deep shelter, I do not care for it — it would be banal at a banquet of words; it is only distinctive on a white cloth. I write it on the whirlwind. There are no words with the same meaning. But we can entangle them — and the contrast of sounds carries their meaning to another place.

At night, I telephone Vergílio. It is his birthday. Seventy-eight, I believe.

— Vergílio?

— Gabriela!

— How are you?

— Not well. I'm losing the joy of writing.

— How?

— I'm old, so exhausted, my mind is fading… There's nothing left to write.

— That isn't true. You will always need to write.

— You always tell me that…

On this end, I must have laughed.

— And laughing, no less. Have you been writing?

I tell him about how everything suddenly stops and begins again, about the fragilely necessary objects, the white cloth, the word *pressing*, and the whirlwind. I sense he is listening intently.

— That's funny, that whirlwind is just like me — he says from that end, and suddenly stops. — I've spent most of my life in a whirlwind, but I sometimes think I've been a white cloth.

_____ today, with the window open, I am an atmospheric phenomenon, I and the fog which rolls to the right side and, at this very instant, begins falling as rain. I cannot settle into an introverted state. Augusto now dwells within a great inner reserve, creating a vast zone of silence between us, which is transformed into an affective fog; I have always known where to find him — where to cast all my vitality, and find an echo; only the passage through the metanight, which I have, as of late, begun attempting to write in *Lisbonleipzig II*, will be able to give him, for the moment, his true meaning. But, within the metanight, I feel a certain poignant happiness, or an unhappiness that illumines. This house, which in its finishes, its furniture, its construction, is beautifully blue, did not seem to have been made to embrace such a silence.

_____ I go out to buy white thread.

I head toward the supermarket, where I know there is a store selling small items — buttons, thread, needles, feminine trifles. I go in. There was a woman in the clerk — I read it in her eyes — a gentle woman, wholly subdued, "no longer any ideas in her head." Yet I was drawn to her, she who had a quiet banality without any need to be cruel even though they were cruel to her.

— You have to be self-sufficient — said her employer, in front of whom were standing myself and another customer — You cannot constantly be asking me questions like a child.

I leave, accompanied by the silence of my language. On the way back, Augusto (atmospheric center) whispers a phrase by Deleuze into the mind of my ear, "Loving those who are like

this _____ when they enter a room they are not
persons, characters or subjects, but an atmospheric variation,
a change of hue, an imperceptible molecule, a discrete
population, a fog or a cloud of droplets." I pass by the
Miradouro da Correnteza, and over the mountains, I see the
morning fog lingering. I lean out over the valley.

I am in Toki Alai (that was my dream during the night), on
a foggy day such as this, and my essential concerns are three: to
feed the cats, to also feed a chicken, to spread out a blanket
beneath the roof of the front porch, which will serve as a bed for
a large dog that is now there. When an automobile passes by,
and the gate is open, the large dog rushes in, lunging like an
authoritative molossus, then the garden returns to silence as the
humidity falls, and I can clearly see the dog's body, agile,
slender, mouth open and ready to bite, a protective warrior.
From the inmost part of this house, I call him the *dog of the rule
of silence*, and the light that passes across the forehead of this
man — the other in this dyad of tension and harmony, this
conjunction of two contradictory and complementary natures,
whose singularity nurtures my own — *my ambo*, as I refer to
him, persists.
    I give the *dog of the rule of silence* a large bone, still quite
meaty. But now, I am awake — yet I haven't stopped thinking
about him. There is no longer any mystery, as the dog stands
there for a moment, leaning out over the valley, and I see him in
the text, just like Bach, Anna Magdalena, Baruch, Infausta, or
Aossê. I see him even more clearly, emaciated by the struggle. I
find he bears a great resemblance to Grandmother Maria's
Alsatian wolf, made of porcelain, which she kept among other
animals, including the sheep, on Rua Domingos Sequeira, on

318

her dressing table. I remember Jade, from *Loving a Dog*, a small book I wrote, and I know the dog loves us. Just like the other animals. I hear his footsteps within the metanight, carpeted with grass from the garden.

"Who is it? Who goes there?" I ask. Were book and everyday life truly so separate? Were they so far apart, words so distant from one another?

And then I enter *The Music Rehearsal* (about the metanight, which I now know is a fierce struggle against abstract representations that lay bare the spirit. Images tumble down from the horizon and, heedlessly, attempt to breach the ring where the flame burns …) _____ a solitary thread of thought, which suggests to me that, I and Augusto, we are equals in the presence of the solitary Nature. I am not sure what we are to one another. We are an *ambo*, but what that truly means is still cloaked in mist. I light the candle of tenderness for him. Here, my *ambo*,
take the candle of tenderness. With it comes the loyalty that never goes out _____ and the freedom of my space ascends the mountain _____ these nearby roofs _____, where there are birds, more precisely, a great number of swallows.

This dense fog falls steadily over them and I, within the accepted rule of silence, feel neither alone, nor despondent.
— He's awfully quiet, isn't he? — Vergílio once asked.
Augusto sleeps. I also ask for a restful slumber for our ills. It was almost unfathomable how the wind of greed swept away Senda, his entire team, and his project.
— Was it terrible?
— He says very little, if anything. What I know was mostly

told to me by others. He wants to mend the atrocious din of the metanight with silence.

It was almost unfathomable how the tension came back upon us and wanted, heedlessly, to steal us away, in order to separate and dilute us. But stronger than that voracious point was the text — the faithful Book, the one tipping the scales, an expression which often occurs to the *dog who does not fear the imposture of language.*

— *The internal equilibrium,* as I call it. When he wakes up, Gabriela, tell him that a possibility at life is measured by the movements it traces, and the intensities it creates.

"Time passed successfully, this morning," I tell them.

"It was not time wasted," they both agree.

Our life is a steady rainfall, as it is raining now. And it is not a comparison, because the proximity of everything is great, and nature — the same. Dog and book, fear and autonomy, root and strength, companions and comrades. There is nothing sweeter than
a solitary place, freed from fear,
or when fear frees it.

5 OCTOBER 1994*

"It is always a terrible night, for those who bid farewell / to
oblivion."

The Angel of Eros burned, leaning against the chimney; he
spoke softly; he repeated, in *time*, the same sound. Gazing at the
rain, my body had the desire to put out all the lights

and if someone were to come from outside and
knock, innocent of this world of flame, at the door,
the angel would inevitably sense he was alien to the *place* and
the flame. Because the flame is, like sex, an affirmation of one's
own volition, he contemplated himself in it, burning: flames
were rising from the fire with full consciousness of deciding; to
defend oneself from non-being, I thought, is shared by him and
the animals, and the stones, and also the "night sacrificed / to
dread and joy."

Because, in the end, everything that was happening   "a
wave that opens up / in the body" was happening within me.
Someone
knocked on the door, a long way off, exactly where the great hall
began, and asked me in that voice
with which young people are hesitant to ask questions:
— Is this the court where Eros comes to fetch his Angel?
— he asked me, placing a foot inside the door, and adding that
he only knows the shattered night of the practice of love: — But
I sense — he says — that other riches are emerging.   I think,
to myself, that if a bee were to seek out my lips,
where I would try to find out whether it was landing to sting
me, or speak to me, but I tell him only what the poet says: "They
ask so much of those who love: they ask for / love. They also

ask for / solitude and madness."

In the room — where I am alone with the flame — and Eros (man) is sitting, or Eros (woman) is sitting, in the chair where I usually put my feet,
      the silence is made of stone/darkness, illuminated.

I finally have the time to contemplate the encounter between the Angel and his Eros at length. It is my body which lights the flame _____
the moment has arrived when I will no longer follow it with my gaze. If the flame leaves the window, my body will return it to its *place*, so that it does not consume the opening of the window, and then the outside air and, finally, all the breath of the Universe; I place my writing hand on Eros's knee, a hand for work, where the writing, invisible, becomes lost, and roughness is the new force which has now been set alight; Eros extends the gaze of his hand toward the future that will be his creation, and rests it on the Angel. — Why will dawn come tomorrow? — he asks him. — Why will this storm from October to November persist in its mad days? — replies the Angel.

The rhythm of my breathing slows, and all the minute details of this dialogue, with table, carpets, and chairs   are *elsewhere*, between what will die in me, and my gaze. "Infinitely strange young woman," I think.
    — How infinitely strange you are, O Visitor — says the Angel — so infinitely different from what you believe you are. You burn villages, rob and kill, and gladden the world, and terrify, and burn the reticent places of this world.

— If you have a glimpse of who I am — says the young woman — and of who brought me to look at you, in this place in the room,

take away my voice, and give me the art of enduring, of transmuting my body, of having hands that flourish.

In the room, where I am alone with the flame _____ .

<hr>

*   The sentences in quotation marks, as well as the altered sentence beginning with "You burn villages..." are from a poem by Herberto Helder, entitled *Place*.
    It started out as a hoarse voice from behind the screen. It was late afternoon, in a gray, rainy Lisbon, in 1964. In the room, shadows fall. Behind the screen, the voice slowly illuminates the rural image that appears on the cloth, in another *place*, whose name I didn't know at the time: the *voracious point*, "the mirrored end of the earth," as the poem said.
    (The date I have given it today is the day I sent it to *Jornal de Letras* to be part of a dossier on Herberto Helder. In actuality, I wrote it a year earlier, on 7 November 1993.)

———————————— today I saw fear in a swallow: I would prefer to see it in myself. A swallow motionless in the angular corner of the kitchen, its eyes glazed over with helplessness, is not an aspect of defenseless nature that I would like to see.

But I saw it.

And, in the mind of my body, which was in my hand and in my gaze, the figure of the monster of the metanight appeared, aquatic, viscous,

which dwells in the far reaches of the earth,

and comes to us

to

save itself in the human,

if there are humans who so desire. And if there are, there will be fear, language, beauty, and thinking.

The trilogy of the beautiful, the thinking, and the living, which hides a *fearsome* in itself.

This kitchen, entirely windows, can elicit monstrous forms, in my mind ———————————— unsuspecting swallows. But I was given the gift of striding toward monsters barehanded. I said to it, picking it up with a revulsion made prehension:

— Go, beloved swallow.

And, in a feat of flight or magic which occurs, under the upward gaze, in all species, the swallow retrieved its winged body, returned to the image of Oscar Wilde's *Happy Prince*, and took with it the deep fear of losing my identity which had seized me earlier in the morning.

And, today, in *The Music Rehearsal*, I wrote:

"And the young girl, before she can throw a new stick in the direction of Baruch's spirit, finds herself struck, unexpectedly, by the fear she had seen in the eyes of the boy who was about to be cast into the emptiness of the cliff. She sees it in herself. Another child, eyes glazed over with helplessness, feet retreating _____ about to cling to the last, nonexistent ledge _____ is not an image of a helpless human that she had expected to find. But *she had.*

She takes a deep breath to counter the effect of the image. And, in her clear mind, in the swiftness of the leap and the hands with which she intervened, appears *the form of enchantment and fascination* _____ (Baruch's spirit, meditating to himself, tells her they are the *attributes of thinking and extension*), but *what* she sees emerging is an aquatic, viscous monster, emerging from the far reaches of the living and the conceptual, which is revealing itself, through regressive unfurlings, to the uncertain part, as a relationship that cries out, pleading for help from the human. '*Save me,*' it would vociferate confusedly, if there were humans who wanted to make the gesture."

_____ published, *The Unexpected Encounter of Diversity*. I organized, once again with Crisante's invaluable assistance, a reading event at Casa Fernando Pessoa. Manuela Júdice lent me the most support, in a spirit of great collaboration.

Next, António Guerreiro would also like to organize a Colloquium about my text. I do not know if anyone will want to take part.

I was happy with the event. I remember the reading by Eunice Muñoz, the words of Eduardo, and, more than anything, the quality of the silence during the readings. Afterwards — we went out to dinner.

"You're imitating *Current Account...*" he says to me.

"No. I am lowering the veil of the text over the event."

Dinner at the Chinese restaurant, on Rua Coelho da Rocha — a number of friends in attendance. I sat next to Vergílio, who when he interrupted the conversation with Christine and Sandra's youthfulness, "messed with me," apropos of Spinoza.

— What if we spoke about *The Unexpected Encounter of Diversity* instead? — But he refused. Yet in the end, he and Augusto grappled with the great question of his life as a writer — the nature and future of the novel.

As I talked with Regina, my mind had returned to the text: my involvement in the light is a question.

_____ a large square translucent handkerchief (virginal and gardenal) covers the round abat-jour lamp on my desk, and gives the room a garden light, which I, sitting in the

floral armchair, reencounter upon the furniture. There is no interstice of a book which does not have that light, and I rely on it to heal myself of the rarity of moments when an absence pains me. Undetermined — *one*, undefined, and not unifying. I use the energy from the color
of that light,
my eyes taste it and, having risen up before it, give it as nourishment to my other senses.

Active participation, in the light _____ the aesthetic secret of that light makes me think about the subtle thread with which it is connected to my thinking. I will ask it why it is taking me like this _____
and who is it?
I know it returns my question, murmuring
"Now it's up to you,"
and I accept its path in the lamp, and "I'm going to write a text without a shadow," it would say in reply.

And so the light fades in my room. I will soon have more information about the receptivity of the lamp. But, in anticipation, I know that neither he, nor I, want the formal definition of the meaning of *our* writing to interrupt the act of writing-now, or even interfere with it.

— What did you talk about? — I asked Augusto.
— With Vergílio?
— Yes.
— We can talk about it later, if you want. I was left with a stronger impression, which is, by far, a greater priority. Today, during the readings, I understood how those texts had readers,

and that readers are: people who read, who look for meaning without belief and without a mentor. I felt they were protecting you — which is one way of being benevolent. That a faint, indelible sensuality was circulating between the people...

— A kind of sex of reading?

— Yes, I didn't feel possession, but rather appropriation. But what struck me most was discovering that we were performing an aesthetic act, an act of conscious beauty. It was vast, without ever being imposing, or impeding. We took what we wanted, and took what we could. For a moment, we were neither powerless, nor thieves. That was what I felt most strongly.

— And Vergílio?

— He must have felt something similar. But in him, those feelings are at war with everything he knows. He felt fine, but ever cautious. With him, I'm often almost certain that he uses his thinking against what he feels.

_____ nothing is swifter than melancholy; it is insidious in its attack, unexpectedly resurfaces before our eyes, and the whirlwind is such that it vanishes without any clear lines. The primary, determining fact is that our form, the form with which we are receptive or act, is a body, all affect is born, persists, and vanishes in that form; the physical separation of bodies can sometimes be the most remarkable fact: against which the concept loses strength and patience. It is useless for me to want to be reasonable. When I lapse into nostalgia, it is utterly upsetting.

The reality of pain, until I long for death, is not in the physical separation (what is most of life made of, if not *present absences?*), but in the simple effect of images that do not overlap.

I'm not going to ask, "Who is missing?" It is I who am missing, the fragment over which I sigh, which is hovering outside of me. *I* who wanted to be *him*, without being able to, like _____ like a remnant of a sentence that is forgotten.

But when I write, I feel the parts in my hand (more than anything, the *sex that reads*), and the nostalgia which, in the end, is also the absence of power _____ is undone and the unsutured, though interrupted, scene of our conversation unfolds.

The fact remains that literature, or what have you, is of little interest to me: what interests me is proximity-overlapping. And I cannot write if I am not proximate, coincident. With my gaze on another. Gazing into the gaze of the unending gaze. Seeking out gazes, encompassing and liberating gazes, entering into

paradoxical gazes, emerging from them, suffering for seeing,
smiling for seeing even more. Interweaving gazes,
causing
the images to overreach themselves,
until they swoon in *their* possessive but not cannibalistic night.
    For each image, craft a tale, disarrange them,
observe the creation without understanding it
except for a gaze,
one final gaze.

        Cast a beautiful gaze full of those images onto one
newly born, or someone who has just died. At this moment,
I know,
by a grace of the unending gaze,
"There is a child of mine yet to be born,
a child who has just died
and returned."

    — Then what did you talk about?
    — I already told you some of it yesterday. It is sometimes
difficult for me to talk to Vergílio, because he almost always
moves from the general to the particular. Since we know very
little about that general, this means that the general is not
actually substantiated, nor does the particular acquire strength.
Much to the contrary. It loses the strength it has, and becomes
diluted. I know the only thing that interests Vergílio is his novel,
and the crossroads at which he finds himself, but — rather than
addressing the question directly — we take a long excursion
through the crisis of the novel in general. Which, after that
event, I must confess was particularly arduous for me.
    — But you seemed so, so attentive…

— Vergílio deserves all my respect. He is someone. I'm very fond of him and his problem: I'm bothered by the way he approaches it. Vergílio's question is not the crisis of the novel, it is another reality entirely. The crisis is — in him — a concept-simulacrum.

For example, he made very pertinent technical observations about your book. It was obvious he had read it. For him, your book could be seen as an ironic way of showing how the novel-form is constructed, and how it shapes and directs the reader's gaze. Every novel is made of fragments from which the author erases the date. The horizon of every novel is the autobiographical, where the author hides in order to spin the threads of their story, as if they were someone else, as if that adventure-problem were not their own, nor they a part of it. Every novel — to be savored — has to be propelled by either the drama it inherited from Greek tragedy, or the enigma it has drawn from myths.

Yet he observed that you, sometimes years apart, do not erase the path of your trajectory. Everything is a fragment; everything is dated; nothing follows a chronological order. It is often necessary to wait for the past in order to understand the future. Other times, it isn't. Time does not guide. The guiding thread lies in the logic of the encounters. The figures in the text, who have traveled a great distance, do not pursue an enigma, nor do they live a drama: they are focused on living consequential affective-mental experiences. He observed that, without the slightest trace of confessionalism, you make their pursuit your own. And, more importantly, it has not escaped him that both body and thinking are engaged in that pursuit.

And this is what truly interests him. Vergílio's question is to understand whether your text is possible, whether there is, in it, a kind of assurance of truth, such as that which faith has provided for belief and experimental science for reason.

If there is...

— Good Lord, what does it matter what the foundation is?

— The trouble is that this is what most ways of thinking are searching for. In any case, he follows your text attentively. It would take too long to explain the reasons for that attention. But I know it's true. He is a kind of fellow observer — empathetic and critical — at the same time. In *A Kiss Given Later*, Témia was looking for a philosophical companion. Well, I think he is your philosophical companion. In practice, he doesn't care whether your text continues, or replaces, or recasts the novel. What he wants to know is whether it produces a certainty that can underpin a volition — as he did with *Apparition*. Vergílio's famous "blood evidence," establishing a new "internal equilibrium." For him, your text produces equivalent or superior evidence, but who knows exactly what kind... Which is all the more curious — enigmatic evidence.

Today, I am unable to interrogate — it is I who assert:

I could
write about the problems of the time we live in, but I could only
speak about them from my own, my own time, un-dating, which
is how I brush away the fact of those images

which, to those who
take this path,
    ceaselessly speak to them of their *unreality*. The world. But
which one? In my own,
powerful existents struggle
against perhaps unfeasible realities — the "it is so" of the cynics
against Eckhart's "let us have a common love."

All I have to do is cross the street to find our time, all I have to
do is turn back to find myself in my own. Somewhere, in my body,
between crossing and turning back, was the collision of images.

From the television I watch to the text I write, the distance is
unmeasurable.

I do not need to press the button to find, in the texts I write
to be read, indelible, their own images, not ephemeral — if the
eyes of those who read them are also indelible. In the trace of that
indelibility, gazes are shaped, which are mirrors for the real
images of all the nomadic territories we create, and keep
exchanging between them and ourselves.

I remember, apropos of images, a line from a song I heard
years ago:

"If only I were the one you're thinking of, the one you love…"

Today, I am unable to interrogate — it is I who assert:

> that I hear the hoofbeats of horses in the street;
> that I'm going out;
> that I'm going to comb my hair;
> that I'm going to put on my coat;
> that it is a cloudy day;
> that there are so many others (not *the others*) who
> exist, want to be real,
> and not die.

I assert that *going out* and *not wanting to die* seems to me, suddenly, to be a kind of constitution of images, as if there were in them a certain conscious and imperishable matter beyond the body, which asks itself how to bring what is current life into the invisible not taken by death.

I am unable to question. To write, I have to know, to the greatest of certainties.

I open to the first page of the book,
where I was led by memories that came alive for me in the
street, a barouche passing by at a trot, pulled by a pair of white
horses,
and an automobile, no make as far as I can tell,
where I see, in the window, the head of a dog — a cocker
spaniel, like Jade;
today, I have fallen into a deep depression, for they have made
me realize that my texts do have the eroticism they proclaim,
when I know
there is only
the libidinal flower — without classifications, or dramas; I do
not deconstruct the Angel when I write him — the movement
is another; and so, at this moment, seeing myself bereft of Eros,
I have lost the north _____ where is Agape? I tremble
as I write this word,
    I am struck by a pang of nostalgia, and I know my struggle
against death (death is not a noun) is to weave the enduringness
of now-impossible presences into a text, to capture their
question "Why,
when you were alive, did you feel so much nostalgia,"
and why do I now have so much nostalgia for you?
    There is no equilibrium between *Loving a Dog* (Jade, who I
see running, radiant in his absence) and the provisional
presence of Vergílio, my philosophical companion, except that I
followed an ascending scale of incandescence, that of the dog
who runs ahead or behind, within the shadow of someone
_____ and I saw the birth of an inhabitant who went into
the shadow of writing, of a presentiment, of the internal

equilibrium. Confronted with a work, and the memory of the anguish of writing it, even though, paradoxically, it is joy, I was struck by the sources of my knowledge about Vergílio when, for the first time, we met face to face at the Sorbonne, representing Portugal with other writers and poets like ourselves.

The amphitheater, so vast, was pure open space; but, pitch black with people under spotlights, and the strangeness of the statues in the distance, I felt as though I was about to plummet with my body, and the double body of my text _____ into an inconsolable abyss, in which the stones at the bottom — and the ones nearby — were human heads. We spontaneously confessed our fear and lack of confidence to one another. And confessing it gave that same fear a sort of shining nimbus of protection. Stretching out under my feet was the solidity of the text — the unsutured robe of my inmost and outer reality. Text and text. Fear and fear. The mortal unknown was present in the amphitheater. But enfolded in the same sex that reads, the adversative and the adverse filled with light, although I know that light is a poor word _____ it was instead a shawl, a Jade teaching the child about the mission of
Humans

_____ to interrogate,
to confront, barehanded,
the overwhelming image that comes, and is going to submerge us. "Vergílio, we didn't close our eyes, remember?" and the image recoiled: — I am you — it said to us: — Speak. — And we did.

It was my turn for a birthday. *Once again*, the need to be in motion, perhaps physically relocate, get rid of furniture, objects, clothes — lighten the load for the sake of the signs and images the text brings me. It is, in the end, the only place in the body that truly moves. When I was born, everything was related to space and time. In mid-life, Vergílio spoke of the internal equilibrium that demanded the absolute of the self and the question which remains unanswered _____ whether there was a bridge of time over space.

— Gabriela, will someone be waiting for me?

I do not know.

"If the question is one of knowing," is what I reply to myself today. — I am traveling over that bridge on a laden donkey, the horizon is vast, the sea is within, and life, paradoxically, I do not know whether it has a duration, or not. But if the question is one of desire, of vitality, then I say that I will stop the donkey, I will throw the objects over, down into the depths which shelters them, I will lean out over the bridge, with my free donkey, at my side,

I will lean out over it on my limbs and hooves and see the images floating, mine as well, finally emptying into the sea.

I mistake my head for a snow-capped peak. I catch sight of it and mistake it.

— Your writing is changing — Vergílio tells me, referring to *The Unexpected Encounter of Diversity* and the text I sent to the Parliament of Writers.

— Perhaps the equivalent, in verb tenses, to the infinitive, which bends and flexes without thinking about death, or making metaphors.

I am lying in the bed I bought when I was fifteen years old, which then departed with me for life, selecting the poems of Emily Dickinson that I will translate. Augusto writes another preface and organizes the next meeting at the art gallery Monumental. We listen to Gregorian chants. Sandra and Anabela have set up their small distribution company. Christine is looking for a path in the text. Lurdes's father is very ill, and she is worried,

while I conjure up figures with beings so diverse and different, so irreconcilable — passersby from disparate backgrounds — until some are simply disappeared people, and others *present figures*.

_____ I was translating Rimbaud, page 259 in the book,

"These are cities! A people for whom these dreamed Alleghanies and Lebanons were produced! (...) Lovers' festivals echo across canals suspended behind chalets. (...) On platforms, amidst chasms, Rolands herald their courage. On bridges suspended over the chasms and the rooftops (...) the burning of the heavens raises flags. The crumbling of the apotheosis overtakes the celestial regions where seraphic centauresses amble among avalanches. Above the highest peaks, a churning sea, laden with Orphean fleets sea and the murmur of precious pearls and whelks, laden with choirs of waves and the murmur of precious pearls and shells, is troubled by the eternal birth of Venus — the sea sometimes darkening with deadly lightning. On the hillsides, roar gatherings of flowers, tall as our guns and goblets. (...) Up there, their hooves between waterfalls and brambles, deer suckle on Diana. (...) Venus penetrates the caves of smiths and hermits. A band of belfries sing the thoughts of the people. (...) All the legends evolve and an unbridled impetus moves through the town. The paradise of storms subsides. (...) And, for an hour, I went down into the bustle of a Bagdad boulevard where different bands were singing the joy of the new work under a heavy breeze, circulating without being able to elude the fabulous ghosts of the mountains where we were supposed to gather. (...)"

when it became almost impossible to continue translating because my own text — another text — was

faltering between the lines and provisionally replacing
Rimbaud's (and even revolting against it), I wanted to go up the
typewriter; the four rows of keys, arranged in terraces or steps,
seemed to be the entryway to my own morning, which today
was the morning of the rainbow,
rather than the *white-blackbow*,
(Rimbaud's *A* and *E*, or the ELA in Gabriela, the hanging part I
lack) and which usually almost always settles in my vision when
I awake.

I have always been called Gabi, by those close to me,   I
now long for my entire name, to recapture all the colors of the
name I was given. The colors of the woman and the man, the
libido of the vitality which asserts and neither divides nor
separates. Although it was not my usual habit, I had gone to
crack open the window and it was raining, the Sintra sky, so
sensitive, was completely overcast, and behind the Palácio, like
an errant castle or a haughty I, an unbearably heavy cloud was
passing by. Then the rainbow was loosed, and I stood gazing at
it between the text that was heading toward the house and the
ever so physical question, "Why, for so long, did they take the
colors of my name? Why does Rimbaud lack colors?" Against
this unstable, colored background, the cloud drew nearer, the
text arrived, and I found myself thinking about the present
circumstances of our own lives, and how Toki Alai was in
danger. I pushed the pages aside, and wrote down the dream I
had yesterday,
which had ruined, brilliantly,
many of the remnants of my depressive sorrow.

I was — that is to say, in the dream — in a kind of temple
in front of altars engulfed in foggy hollows, and a tall man,

dressed as we were, affectionately placed his hand on my
shoulder and gave me a fleeting and somewhat radiant caress on
my thigh. Then he disappeared to officiate, and I saw a fragile
woman emerge, dressed in a skirt and coat, with the lightness
and joy of a happy soul, who immediately became my
companion and had a close rapport with me.

Yet there came to me now, in the clatter of the typewriter
keys, the first scene of the dream — the Prologue _____
it had been an expansive golden place, between two rocks
where large animals ran, and played, and fought undisturbed in
the serene gold breeze, like the third color of the rainbow it
made. There were bison, buffalo, bears, and other animals with a
name that ends in ch, which I cannot now recall the name of. I
only recall the image of the word that does not correspond to
how it is spelled. I knew it was their colors that distorted the
spelling of their names, as if they (the colors) were behind the
phonetics, which was a kind of chromatic sound. I was in the
dream writing (dreaming to write)
that the officiant should, logically, go on a safari — the green
arriving after the golden yellow — and to prevent him from
leaving on his own, the woman in the skirt and I — I in the
lead, and pulling with mental energy for her — went down the
steep stone slope, covered in writing, and jumped into a car that
was there waiting for us. The woman was in the middle, I on the
right side, next to the window. At the other end, a third woman
appeared, who when the (alleged) officiant moved closer to the
window, said: — Yes, yes, that's all very well, but I'm the one
who has to put up with him. — It was Regina, referring to her
husband Vergílio, distressed by having to care for him, and not
being the one to whom he addresses his craft of writing. I know
all the women who emerge within her are that woman in the

skirt and coat, but I cannot tell her that she is her, for all language is grounded in names. It was she who refused him the photograph, so that he would seek her out — two distinct people and a single figure. The name excludes what the verb accepts and says.

And, through the rainbow and the weave of closings and openings cast over Sintra,
a piece of cloth — blue as an *O* — spread out on the table,
open, which was a new shawl of the mind born from the first,
the plan of the city from my books,   rather, from a
luminous scene that rendered, with the initial appearance of a
hovering cloud,
the text,
from which fell books, cut with scissors, or a gardener's blade.
          You, at the age of twenty, were writing. "These
thousand interrogations / That put out branches on their own /
Bring with them, in short, / Ecstasy and a bender." But I know,
today, that it isn't actually true — these books I'm speaking of
are the books for this part of my life, a phase of making a living
— me, in Sintra, and you in Abyssinia — of fulfilling
obligations, of calming the objects that were afraid of being
broken on the shelves and furniture, and encouraging my
philosophical companion to truly leave, undaunted, always
keeping my promise to continue to exist and to evolve with us,
in an enduring, lasting way. This, then, is the tree of texts
divided into books, with Prunus Triloba depicted behind it, in
india ink, the books existing, but unfathomable, and still barely
attached to their land
(the land of that tree: ink, an indigo color, or an image of an
intense blue). And I saw that

_____ there was the absolutely necessary continuation of the *Diary*, letting us see and read the extent to which everything grew from the same trunk, and which finally appears under the *old and lucid* name of Herbais: *Inquiry into the Four Confidences*

_____ there was *Joshua, Companions and Lovers* (largely written in Herbais and upon arriving in Portugal, during the six months in Mucifal), which begins with Ursula contemplating, inside and outside her window, the *material affective pulsation* of this land with all of you, incandescent and intense, like the violet and certain part of reality. A way of saying that the canonical and apocryphal gospels intersect in tone and will find rest in another paradox encountered beyond _____ how to cease existing "In the name of," and communicate in the "Verb that has existed from the beginning." Ursula also asks herself the question

"Why did they hide so many colors from
Joshua?"

_____ there was *Vergílio*, which is not the name of a book, but rather a path, as the dream indicates:

— Vergílio!
— Yes?
— Should we change the color and letter of Rimbaud's *A*? Do you remember what he wrote? "The star wept rose in the heart of your attentive ear / The infinite rolled a white target through your body, from nape to kidney / The sea dewed red on your copper red breasts / And Man bled black onto your endless flank."
— He identifies the black *A* and Man.

343

— Yes. And the white target with the infinite. But in our language, the white target is circulated by the verb, in the white, reaching the target.

— And how would it look?

— *Há. 'There is.'*

— And the color?

— We would go-and-see.

_____ we would see;
we could spend a few days without leaving the house, solely
being witnesses to what goes on between humans and the text;
the text, without humans devouring its reality ("the solid state,"
he says) _____ is happier.

 — Then what is the purpose of readers?
 — To plunge into the text and its happiness.

 I write plunge, rather than *learn* because, as I moved
from left to right
the transparent vase made of blue glass, because it hindered my
access to the typewriter, I entered even more fully into the
reality with which I began; and, seeing what I am saying, the
explanation fades and, if it returns to me,
it is open for me to see further — and indelibly —
until it is overlaid by
the next circumscribed ink.

 Let the explanation say ("Can't you explain later?") what I
am writing in other words _____ the text accepts the challenge
and, devoted friend, becomes motionless, opening up the
innocent blue eyes that were forget-me-nots in paradise.

 — The text is, then, the art of the verbal, of the gaze, of the
confidence, and of paradise?
 — Of the verbal and the gaze. Of paradise, perhaps.
 — Perhaps?
 — It depends on the gaze. It is the art of the *hú*, of the
'*There is.*' Of what '*There is*' between.
 — And the confidence?
 — It is what we are undergoing… what 'There is' between

the gazes. Do you want the tree or the confidence?

— The tree.

I sat down beneath the tree, carefully examining how the leaves were arranged. "So many people, Good Lord," like leaves. Counting would be futile. There was, in actuality, a well nearby and the unfathomable, with the reflection of the leaves, was bathing in its waters. "How does the divine bathe? How does it plunge?" I asked. If only I could watch, without, for the moment, being inside, or entirely outside. It then occurred to me that I had a great tendency to clothe philosophy in its own landscape, and that philosophy, without that garment, was a dead part of the unfathomable. If I could bring the linden tree home, fragment it into a thousand pieces during the journey, and if my companions saw me at that instant, what tree would I give them? What vision would I have of them, and they of me? And when I pieced it back together, would I not then have "the single image I didn't have before"?

I never saw the linden tree, but rather a myriad of living leaves, at the moment when my heart suspected that the divine plunges into the unfathomable to bathe. And my companions, and the linden itself, do not want me to disincarnate them with the sharp end of the word. Instead, I leaf through them. I look at them,
and they yield to my gaze,
asking for another,
a second gaze which is a kiss. They do not ask me to disrobe them, but to be with them, giving them leaves.

It is truly strange what is happening here, crowned by beauty. *And invincible.* Two shepherds of beauty arrived to

dismantle it. They began to speak, explaining it. By and by, the
leaves fell from the tree. They didn't actually fall, but
they fell,   they became transparent outlines that allowed the
other leaves to be seen, with no loss of position, nor meaning.
But the green collapsed,
and that pulsation which is the winged utterance of the trees
faded, feeling shifted into another orbit. It is outside that it is, it
is inside that it exists.

    I sat down between the two shepherds — and I myself.
There was a breeze filled with a solar brightness,
and I stared at the faces with the intensity that is my own. I saw
them distinctly as loose lines crossing one another

            and I longed, no less intensely, to see a nest appear in
the tree.

    Then, a flock of birds from scattered places took the very
fine lines in their beaks, as material for building nests, and made
nests that were difficult to describe — but easy to enter. New
birds landed delightedly on the tree.
    — Would it be a nest, or would it not be a nest? — I asked.
"I will know for certain if there is egg laying."
    The *object of love*
(the name I also give you — philosophical companion — when
I offer you my gaze and speak to you in the third person) came
running up, panting, and I saw, at the fringe of the landscape,
that it was a true human being, with whom one could share
confidences. He climbed into the nest and took the forlorn and
attentive position of a bird laying,
there being no contradiction in the two overlapping attitudes,

but rather making it possible to communicate the verb — to lay, laying, laid — to other birds.

"My form in this form…" he plunged into the silence of the waters.

"That story about the birds, the other day, was what? An allegory?"

"No, a confidence: one of the places where the world begins."

"One of the places from which immanence wells..."

"Yes..."

"...made of weak threads and strong threads. I know that the world begins in the strong threads..."

"   and then unfolds, like a piece of cloth, in weak threads, in fine designs — largely imperceptible."

"Yes. Yes. But Gabriela, I've noticed you are less on the side of emotion..."

"Many weak threads only appear to be weak; our life is made of many weak threads. When you approach immanence, Vergílio, you do so, first and foremost, from the side of the sublime — you compel. But, on another subject. Do you want a house or a dog?"

"What are the four confidences you mentioned?"

I'm going to say it very quickly, and then I want to go with you to another place in the world, where to write the text is to dance it to the rhythm of its fragility and beauty.

The first confidence
is that we are nothing _____ ("Don't be angry"). *The self as name* is nothing. There is a place of bondage.

The second confidence
is that our actions, even the transhumance or transplantation of the blue of the vase, are less than we are. There is a whirlwind of intensities summoning us: they are Rilke's angels, or Walter Benjamin's legions of evanescent cherubs.

The third confidence
is that there are no contemporaries, but threads of present
absences; there is a ring of escape. In practice, it is an infinite
scene — the place where we are figures.

The fourth confidence
is about desire and the loathing of identity. There is an Edenic
place. ("No, don't say anything"). Indeed, we were given a
name, the name we are called, but it is not consistent — it is a
verb.

Our verb, for example, is to write.

_____ let's imagine I am in
an open house. That as we are doing now, I converse with
figures, transforming myself into all-encompassing action
_____ the arch of the door through which I pass, the
light from the end of the hallway in its lamp, the carpet on the
floor. I think no one else exists,
apart from the doors
which open onto nature. The upstanding nature I see on the
path alongside a trail, when I step into my room. Since I'm a
long way from writing what I feel, I push the door open after
feeling its seal with my hand. The photograph album of the
house is on the dining room table. It is open to the portrait of a
window, and I think that

I do not think,
and I see that I think.

This is a serious lack — seeing what you think. And I think
that the house vibrates in the voice of children when, in the end,
the place where it vibrates is the part of my affect that will
become thinking. I transform it into writing by running down

the hallway, but leaving behind my presence in the room toward
which I gaze — imminent and serious — with the roof holding
up a bird,
which has the clear indication of a sparrow.
    — Vergílio, where does the desire of this bodywriting
emerge from, where is it accomplished?
    — Where is it accomplished from, is that what you're
asking?
    — Yes, that's right.
    — From the heart of fleeting joy.

    I rush down the hallway writing in that joy, before it fades,
as I ask him to:
    — Open the door.
    — The one to the living room?
    — The living room has no door. — The hallway laughs at
our imagination.
    — Open the door.
    — The one to the bedroom?
    — The bedroom has no door. — The hallway with no
doors echoes with laughter.
    — The one to the commonplaces?
    — Yes, that one.

    He moves toward the kitchen with no landscape, no
passageway that can be named, opens the cupboard, pours the
coffee into the cup — and is surprised it is hot in the cold
cupboard.
    With the door open to the commonplaces,
amidst fleeting joy,
he sits down in front of us, at the table _____ an utterly

black face with a daring equal to that of its own gaze. It is rare. It
is rare that the black A can gaze at her. It is rare that she can
return its gaze — you do not return what you almost never
encounter. But if her intuition is accurate and serious, and the
time and place are right,
like a hill poised to watch the sun rise,
then that face will arrange an encounter in the unheard history
of the house, when I am alone
with my hand,
gazing at it in the shadow on the wall.

    — Gabriela, what if I had seen your black face? — Vergílio
asks me
    — Where the brown eyes aren't prominent, and the
non-place exists?
    — Yes. — I move in that direction, toward my black face
— the face of my death and the anonymous crowds to which I
do not belong.
    — I do not belong to the black *A* that has this world in its
power.
    — It was a face I have traversed. It is a struggle I have yet to
conclude. You know, Gabriela, everything is admirable — even
a simple truth: the beginning of humans has no color.
    — If I write it down… — I reply.
    — If I scarify it in music… — he continues, in a
monotonous tone.
    — If I find it on the street of windows, as if it were a refrain.
    — If I intone it with my throat, imperceptibly…,
      we will always be spinning around, in the reverse of the
black light
this simple and elemental unrelenting reality.

"I was exhausted, and I wrote," he says. "I was full of energy, and I wrote," I reply quietly. These are the two states in which we can take turns writing; in the interim states, we need to put our hands together.

— I write so that the strength of the mansion will come to us, from the 'There is,' from the *Há* of the world — he says.

— I write to spin from *A* to *Há*, to whirl with the vibrations that rise and lift us up to the place where we can no longer descend, nor evade ourselves — the 'There is' upon the 'There is.'

_____ and so, the creation of the world encompasses us; and encompasses our equals, even the most obscure.

— All the unutterables, all the *if-I's* that were my knot and are, in the end, the thread I stretched across the universe — says the philosophical companion.

All this takes place in the kitchen. By the light of a candle — a light which transcends the tangible light of that face and puts it out, in order to bring it back larger, more tarnished and scarified in the sun in the background. "Our dark face, Gabriela."

I say to the face: — *Everything is a question of opening your eyes.* — Open your eyes.

He says to the face: — *Of tilting your head* — Turn toward eternity.

I say to the face: — *Of fragrant scent spilled.* — Forget the feces of gold.

It says to our face: — *Of the humiliation of writing.* — I baptize you with oblivion. — Have I ever humiliated you? — asks the *black* — or tarnished? — *A*, turning to Vergílio, utterly amazed it is having coffee with us, in the kitchen.

— How can I, if you are me? — replies my philosophical companion: — Don't you remember your other birth, the most ancient one, when I was perfectly at ease in your body and your russet color, in other times, in the middle of the Attica desert?

— Yes, I had forgotten.

— Come and meet me, and call the dog who will enfold us in his keeping.

In place of the hound came a tiger. It lay down in the blazing sun. And when the sun bloomed, it ate them both — flesh of the same human flesh. They were thus rooted for eternity in the same house in that lost Attica. An old Greek face interrogating the being, at the edge of his dog.

I look at my guard dog made of porcelain on the desk — a descendent of my paternal grandmother. If he were a living being, he would bark as I run down the hallway writing. "Who is that running beside you?" he would ask. He looks and gathers the pages with his mouth and paws _____ beneath him, in his animal grandeur, excised, with the utmost accuracy, according to the shape of his own truth.

I say to that dog, opaque and motionless:

— Be quiet. The face of my death is rising from its tomb in Attica.

He growls softly.

— Fear not. It comes with a *Younger One* who runs the dusty roads, asking questions of the dog who accompanies him. He dances on light feet, and hurls his favored cry into the air: Yové! Yové!

He is a Man.

_____ the confidences.

And it was then that the *Younger One* appeared, piecing back together, before the face was shattered, its virtual fragments, strewn along the hallway.

With the simplest gestures came the meaning of the simplest gestures, and the growing soul was once again at the center of the prayer — a new place outside which I still don't know how to define, it simply shines when, at night, flipping the switch, I want to turn on the lamp that shines a circle of light upon the incongruous objects on the bedside table — the jar of Vicks, the aspirin, my father's silver cigarette case, the pencils, the cream, the paperweight.

As I age, there is the growing soul, which allows me not to age, and youth unfurls _____ it is only a fleeting sign of youthfulness that does not age; then, reality lingers, a woman in her form, a living manifold figure, recapturing all the colors with which her creation of being was conceived, and I know that, in this way, it is possible to clothe the human. But it strikes no fear, not even in itself, most notably. All the beings arrive, and I think about the donkey that accompanies *the Younger One* ("Where do you see him?"), and its ears. A being so long ignored that it left almost no trace. But its caricature — a sign of all the faded colors of the human — constantly appears on faces, as its inverted image. A true trail from self to self, as is the work of creation; where power has taken away the colors of the human, resentment has darkened the emptiness, and immense daubs of evil and stupidity appear.

And yet,
O hand that writes cast in shadow,
I distantly feel the sensation of having been a horse. ("I was a dog"). My first sensation is that of morning, when the night no longer slumbers, nor dreams. The bucket of water flashes under a few pieces of straw, from one image to the next, and I am beating my hooves impatiently, as befits a horse which has an unending hallway to run. I am waiting for *the Younger One*. A swallow flies past, glimpsed amidst the pear tree through the half-open door. I am awake, watching over the other horses that are still sleeping, rousing my day, for I only desire resolute commands. I can hear distinctly and clearly, but I am not yet able to write, being neither man nor woman, only a flicking tail, and a whinny in the morning. Wherever my run is lies the narrative of my adventure _____ what I will have to say when, in the hands of the butcher, the creator at last wants to hear me. And I will say

_____ I place my hooves between meditating and understanding, a confluence from which will be born the metamorphosis of my surroundings. But I find I am already thinking, insisting on the beginning of the day while time changes radically, because the human pulls me toward its nature. The horses stop at the entrance to the garden, in front of the carts that ferry god's faithful to the top of the mountain. They scent that a text is swaying as if conveyed at a trot, and tethered to the barrier, they sense it is going to dilute them in the vortex of thinking ___ a sign they have little time left

before they become nonexistent or human. Both perspectives
terrify us and, standing in a circle, we demand
the creator keep his promise to listen to us, and we tell him
that only one man enters the stable, which is deserted

our straw changes
our face changes
our water changes
while day breaks on the night that is ending
("Yes, there is Night and there is Day, just as you made them")
we are all one, scoring long furrows with our hooves, gleaming
horses preparing to break into a trot and express the command
which reveals space in its movement
we wait for the obstacles to be cleared
we separate into groups of four,

and they separate from me — I light the candle. *The
Younger One* reads them the text about "the most beautiful
mission of the horse." Multiple beams of light are cast by the
candle — multiple beams that strike their eyes. But they do not
blink. It is the obstacle of the candle which the horses are going
to clear _____

and no one says anything. Other than, today:

"The mares that carry me, as far as impulse might reach..."
— Gabriela, but that is the beginning of Parmenides's
poem!
"... were taking me..."
— Yes.
"... when they brought me and placed me upon the much-
speaking route of the goddess,

that carries everywhere unscathed the man who knows

thereon was I carried, for thereon the much-guided mares
were carrying me,

straining to pull the chariot, and maidens were leading the
way…"

— Let me translate.

— Translate.

"Daughters of the Sun were hastening to escort me, after
leaving the House of Night for the light, having pushed back
with their hands the veils from their heads."

— They tied the shawls of their minds around their waists.

— Quite possibly!

"There are the gates of the paths of Night and Day, and for
these Justice, much-avenging, holds the keys of retribution

coaxing her with gentle words, the maidens did cunningly
persuade her that she should push back the bolted bar for them
swiftly from the gates

and these made of the doors a gaping gap as they were
opened wide, swinging in turn in their sockets the brazen posts

straight through them at that point did the maidens drive
the chariot and mares along the broad way…"

— Do you know the names of the young women who are
driving you?

— Who are driving me?

— Isn't it you, Vergílio, who are riding in the chariot, to
meet the god?

— First of all, it isn't a god, but a goddess. Justice. Second, I
don't know if it's me. And if it is?

— If it is, they are named Barbara, Monica, Sandra…

— Onward!

"…and the goddess received me kindly, and took my right

hand with her hand, and uttered speech and thus addressed me:
Youth
    it is no ill fortune that sent you forth to travel this route (for
it lies far indeed from the beaten track of men),
    and it is right that you should learn all things —
    both the steadfast heart of persuasive Truth
    and the beliefs of mortals, in which there is no true trust."
    — And... if I am the Youth, then who are you, Gabriela?

_____ he is explaining and I contemplate deeply,
not averting my gaze for a single instant; we are eating
toast, he found the butter salty, scraping at his tongue. I
contemplate,
absorb,
without making any judgments, it only
seems to me that what he says is a kind of dismantling,
perhaps slightly painful,
of my contemplation.

    — Why should I be *the Younger One* — when I am old?
    — Vergílio_____

What I know how to best encompass is space.
    — Don't lecture me. Why are you looking at me as if there
were someone else…? _____
Who constantly revels in space, and gallops?
    — I'm sorry! I am irritable and perplexed! _____

without wounding, or biting. Without biting me, is what I
should say.
Revels and recreates.

I contemplate what he is explaining to me,
"And at last, the entire body in a single piece spun
suspended from the highest bar, and remained motionless
for an instant, high above,"

and I feel my contemplation transforming,

"Lightweight. High above. Then it spun again, a god was spinning it in the air,"

penetrating the fear, shattering it, for what I contemplate has a vital expansiveness that bites this restrained suffering, "I clapped my hands, they echoed through the space of Olympus,"

and causes it to meekly leave at full tilt, in a contradictory rhythm.
"Man always has, in himself, another of himself…"

As if a dog, leaping back in fright, were to unintentionally collide with the new thing in front of him. The very air on the path is constantly changing the direction of his paws. But the universal figure of the dog walking is not dismantled. And he is as real as Jade,
the dog,
my fellow being and my counterpart,
who accompanied me.

— We have to give the dog another name — says my philosophical companion.
— There is another dog to come, isn't there?

I laugh. I am happy — it is *the Younger One* who is speaking, the other of him.
— Where do you get such certainty, Gabriela? — he asks me, affably.
— All I know is that I don't know the form of knowledge you are referring to, Vergílio — I reply.

How can I tell him I don't know, that knowing-knowledge
dulls, that I fear knowledge, plans, and explanations, that
humans do not possess the body to imagine the universe, the
ultimate ends and initial reasons, but they are here,
wandering in the 'There is' that 'There is'?
Vergílio,
we are not companions in knowledge, but rather wanderers.
Beauty overwhelms us. We do not want to be annihilated. We
want to see. Utterly. Irremediably. And with no return. Isn't that
what we have?

If I lose the thread of the different events that give a
semblance to my life, to its air (area, aria, aridity, rarity),
the multiple and routine images of the world suffocate me
_____ and life is lost — the threads, the evolutions and
contradictions of my breathing.

I am the *girl who comes out of the text*. I can only ever write a
word and interrogate it, and then I can proceed,
continuing to write and come out, as I am going to do now from
the house to go to the bank. My outing holds what I think. My
body holds what I am, the place where I'm going holds where
I'm going.
I stand up,
and it feels, at the same time, natural and strange to be standing
up with such an intensity and awareness of myself — and
come out of the house.
The hours repay me.

— Wait for me — he says. — Take my point of view with
you, and I'll take yours.

I smile again, and ask him:
— Is it an exchange?
— No. It is a taking in order to experience. You'll take *the Younger One*, and I'll take *the girl who comes out of the text*. We would go-and-see, as you said. Or rather, we would see ourselves in figures. I want to know what it's like.

And I saw, as Parmenides had seen, a burning field, and even as it burned, how birds came to peck at seeds and grains of wheat, and drink cool water in the circle of the fire. A bird and a bird of a different color rehearsed figures of flight and a reading of landscapes, and
both,
in their absence, raced across the land, staggering with difficulty, their hearts that strange color; it was affecting to see the burning moonlight accelerate all modes of locomotion — the most daring — in their bird bodies.

> *Apart from flight, what else is there?*
> The key to reading the burning landscapes _____

I asserted

> that there is else,
> irrefutably.
> Object of my creation,
> and my creator,
> it is *irrefutably* that I am writing to you.

— I will translate — he said, as if in response:
> But do not fail to learn the way in which
> the diversity
> that reveals itself
> must appear in such a way as to be received,

by extending to all things
the realm of its manifestation.

_____ Only today can *yesterday* be written.

Sitting on the stone wall at the Volta do Duche, *the Younger
One*, in a voice like a flight,
would continue to read Parmenides's poem to the girl who had
come out of the text; indeed,
          a figural adventure was soaring over an entirely green
universe. Two birds and many colors were flying — although
blue was predominant — rehearsing complex choreographies
of the 'There is,' of the há.   Even the cries they loosed
in the air hanging over the valley seemed to be the cries of
gulls   *há há há*   anticipating a storm, an
atmospheric whirlwind similar to those that bring the new,
which can either be a catastrophe
or a beneficial mutation.   When we went into the
kitchen, where the garden of figures disappears and
begins,
we, and our lineages   in the sense of almost being a part of
our hands   were there, at the green door breathing in the
blue, and,
directed by the voice,
we occupied transparent places. On a page, on an anodyne object,
on a chair, on an orange placed on the floor, on the small table
in the hallway. Other humans were outside the house, moving
along the street, but we, there, had had an encounter with
meaning
(knowing what is being said, ignoring what it refers to)
(and he says — Say it differently, say that we met in the gaze of
the 'There is'), both of us knowing we are going to write

because,

because there is an experience in pursuit of its geography, in the
understandable of the common language _____
_____ other humans were moving along the street and
speaking,
unaware they were witnessing the revelation of color as the
shore where rhythm ceases.

    — Gabriela, how are you going to speak,   now that you
have come out of the text?
    — Vergílio, how are you going to speak,   now that you
are *the Younger One* as yet unwritten?

    "Come, I shall tell you, and do you listen and convey the
story,
    what routes of inquiry alone there are for thinking."

    — Vergílio, listen.
    — I'm listening.
    — No, it's something else. I'm not referring to
Parmenides's poem that you're reading to me. There's
something else I wanted to tell you.
    — Then tell me.
    — No. I can tell you later. Please continue reading.

    "The one _____ that is and that cannot not
be,
is the path of persuasion,
for it attends upon Truth.

The other _____ that is not, and that needs must not be,

that I point out to you to be a path wholly unlearnable,
for you could not know what-is-not."

— What did you want to tell me? — he asks, interrupting
himself.
— Don't you think it's the eternal war of the Greeks
between the solid and the liquid?
— Yes, I do. But that's not what you wanted to tell me, is it?
— No, it isn't. Not as such.

I spread out an unironed piece of cloth on the small table in
the bathroom, replacing the prior, also white, but now dirty and
soiled; I found I preferred the clean to the smooth. "This isn't
the first route," I thought. I hear a young woman from the
Orontes Valley knock on the door, and ask:
— May I come in?
I look at her with clarity, clearly. She already knows what
that gaze means. It means *clean*, I say again with the gaze she
receives. And she sits down, talking about *the Younger One*, and
telling me how much she would like to be a Mother, but of No
One. Which I fully understand, under the effect of the reading
that emanates from the poem. And I say to her:
— Isn't that the other route?

And I thought, "A verb is stronger than the name." Perhaps
she will be the Mother of *the Younger One*, who is emerging
from the book. Or in the Book? I do not know. But if that
happens,
if that 'There is' were to be,
she will have to be an Evanescent Mother, for she tells me

she would fall in love with her Son, also with the brightness
closest to the libidinal force. According to the *Inquiry into the
Four Confidences* that I have been writing, "Maybe so." But if that
happens, it will be a 'There is' of remarkable brightness and
beauty,
which
does not wound
anyone.
And I thought,
"We have to take a different route"_____ the route of the
'There is' which has an aura.

    — An aura? — he asks me.
    — The clean white on the pressed white. I have always
been fascinated by the Transparent Rabbits.
    — Yes. Since the 'There is' is exterior and anterior to
worlds, 'There is' and 'There-always-is' are the same,
as here and there,
as 'There was,' 'There is,' and 'There will be.'
    — I certainly believe so.
    — If that is the case, then between 'There was' and 'There
is,' for example, 'There will be' an overlaying. We may not know
anything further from it, but we will witness an astonishing
effect of beauty absent nostalgia.
    — Isn't that an aura? *Apart from flight, what else is there?*
    — Gabriela, how are you going to speak,   now that you
have come out of the text?
    — I will interweave the canonical with the apocryphal.
And Vergílio, how are you going to speak,

now that you are *the Younger One*, as yet unwritten?

— I have so much to say to Sandra, Gabriela.

— Not to Regina?

— Her? Oh, I've never been able to. I'll just hold on to the other name to gather courage.

And to make certain my philosophical companion would never lack courage, I had the impulse to tell him about the fourth confidence. But I kept it to myself, for a time — the time that was to come — which would demand the utmost courage from us.

If I move the blue transparency of the vase from left to right, I set the blue in motion,
I destroy it and reconstruct it in its reflections _____
light,
objects
seen through the transparency of the mist of that same blue,
dance with it — which was its unfathomable and unexpected
— and create the text-path which leads directly to the heart of
the confidence.

But

all this   in its seeming brightness and weightlessness is
inmost, and
leaves much suffering unspoken.

Unheard and poignant,
it is our heart's most genuine offering to the secret of the
'There is.'

——————————— when the canonical is interwoven with the
apocryphal,

love becomes an elusive indescribable — it circulates,
proliferates, is ever-present, and yet,
it remains unable to gauge itself.
It opens up without being able to eclipse itself in openness.
From him, Joshua, I know the effects, I know that an intensity
has passed, will come, will not desist, will not abandon,

it turns on itself
or "Ursula turns on herself against herself,"
shatters and changes names,

what we think of as *I* is rendered voiceless, empty-handed, only
the one who is summoning it insistently broaches the name we
have forgotten. "Is that me?" and, like a dog overcome by fear
and expectation, we turn our faces away,
and we see that an absent one has arrived with a stranger, in the
form of a stranger. He calls out, we perfectly recognize his form
of being absent, "He is not my master, but I recognize his voice,"
says the dog,   and we draw closer ("just like that") to this
dis-known,
in a form
that is known.

   I write without any romanticism, drama, or solace
(— There is no good news — says *the Younger One* to the girl
who came out of the text) ——————— its flame burns and

scorches, but without that muddle, how can we think that 'There is' what is, when 'There is' and only is a wind that stokes the flame? We are the question from the flame, are we not? We are *the becoming* from the water. Whatever the world may be, we will always be, for as long as there is 'There is.'

_____ Sandra,

Good Lord, now love is filthy. In a basin. Filthy, how is that possible? You shouldn't think of it as a question, it's more of a non-question, or the astonishment prior to the question, the pure place of dis-comprehension. A death,
carried by a voice,
bringing it closer to us and sullying our gaze?
That solids exist, they exist,   just as vegetal nature exists. We need only look at how the wood of the tree decomposes.
That liquids exist, they exist,   just as animal nature exists. We need only look at how a body dissolves.
But isn't it necessary, my love, to make the evanescent, real, and vaporous nature of the figures
we have always been,
those magnificent animals with their vibrant howling,
on the verge of extinction,
more intelligible, more perceptive, more ferocious, in short, more irradiant?
With her eyes, the girl who came out of the text ("Don't be jealous! There's nothing like that between us!") tells me yes, but with her mouth she utters:
— What an incomprehensible thing to have lived with a name of our own.

_____ each of us will write what
we have seen — "will ex-scribe," as my philosophical
companion says — and, like different planetary paths around
the same sun, we will be in conjunction at the circus in the
Herbais stable, nine months and several days from now.

In the *'There is' that I have chosen,*
my backbone is exultation. Writing
is within the fold of paradise, which is also a hedge where I
enter through the air; my material constitution is fragile;
indeed, my feet are my only matter that is not
relentlessly cut through by the air,
which takes away images,
brings images, and is
very often,
pervasive with the scents that sorrow bears.

Who was sorrow?

_____ in the 'There is' that I
have chosen, my backbone is exultation.

My reflection today, interrupting the writing of *Joshua,
Companions and Lovers*, and the translations, is about the
obstacle,
and the place of mixtures, separations, and rhythms. About the
practicalities of entering and leaving paradise, unsettling places
of images, as if, on either side of that threshold, there is a
shifting mist that gives the images a color opposite the one they
truly have. Ever a limpid brown gaze, close to the underlying
structure of jubilation.

Explaining,
in this ever so subtle area where not even the word exists, and
so I wrote it in italics in order to emphasize,   in this
case,   that explaining is a hypothesis _____ explaining,
I was going to say,   is the faded trace of jubilation.

If, at the exit to paradise, one foot nearly outside, a dog
runs up to me,
I pull back and think,
"He's going to bite me."

But, at the entrance to paradise (and the only secret is
entering), when I have already crossed the threshold, and am
standing still,
if a dog leaps toward me, I say,
"It's Jade, my dog who disappeared for a time,
he's going to kiss me."

Senses and directions are so important — the bare tree we

leave with, the linden tree we enter with. "A bad image," I
thought.   A bare tree is always a luminous weapon.

   I stand still deep within the text, intensely visualizing the
Edenic text — seeing its indentations, its margins, its
geography, its smudges, the irritating unbroken lines, and, at the
exit, its isthmuses: *everything forms image and play.*

   The word *play* should not scandalize, I don't think. If
everyone chooses their own 'There is,' for whatever reasons they
may have _____ it is always a pertinent inclination and a
desire. A preference, and a certain *bodily spelling.* Yes. Because
what affects me is the "perhaps it will do," as is true of twine and
wrapping paper, which we save for an occasion,
for the eventuality of "you never know."
   When all those seemingly useless belongings become a
body within us, it is easier to enter and leave paradise. The body
has learned the way, and knows that, in passing through that
mist I spoke of, it changes its own color and name. But it is not
grieved _____ because the dog runs toward it, simply to kiss it.
And calls it by the name only it knows _____ as if it were a
password.

   Or is it?

———————————————————————————————— the irritating
unbroken line.

It is simply a fold and a rope. The text folds, a collage effect.
The text suspends its meaning, waiting for a precise phrasing.
There are sentences I have only completed years later; there are
sentences which, at the threshold of the worlds, should not be
written in their entirety; there are sentences whose referent of
meaning will always be obscure. If I intended to write a text that
was always clean — I would remove the line. Where I did not
know, I would write nothing. But how would I know it was
there I did not know, or it wasn't even my place to know? The
text is clean, and ready to be mended. Where the line is erased,
you can clearly see the rubbing of the eraser. Leaving a trace.

I believe, in this way,
that a door opens onto my text. Another,   opens at the
bottom of the stairs — everything remains illuminated, until
that light fades. Whether it is day, or night. Or now. It is the
lamp which tells the time, not the bell of the church, like the
one I just heard, synchronous with my thinking.

Today,
I was forced to say a strong and radical *no* to someone. I was
with myself, entirely outside of myself and my fear. My body
became more immortal, more universal, more expansive — a
presence of aspidistras. The few I's in my name put away their
claws,   certain that *the other* saw a flaming unbroken line
drawn in the space of the relationship.

What I saw

was my slave (— Who? — asks the philosophical companion.
— My mind and my interests — I replied. — Ah! those
quarrels — he concluded) taking the chains off his feet on the
banks of the river, above the tops of the trees; he is vigorous;
moving toward old age,
his chest bare,
and he uses his deft fingernails in his efforts to free himself; he
washes in the river as the dog barks at him
and looks back with longing,
wanting to stand in the shadow of my body.
    I make no gesture
neither to welcome him,
nor reject him.   May he go where he needs to go, and may
life be kind to him.
    Yet I recognize that a certain beauty emanates from his
attitude
which has nothing of the future. He stands up
and sets out on the path I lay for him. If he becomes lost,
I will not become lost. I have never trusted him. I have been
throwing pebbles on the path for a long time. I know he grows
angry because he feels dethroned
from a throne I did not worship. I observe, incidentally,
that obedience to certain laws of the text is
an angle infinitely more open than the freedom promised me by
reason, held between the two sharp ends of the compass of
coercive force (— You don't believe in anything, do you,
Gabriela? — he asks).

    I threw myself into the river that crowned the trees

without being sure I could swim.
I swim over the *shawl of my mind* (— If you would like
to come, bring your own),
but it is with my feet and arms that I mark the direction
in the celestial heights, while I see my naked slave
moving away:
the secondary garments soaked in sweat,
under his arm.

_____ I thought I had another
understanding of the world,

and I never wanted to place it on a metaphysical plane, in any
way. I do not want to think concepts, but to *make volatile knots
of images, thoughts, fascinations, and signs*
which allow me
today,
to make my way and take pleasure in my path; the cherubs that
appear dancing in the scene of the text change every day; their
song of praise is always one of praise, awe, and beauty, but it is
never the same; and yet I do not understand angelology. I write,
and so often speak of text and affection
(that it becomes irritating)

as Rilke speaks of roses and angels, of stones and seeing,
as Dickinson speaks of circumference and birds, of closing her
eyes, and
not of death ...

   You might say we all have a mania — and it's true — a fold,
an insistence,

   but it is what we see
and, in a certain way, it is what we have come to know, even if
we don't know whether that knowledge, apart from modifying
our body, will serve any other purpose. Speaking of myself, even
that faith-hope was something I had to cast off. It is part of the
garments he carried, under his arm, the slave

379

who moved away_____ without the slightest remorse from me, it's true.

Today,
it seems to me that the origin of my understanding of the world has always been the
viator bush,
and this morning, I found myself returning to *Loving Cause,* and the imminence of its garden. But emerging from it, the reality was already entirely different, as if the evolution of feelings and relationships were only natural. Mere stages in the evolution of a species without any problems of meaning, of being or not being, of classes and typologies of immutable behaviors, but with a place to set out the bare facts.

Within the array of colors, what color would they be, if I didn't have these physical eyes?

What scent, if I didn't have this nose? In other worlds, how would I identify them?

It is of the body — more than the human body — that *Loving Cause* speaks.

There is hope that it will rain, today.

But there is no hope that my mother is going to live.

Nor is there any hope that the rain is going to reach the deepest part of the roots. This is how this day progresses, evolving through its hours, through its knots of fabric, which may have their origin in the plants that settle, alive and green though thirsty for water, in the places where they breathe turned toward the sun.

Augusto will speak about Kafka at the Lisbonleipzig
meetings, on Friday, and I think of the pleasure Kafka would take
in drinking this water. Or maybe not; the pleasure would be all
mine, watching him drink it, enter *Loving Cause*, and tend, in his
own way, the *viator bush*. Augusto argues it would be better if he
didn't:

— Everything you write can be seen as a pursuit — in
reality, endless practical pursuits, almost one for every day — for
viable paths out of entropy. Whereas Kafka thought that entropy
was inexorable and insurmountable — for everything and
everyone — even though, momentarily, the place each person
occupies in this grinding machine was not insignificant. Some are
the meat itself, and others those who eat them as sausages,
although both end up as scraps and detritus. He could not
understand how his own father could have caused him to be
born. His cry, "Father, can't you see I'm drowning? Why do you
do nothing?" would have been utterly incomprehensible to the
viator bush in *Loving Cause*.

Even so, another garden would have been cultivated _____
Kafkaesque, albeit with Kafka blooming once more on a wall.

No rain, but it is a day of introductions, someone
puts a key into the door of knowledge and opens up a new
garden — yes, it's true — full of snares, where you have to walk
without innocence, on tiptoe, raising your hands so as not to eat
the fruit of the Tree of Everything and Nothingness. There is
another way to unravel the knots of intensity and recognize the
unknowable. Not the invisible, as Rilke called it, passing through
his orchard,
nor the space of the invisible, which Vergílio has spoken of for

so long.

The unknowable has no way of being thought, it is *the tumult of images emerging* from the horizon, which strikes the flame that lights and ignites the core of the ring.

There is no way to gain the experience to confront them. Either they will bite, or they will kiss.

I never lost _____ as much but twice _____

I continue, in my text, this text by Emily Dickinson, for, quite by coincidence, this fragment was already written on the top of the page, which I — translating it into Portuguese — had set aside because it was placed too high, on the paper.

This is the hour when I write to the sun at my side.
Between six and seven in the afternoon — approximately — my desk is surrounded by a light that returns incandescently through the window, bringing my hands very close to my heart, and my thinking. I feel outside, as though I am
physically outside,
including trees, poets, animals, affections, the outside itself
(those outside me entering into me),
until the light fades and the twilight turns my gaze to the
paintings in front of me,
and they are real.
I am in my *territory*,
beyond the brute, reactive force that ravages the world, or rather,

looking at the shadow that falls on my worktable.

To identify our own strengths, not to
disentangle them from the others that do not
belong to us. Today there is no front line, no
identifiable masses of enemy maneuvers; no
fixed positions. The perimeter shifts from hour

to hour. Erratically. I wrote the other day that the angelic presence is one of beauty, praise, and awe. Many of those I meet have a sense of this angelic presence, although for reasons I do not understand, they only perceive the element of awe. They flee, a conditioned reaction of identity, when it would be possible, I believe, to work on the reaction: rather than fleeing from awe, to embrace praise and beauty. To draw on the strength of the angel, as I see being practiced in judo, surfing, and certain extreme sports.

I discover the territorial part of beauty and want to enter it, opening up the gate of the territory that the 'There is' has given to me to explore. Not only to me, nor me particularly, but to the paths that the sun, air, wind, and water reach.

It was a simple day in the extreme,
but I wouldn't trade it for other globes, no matter how resplendent they might be,
as all the realms that play the game of beauty are here. Only simpler, today. The noise of my typewriter and that of Augusto's computer, softer, are like footsteps,   and so we possess the land, from one shore to the other shore.

In the meantime,
the porcelain dog lying behind the typewriter has his mouth open. There are a number of objects, and animals and books predominate, mute species. Only the dog heads toward a fountain — I can see, isolated, the Fontanário das Sete Bicas, in

Alpedrinha — and drinks water. He chooses
one of the different basins to drink from
and I can clearly see the hallway of the sentence accompanying
him, for this is how
the text acts _____ the text moves down a hallway lined with
rooms or mirrors that multiply the space, until it finally goes
looking for the
water,
which is guarded
by the dog that drank it.

Today, the sun no longer returns _____ it still shines, but
only in the gray of the light, behind the Palácio da Vila. It wasn't
a day that needed to be mended. It was not born creased — I
didn't feel the absent-presence of someone who spurs me into
the act of searching, which has always accompanied me. It was
born smooth.

The television news is now descending upon the surface of
the world, and the spot of sun is no longer spreading, although I
always continue
along the same path,
moving from what is near to what is distant,
returning reality to me,
that is,
returning the color to my gaze. The sun
has set, is no longer visible, not even its orange face — it is the
moment
when I want to fill my brain with reasoning,
to voluptuously make a fool of myself,
to squander knowledge, in order to, tomorrow, better grasp its

details and solidity. Then it's time for the telenovela. It's always
similar to standing on a *theoretical mantle,* on which I attempt to
dis-distinguish, as on a geographical chart,
the signs of the slightest circulation of my own opinions,
and untangle
the volatile knots I have made
in the immense circulation of the waters. An inglorious task at
which I will never succeed. As I sit watching those storylines, all
supplied by a century and a half of novels and theater, I
recognize there is a certain childishness about this game of
mine. About the "attributes of God,"
Vergílio thinks, so often. They will be *there,* perhaps, but God is
a destroyed word — like the words Love, Power, Ambition,
Intrigue in telenovelas. I look at them and see only a trace left
by so many generations who thought they were exiled from the
'There is.'

   This is not the thinking of the dog, which
appearing from behind the typewriter, an image emerging from
within,
carries in his mouth the fragment of knowledge intended for
me. He does not bark, he waits for me to serve myself as I serve
him. And I recall the way I began the day_____
the light coming in through my room,
going down the stairs,
feeding a stray neighborhood cat, and,
losing this sentence at nightfall because the phone rang. It was
Vergílio.

      — So how are you?
      — I was thinking about the attributes of God.

— Oh really? What are they?

— Water. Water in a dog's mouth.

He laughs, and changes the subject:

— What are you writing?

— *Joshua, Companions and Lovers*. And you?

— Those letters I told you about — he replies. And, without transition continues: — Do you know who called me?

_____ I come in and,
among my papers, I found the letter. I can't place it. Then I
remember Christine's handwriting, and the period of *Tales of
Wandering Evil*. I recognize it. I keep it outside the envelope,
and put it in a prominent place in the house. It astonishes me, as
if it were making love to me, when, in truth,
it makes me aware of the deep meadow I once was, and I think
about the carpet in the living room, where I sit with the strange
pleasure of rising up into old age. I was *there* — in that *dwelling*
— which elicits this *state* in me today. The dwelling is enduring
and ineradicable; even empty, it remains. The state is fleeting,
without being a memory or echo, it is rather an absence whose
presence has weakened_____ like an image whose taste no
longer pervades us. But it is *here*. The dwelling still sends out its
aria, the words are ever sparser,
intended for a letter which never finds its recipient. Dispersed,

> it insists on conversing with me in
> its fragmented parts,
> attempting to recapitulate our lives,
> mine,
> that of the letter,
> that of that dwelling,
> in a single life.

    It will never be anything,
other than a body in transit to its image state. It will not lose its
colors — they will be even stronger, but faded and with no
impetus in its arms or dryness in its mouth. It will have some
other thirst — a thirst I do not yet know how to slake.

The life of the letter provides a meticulous account of witnessable events, attempting biography. I evade that way of thinking, and attempt another
path _____
I un date and gather together the knots of the visible in close proximity, so that their strength is not dispersed.
If the path of life forgot me _____
and I, in the end, came across another perspective,
this dwelling would not be, like all lives, a vague plot of land on the map, but a place in the geography of the 'There is' of the worlds,
that *letter of colors* depicting the outline of a country, which a certain light enhances.

But the word letter I first used did not have this meaning, it was the actual contents of the letter which I continued to read in my chair after I got up from the carpet, and understood, to tell it,

that I had reached the pivotal moment in my existence, where, as Christine had predicted, I was going to accept my black face reflected in the depths of the window looking out over the city, as if in a mirror.

The letter merely transcribed in French — a translation I had requested from the Sanskrit — a short passage from the Upanishads where Nachiketa asks Yama, king of the dead:

> "When a person dies,
> there arises
> this doubt —

he still *exists*, say some
he *does not*, say others —
I want you to teach me the truth:
this is my third boon,"

to which she had added the following comment, written in her own hand:

"Gabi, I do not want to witness your death. Christine."

4 JUNE 1995

_____ I opened the
window,

heat rolls in — and I have
the impression that I have moved my room down to the
street _____
it is
among the passersby, who, passing by, do not notice it. For
instance, they do not notice the seven sources of light that
illuminate it. But I notice them, those passersby and the 'There
is' of this dwelling, within the confines of my consciousness,
for
"to every eye corresponds a perspective of the world."
But every eye can also *blot out the world*, and
is it this way, or that way,
that they are passing by?

    — That way? — asks my philosophical companion.
    — Yes, the one that, next to Beauty, allows enlightenment
to remain — and so learns impregnation.

_____ conflicts ebb and flare; little more is revealed by the nature of my worktable, with two electric lamps, two candles, an old oil lamp — and another blue candle — which I forgot to mention. Six sources of light, and a seventh, a candlestick holder, with a candle made of genuine beeswax.

Seven sources of light, then. Such are the dwellings that many mystics have described in the accounts of their experience.

_____ but the nature of my worktable is not mystical; if it were, it would join with God in a movement of its true wooden nature; as such, it only joins with beauty, and uses the sources of light to enter into communion with the sun. Incapable of ascesis — but not reading — it follows the variations in the signs _____ be they color, sound, or something else, and tells me that there is a present, made of _____;

so, for example, today, in the swing between darkness/brightness, we crossed, she and I, a zone of light where light is absent:

the linden tree in front of the house finally cracked, men from City Hall came to cut it down and took the trunk to make firewood, leaving the branches and leaves behind on the ground to be run over by automobiles. We continued to cast lots for the mantle of the trees, for they told me the linden tree had not cracked, it had simply insisted — a crime against humanity — on growing toward the roof of a building, to which it imparted a particular beauty.

And so the linden tree was the first victim of the absence of
elucidated volition. The one that is rowing is the zigzagging light
of the candle,
the howl of the wolf resembles a stone blocking its throat, and
I ask myself
why I see stones and animals in people,
and trees and humans in figures, and how there is, between
these two natures, a deep sense of identity as a *viator.*

The ones who cut down the linden tree, my worktable tells
me, move like an omnipotent, cruel, and stubborn child in the
'There is' that they have not chosen,
nor understand,
because their head is not covered with the shawl of their mind.
They dull the colors and keep the façades of the buildings faded
and dirty, kill the animals that pass by, and fill the streets with
automobiles.

But my worktable tells me even more: the battered and
slain linden tree is the dwelling place of sorrow, and I,
who am writing,
dwell, at this hour, in the dwelling place of renunciation.

Indeed, to begin writing, I had asked my desk for a name.
The name of an existing — and ardent — figure. Without the
names of the members of the virtual community who find their
dwelling in the text,   how to begin writing?

It then gave me a name, Ibn 'Arabi,
who began to write, at my desk, the episode of the palm tree in
Seville.

When I read what he was writing, the knot of problems
began to unravel — the rent for the house, the telephone bill,
the expenses which render the body less bereft of the substance

that truly affects it, money essential for life, bills, standard of
living, interests —
and I was able to gradually begin
to cast the shifting knot of the text. I was then struck by the
parallels with the heavy clouds, the electric current, the
knocking on the door, and the rain finally beating down on the
house
creating an empty space that
will be calm until the next storm. Writing is thus cyclical, and
therefore healthy. It is a sign my body is working, no longer
tired, no longer drowsy, and has crossed the threshold of
darkness where it rests. But — first — I have to ask for names
for the living people and verbs for the figures.

When at last I hear a name, I stand up, shake off the daze,
and go down to the river where those whom I love,
that is,
those to whom I want to give affective relevance in the
intelligent world,
are washing their outlines.

Just like today,
the day Ibn 'Arabi — in order to cast me into the *living 'There is'*
— came from Damascus, where he has been resting for seven
hundred and fifty years, to tell me the story of the palm tree in
Seville.

_____ it was a sunny day.

It was a radiantly sunny day, which in my atmospheric imagination, arrived after several days of rain.

I was gazing at a carpet of grass ebbing and flowing with color, looking down on it from above, near the Palácio da Vila.

Atop the wall, emerging from the greenery and the stones, appeared a lizard, the first, perhaps the last, that I have seen so fully, and so close.

At night, on the phone with Lurdes and Anabela, I wasn't able to describe the exact dance of its entire body, so unexpected and natural, in the sense that it was a coherent expression of that way of existing, but the fact remains that it evolved in front of us (I was with Augusto) as if no one were there, all alone, with it.

A slender body, four legs, globular eyes with the ability to see a reality wholly different from our own.

In its reptilian way — with which I was delighted — it danced,
exhibited its great ease in the daylight,
and with me,
who had never seen an animal of its species take such a self-assured attitude in front of humans.

— A bare fact inhabits the dwelling place of gratitude — I said to Augusto.

— That is the answer to the linden tree which was cut down — he replied.

Only then did the story of the palm tree in Seville file through my memory.

"There was a palm tree on a street in the city of Seville, which had leaned so far into the street that it became very difficult for passersby to negotiate. It was so troublesome that people arrived at the conclusion that it needed to be cut down. They finally decided to do it the following day.

Ibn ʿArabi says: That night I saw the Prophet in a dream, standing by the palm tree. Complaining, the palm tree said to him:

— O Prophet of God, the people want to cut me down because I obstruct their path.

The Prophet heard it, placed his blessed hand on it, and made it straight.

The next morning, says Ibn ʿArabi, I went to see the palm tree, and found that it was straight. I told the people about the dream I had, and they were so astonished that they considered the palm tree to be a blessed being, making that site a place of pilgrimage."

In my city, the dwelling place of sorrow is far from the dwelling place of gratitude.
The two dwelling places are there,
where the linden tree died and
where the lizard danced. But the distance between the two makes the nexus invisible, and utterly insignificant.
There is no blessing.
This is what is said when we speak of an absent God. Our 'There is' is *viator* and *faber*.
But not in Seville. Sorrow and gratitude were one and the

same place. Humans were confronted by the visibility of a blessing. A Prophet assured the canopy, a mystic communicated a dream.

The 'There is' of those people was *peregrinatio*.

Long ago, when I was baptized, my godparents answered "Yes" to the question "Do you renounce Satan, all his vanities, and all his works?"

Today, when I write, I always answer "Yes," but in reality, I am answering a different question. The question of the linden and the lizard is entirely different. "Do you renounce the blessing?" is what I am asked, and what is asked of me.

21 JUNE 1995

_____ accordingly, my worktable is

a vast theatrical incandescence which,
inevitably,
does not even come from candles.

I must rewrite *The Book of Communities*, and I do not know
how to pursue this "must." I undoubtedly have to look at what is
happening as what I have been imagining. *Faber* is that. Not of
the hands, but of the heart and the brain _____ every
human not being able to leave

their volition unelucidated, I said

to Leonarda. This is not the name she was given, but the name
which draws her closer to her true verb. I went with her to
Magoito
on the morning of the afternoon when I saw the lizard that
overwhelmed and surprised me; the sea is blue like a stone
to sharpen the gaze _____ it was the image of the varying
images of the sea. Leonarda is young, practical, with a thirst
for the new, intensely envisioning the companion (whom
she desires) and *is to* come. She sat down with her legs over
the abyss. I did the same, being practical, erratic, and
assertive,
direct truths which I soon had the impression of in my chest.
But my gaze over the abyss shuddered, and I altered my
position, extending my legs over the wall. Leonarda smiled. At
the instant of my change in posture, I felt
as though my bodily thinking had changed. My body had

entered another thinking _____
the light was traveling through the blue,
a serene convulsion furrowed the waters,
I had a dizzy spell,
"I stopped thinking serenely,"
I observed, as I quickly changed the placement of my legs.

    I reacted the same way as a bush. I altered the position of the stalk. I sought the gravity of the earth and, in the space of a minimal and compelling sensation, I moved from the dwelling place of fear to the dwelling place of hope. Confronted with the images from the far horizon, I knew that in the 'There is,' there are only instants, and that my body was a bridge made of breath
amidst opposing currents. And I thought

_____ blue, almost
blue, in the space of *Joshua, Companions and Lovers*, they were
sitting on the sand, and every shawl they wore away from their
necks had sea foam as its edge _____ some were lying on
the rock,
                              layers of sedimentary terrain, and rather
than using what happens,   occurrences, in the words of
their interlude, described in greater detail,

they observed from within
what a being is born with   and read, there, the
enduring signs of pleasure and regeneration. This was the novel
they wanted to be in — and no other.

    Lying on their backs, on the edges of their shawls, they
observed the sea, as captivating to them as
it is to historians,
sociologists,
entrepreneurs,
journalists,
psychologists,
healers of souls

                              the history of the facts of men (only they
are not bare,
but *made of something else*)
        — Of what? — asked Gonçala.
        — Of desire — I replied.

With that bare fact, full of blue and gray tones, they fell in love. They lived among those tones   and
brought them to my room, and I
always leaving to go to them (women), and them (men).
They were ancient beings. We imagined

a space larger than this one and, in the place of the desk, the furniture pushed aside, we sat in low chairs — looking at the entire room. This dwelling place

is one of love.
          — One of love, *pure as they say of the air* — I said to Gonçala and Leonarda, for I knew that, in their eyes, women were looking at the sea. And only that.

I know where the *invisibility* is in their gazes.
          There were no bodies penetrating one another.
          No companions could be seen.
          No one was waiting for someone, or running toward them.
          There was no intimacy, no seduction, nor possession.
          There was nothing of what I was saying.

Gonçala and Leonarda,
nothing
can be said
with
sex, but it is with it that one speaks, like a sheet of paper with a pencil.

An old pencil does not know how to sharpen itself. A sheet of paper, even a blank one, will never read what has been written on it.

It is a secret: the secret of the 'There is.'

I will only tell you: — Nothing is commonplace, everything is figural.

Gonçala and Leonarda,
take your sexes of reading, the *viator and faber sex* and, if you wish, write with it. But place the bare and seductive fact of your body before the baptismal question of the world.

Ask yourselves:

_____ how is it possible to love someone in a world where it is necessary to renounce the blessing?

I saw in their eyes that they saw and failed to see. They saw with surprise that human beings sought one another and surrendered themselves to one another, without gauging for themselves the sex they used and had _____ without leaning it against a question that would anchor it — as the trunk for the tree. They failed to see that the libido was neither a garden, nor an orchard, nor, still less, the promised delight: they failed to notice the confusion of the adjectives.

— Gonçala, there are solar and lunar adjectives, in accordance with our naked body.

I saw in their eyes that they failed to see. Perhaps they needed the globular eyes of the lizard of gratitude, but I insisted:

— The solar find their dwelling place in oblation, and the lunar in patience.

_____ the truth _____ is that I probably have two
bodies _____

I feel them in my own veins as I write, perhaps in the same way
that dying — I do not know —
is like passing into another body, or bringing that body
to the place
where my consciousness remembers.

    I remember, I fail to remember,
I am circling a sentence that came to me yesterday, in Lisbon,
but I do not think it is a sentence, but rather a vortex
surrounding the sex of reading with vitality. Or the elucidated
volition. From my body to another body, from a place to
another place, from a dwelling to another dwelling. And if I see
the sun is here, it is because I am not
in the other galaxy of flesh, or face, to which I should compare
this, which is more natural than nature _____
it blooms and gleams, or gleams or blooms. Because order is
arbitrary in the vortex that irradiates beams of light and bodies.
It is like wandering through a dis-born time. Perhaps the
sentence I fail to remember is, in the end, a forgotten 'There is'
— either because its time has been annulled, or because I have
been sheltered by another space.

    They will tell me I am "precious," that I pay attention to a
detail because "forgetful, who isn't?" But if you want to know,
the genesis began on the bed where I replaced the white
coverlet with another white coverlet — but it wasn't the same, it

was profoundly different, because from that moment on, the entire room was seen
(by whom?)
gleaming, and different. It was just another material through which I had maturely reflected the penchant (perhaps ruminenchant?). I attempt to unravel all
the lines prior to my existence, but without experiencing, rather entering — swiftly — into the certainty of seeing. Who
is here with me? Who appears and reappears _____ waves of the sea in the same space, and at the same instant? Who is moving away from me? Ursula,
who is so near, does not knock at the door to my cell or room, always open, she is at the door, at the entrance to my heart, which I share with her. When she enters, it is Ana in the place of my body, and even, very likely, with my features, who attends to her as I slip away to a corner of the shadow
to write down what is happening. She is going to ask her a question, to be enraptured, but Ana doesn't want her to be enraptured by this reality, she wants her to work on it, to go down with her into the earth that her room is made of
— hers, as well.

There is no doubt that here
the sun and the solitude
are determining factors, they banish the fear so inherent to this land. I, Gabriela, call her, Ursula, one of my bodies, which I have placed on the worktable — or on the windowsill
— without being mine alone.

Who is speaking?
— I am speaking — she answers, haughtily unconveyable.

404

(— Who is she — asks my philosophical companion. — She is a beguine, like your Sandra — I reply: — Another of your bodies. — The body I will receive later? — he presses). As far as I know, Ursula

prefers not to breathe, unless it is in text, rather than having to answer obvious questions. She always brings me meaningful words,

but all this came from the coverlet, and its reverberations. She, Ursula, says:
    — ...I was born in the North, among the trees that stood amidst trees, groves, which surround the edge of your room, or the house where they emigrated, traveling,
Joshua and other enigmatic figures who dared to want to reconstruct _____
    _____ I am

losing strength. A fly buzzes,
breaks through the silent depths that abruptly loom. One of my bodies reaches me. I take the stone. I change places. I do not have the voraciousness of any unknown image. I penetrate it. I give the stone to Ursula, who finds it effective and weightless. Pure material matter.

    And that is how the day unfolds, so that tomorrow strength will be born anew.

_____ I believe that reading

     is the sexual act par excellence. It penetrates,
     spans, transubstantiates. It is the organ of the
     charismas of the *viator-faber*. The mystics always
     wanted to separate them from their organ — which
     has had dire effects — conceding, however, that
     charismas and a union with God were not synonymous.
     Just as sex and love are not synonymous. They are
     potencies, *pleasures*, experienced and effective forces.
     It was important that they remain in the marrow of the
     blessing. But all the charismas were given to the human
     Garden of Eden. To separate them from their organ is to
     weaken free will. They were what hung

over the surface of the waters
the secret of the 'There is.'

    If the pursuit of *beauty* is not inscribed in that potency to
transform it into agape, will there ever be a beauty that pulsates
in the human? Will there ever be an elucidated volition? I found
myself sitting at the edge of the water,

which was a reader with an open body, and I saw the text
longing for it, impatiently beating its hooves on the stone
_____ not that I am implying it is a horse.
    The text languidly formed itself,
creating legs,
feathers,

a tail,
inaudible voice,
absorbed gaze,

not that I am implying it is a misshapen being, or a monster. But
it was longing for its deep mirror,
              the waters where it would be able to distend
and bloom its wounded body, wrapped in linen. Wounded
— but not sick — it yearned only to be able to enter, unscathed
along its way, the body of the waters.

      I bent over the liquid piece of cloth, and understood that it
gave it meaning — in accordance with the fertile place where it
would take it — but I could not imagine then what place that
would be:
      "It is, surely, according to its strength and its consciousness,
its readerly incandescence," I thought.

      With this open feeling at the edge of the waters, the text
flowed, seeking a path in its harmonious misshapenness
through which the *beautiful*,
as if to say "the song of songs,"
rushed past. Its dwelling place was the *metanight*.

      Indeed,
it is night. All the words have lit their torches. I hear the footsteps
of readers in the sand, just as I am, the grains of sand are
themselves alight ——— they illuminate the shores, the surface
and line of the horizon of the creational nature which casts the
charismas of kindness, patience, and intrepidness upon us. Some,
less experienced, attempt to open up seams and depths.

(— Do not dig wells — my philosophical companion tells them: — Look for sources.)

Indeed,
in creational nature — the only one that is enduring and evanescent — we are the singular sexes of reading,   and I slip into my childhood scene — *I water* — looking at the text, which I assimilate into a figure scattered across books, pages, images,
oral histories,
a restless pupil who sees
the pain of reading everywhere.   "I still don't know how to read and I want to read," I remember. It is such a serene anxiety, an arrow of uncertain meaning, a

gleaming nature which runs through the aching nature. "How are children born?" I then asked. But I wanted to ask "Where is my brother, whom I cannot see?"

I was going to translate Rilke, attempt to be the reader of his sources, even
if I would founder,   when I felt the need to write this text. I am always falling asleep and awaking, today I fell asleep and awoke next to the water of reading. The text is an affection of mine, I try to connect it to other people for whom I also have great affection. Perhaps it will be useful for them. But the text, written or read, is the scene where I see reality,
a bare fact at the moment it is interwoven with the beautiful,
and I recognize that I assess the quality of affections with the same measure I use to assess the quality of texts. It is a harsh ordeal, but it causes love to evolve into an intimate and

expressive demand. And I love those who read, unrelentingly.
So I am rigorous in my reading failures, afraid to breach the
water — a thought which occurred to the text. How could I, or
how could we,
a source of text, possibly enter into your water, water
that would not create a thirst for more water? The liquid image
of creation is you.

If it pleases you, drink.

_____ since I need to cool myself down,
and have no pool, nor ocean,
I decided, after my bath — alone at home — to remain naked
for a while, opening the windows,
washing the waxed floor and the white tiles. I wanted, in fact
(the gesture had been, at that moment, entirely too
spontaneous for me to know what I wanted); I should instead
write _____ I felt the need for silence between me
and the book of *Joshua*,

to open the windows and

remain naked, sheltering the image of a lawless animal in my
heart. No garments, nor buildings, nor exercises,
myself overflowing, and the one who I am on a journey
now outside of myself _____ and so I was a *body
without concerns*, so I spent part of the morning, insufficient and
incalculable.

  Between my soul and the water, the body was bare,
incognito in its nature — a work by an unknown author; as I
washed the floor, what came to mind was the classification of
the parts of the body, into *heart, membrane, bowels, nucleus, core,
blood* — a curious classification like the ones Foucault
appreciated, presuming the existence of an anatomy that
ignored the notion of an organism. And, after I dressed,

I pushed the water away and plunged, now more freely, into the
album of writing; this is how I would like to write, honing the

photograph album of the body without concerns, flash after flash, moving the arm handling the typewriter to all possible angles. I call this text *the photograph* _____
captured in the image was a naked woman with her knees on a towel to keep her knees from hurting, dipping — as I did in Jodoigne — a cloth into the basin which served as a bucket; in the meantime, I thought feeling,
I never stopped attributing thinking to it,
and seeing it emerge later on. There was a concept waiting for me, in the hallway. What

is female about it? What is this look? _____ It doesn't sell perfume, or rags, it doesn't direct companies, or children, it doesn't know which is the best detergent for clothes, or which bleach is less damaging, it isn't in sanitary napkins, or in the automobile business, or... What is the look of the *or*? What is depicted in that photograph of a naked woman, writing and reflecting in an inappropriate, or at least curious posture, like the classification above? A man, a woman?
Who cares about
the place of representation in the water
if nudity is the source of the body,
the very effect of writing
before being *told* the sex with which you will read the world?
    And what effect is this, if not the *core* (which for the anonymous author I quoted
is the place of revelation, as the bowels are of vision, and the heart of faith)?

dipping a cloth in the bucket

— There is also a photograph album in *Apparition* — he tells me, halfway down the hall: — Don't you remember?

— No.

— Can I read it to you?

— You can — I say reluctantly.   "Like the portraits in

Aunt Dulce's album…" (Pause)

"They are now utter, absolute nothingness, pure absence, nothingness — nothingness? Here begins your long journey into the vertigo of the ages, into the vanishing silence of the millennia. Yes, you are still living for me now, because I know you." (Pause)

— Vergílio, the copper basins are waiting to be sanded — I try to interrupt.

"Good Aunt Dulce! I remember you not so much by your gestures and words, but by what resonated there from the gravity of it all. So…"

— Vergílio…

"…I forget that intransigent appetite of yours, the ensuing poor digestion, and the magnesia and the enemas, your mouth whetted in convenience, the gluttony with which you welcomed our kisses." (Pause)

— Just a bit more…

"And I have here in front of me now like the specter of ages

and people I hardly know any longer and they are staring at me
still from the other side of life and long to speak to me without
being able and they distress me..." (Pause)

Now the copper pots (I stop listening to him),
the old basins worn out by the time that has embellished them.
There are four — authentic pots of confidences which I will
clean with Solarine until they smell nice, look nice, and I hear
the rustling of wings; listening to those read pages falling
through the open waterfalls along the hallway,

my nakedness dulled with blue in front of the copper; the heavy
blue of the sky breaks the circle that distressed me to arrive at
myself,
not at myself but at what is left of me,
guided by the angels, which, fleeing and smiling, hide in every
line; I let time pass, nor does it — time — appear to me. My
philosophical companion tells me to make an unbroken Diary,
to leave traces of myself behind, before I lose the place from
whence I go to whence I came.

Absorbed in these thoughts and noises, I have not yet
begun to clean the copper pots, but I am going to. It is another
ablution which I will add to that of the water. Why was I
suddenly afraid that this moment would come undone? How
will I live after it?
If my virtual brothers existed in silence, I wouldn't fear
them so much.

I only fear they will drown my angels, or change their wings and
face. Will I still be myself, I wonder, will I still be myself, after

this nakedness?
    As I dress, I see,
in a procession, as if at an investiture, garment by garment

> my vigilant body,
> my reading body,
> my silent body,
> my sorrowful and merciful body,
> my law-abiding body
> my intercessor body,
> my warrior body,
> my paladin body,
> my meditative and contemplative body.

— The desire to live is strange, isn't it? — he asks me. — Only so many years later do I notice the proximity between disarrayed viscera and a memory that is lost... Did you notice how, as it is lost, the need for vision is born? And we can no longer talk to one another, there has appeared, hasn't there, that membrane of...?

— How? — I ask him, as I vest my body.

— Weren't you listening to the text?

_____ I'm going to say farewell,
begin

to say farewell   to yet another of my *stopping places* on this
path, as Gil Vicente said. I sense that

> Vergílio is sitting in his armchair.
> Regina, at his side. He is translucent
> ("Beautiful, kind, and bright," Augusto,
> who was sitting in front of him,
> would later tell me).
>   — Are you leaving already? — he asks us.

I'm going to say farewell, begin to say farewell without
anything breaking or shattering. My philosophical companion is
cold everywhere, except for on the sheet of writing paper; the
fireplace is dying, the trail of fire leads to the page, and there it
endures beyond all consummation.

I simply have to stop once again, and leave.

I came here to retrace my steps — and leave once more. It
is the changing of the scene; the voices change places; they
change texts,
it is the changing of garments — quick seamstresses perform
the changing of loves, *which are always the same.* This, the
contract of kindness that binds us. And knowing it is 'There is.'

The fireplace is above the chimney, and the adjacent tree
burns, and sparks fall on the stage, on the lines where my
philosophical companion — the face of the *Younger One* on his

final body — is lying down thinking about his next body. At what age will it be reborn, in what era will it again cover the slit of the eyes, where multiple images of scattered things came to be set alight?

This is how I write the bare fact of a loosening from all things,
in order to go to the meeting in the courtyard of the School
— which, for us, is a circus or a stage, as I told him — where other worlds teach us that we carry the universe suspended from our own necks — rather than a yoke. Within our dream, someone is waiting for you. Between you and the text is the bed of transmutation. Will you remain on the edge of the stage, or will you bring your stones of contradiction into the midst of the game?

This collar is mine, this garment is yours, you must look for the handkerchief in the midst of the flame, the blooming thunder that roars in the garden. Cold, cold! Look on the left side of the house, by the jars! Hot, hot! Scorching!

— I enjoy going to the Theater — he says. — I enjoyed being an actor. It is, indeed, a Circus. Suddenly, the internal equilibrium is different...

The Younger One steps onto the stage, dressed as Harlequin, and confesses to the girl who came out of the text:

— Few have understood how I attempted to enact an unheard thinking. I strayed so far, don't you think? Why are we born with Pessoa, in this country? What are we doing here?

The girl puts a finger over her mouth:

— That subject is part of non-thinking.

— And?

— It leads nowhere. It is the gray houses in the Game of the Goose.

My hands on the sheet of paper
are alive, they move with my thinking
as it works; they write my small writing,
as I bid farewell to my books. I tell
them, "I'm leaving, I am astonishingly
tired, nothing motivates me any longer."
They assume I'm not going, that I'm
never going, they do not want to grow
old in my absence. They are fibers.
Yet their physical body, made of pulp, will
last far beyond my own. In less than a
fortnight, I will be made of illiterate worms.
This is the end. Move away from the
floor so that I can stretch myself out.

——————— I hear him talking to himself, and getting ready.

An Easter song is rising on the left, from my window, but
the true place of music, in my provisional house, is on the right.
There are no chains, no solace, only irrepressible nature in its
cyclicality. What nostalgia I have for the creators
when they stride toward me
undone in the anguish of creation ———————
when it rains, outside, outside the music.

I want to coalesce with that song in the space where I am,
and feel the insistent reality of my body outside my body, in
which I materially exist when I return.

Take away everything, everything that makes the breeze heavy. Being weightless is the primal condition of my refuge — my focal image, my transparent axis. I am also so far from my hand that I cannot understand why I am still writing. Only because I have vested myself, perhaps.

When he leaves,
I will be even further away from the references of understanding, from the ponderability of things, from the precise and effective segments of the common reading. Augusto, who is listening to me, tries to focus me, without the knowledge of what I'm feeling: — It has been millions of years, and a handful of encounters. It has always been this way, Maria Gabriela. There's no need to grumble. The two of you, you have had a an incredibly rare opportunity. — And aren't you sad? — I am, but it isn't much use. In any case, for now, he's the one who is moving on. And as far as I know, being born and dying are occurrences we're not particularly adept at handling. I'd rather think about him. And, when he's gone, Regina.

_____ Oh, the past! The past is futile. What does it offer me except an unreliable summary of my life? I have been plunging into it for days and drowning,
because everything is happening for you,   my Ink. And the rest is secondary, mere circumstances of our present life, but which affect my body.

And yet, every day, I hold a text on my finger, and I rejoice over it like an animal for whom the door has been opened; it is a rabbit with a soft fur coat, and as it comes out of the forest which I envision above the fields,   it reproduces, then

grazes on grass. It finds shelter and smells the air, ignores the
hunters — and opens up the second door to the darkness of
the house. There it writes itself in utter stillness, leaping from
image to image, and returning me to the source of my thirst. I
am the rabbit,
the rabbit is me — I am naked between the two like a moon.
This inner room is entirely bare of darkness and reflects
all the filthy, *unworldly* animals (who are not of this world and
live here, beginning with us), defended solely by the ringing of
the kitchen bell above the refrigerator. It rings,
a bronze bell,
impels the animals in the house to reproduce,
gives them an invisible wing for motherhood,
shows the Transparent Rabbit the place where my
philosophical companion will be reborn,
around the fire in the hearth.

    I sat with the animals around the fire,   knowing
who I was in that instant, and who it was who did not know us.
A bench transformed into a pearl, along the lines of the text
above,
left me sitting alone upon an image, which held me steady
despite my weight and my heightened sense of pain. It was not
I who was there — you know; I am not nothingness, I live
perfectly in nothingness _____ except that, all around me,
everything is 'There is.'

    — Why rabbits — *the Younger One* wanted to know.
    — Because they're rabbits — I replied, with Ursula at my
side. — When the signs — those bare facts that appear in the
nimbus of colors and hearing — appear to me, they look like

hares with raised, transparent ears, peering at the sleeping hunter. Can you envision lights flashing on and off in the darkness?

— Yes, they are signs.

— Signs and transparent rabbits. Someone is there.

— Someone, or something?

— No, someone. A person or a figure. Who has come for you.

— A lover?

— Who can know? Only by going there _____ and seeing.

Ursula puts her hands on *the Younger One*'s knees:

— There was a time when I believed — absolutely — that the libido was the aura of bodies approaching one another.

— What are you trying to say?

— That there were times when I believed that the aura was tangible.

— Ursula, what are you talking about? As I understand it, the lovers in your reality have other rules. — *The Younger One* senses she is confused, or indecisive, truly distraught.

— In all realities, lovers die — she says to him: — That's what I am telling you.

— But what is a lover?

She puts her hand on her sex, and says to him:

— It is not only the *faber* of this. *This* is the sharp edge of the 'There is.' — And she places her hand on his head as if he were her student. — This — and moves her hand back to her open sex, which he gazes at, mute with astonishment — is nimbus and incandescence, but also killing strength, survival, nothingness.

Even though we are so close, Ursula has never been so audacious with me. If she does so now, it is because *the time* has come. And in a frenzy, she *tears* her own sex, without anguish. It is merely an image of her.

Merely an image where a scene appears _____ two beings running, longing to enter into one another's love, and make themselves _____ (*viator* and *faber*, I thought).

There is, on one side, the scene of death; it is there, empty ("Like the *surface of the waters*," I thought); there is, on the other side, the scene of life, nurtured by a tree. Indeed, there is a tree in the middle, a tree from a house they have never seen, as trees are usually outside, or in gardens. They see their separate love, mixing the consciousness of their utmost pleasure in the blackness, when it emerges _____ and they averted their eyes out of a lack of modesty, one in front of the other. In the middle of the scene that is appearing, an obstacle appears, and although it is transparent, it is the greatest obstacle they have ever encountered, and it causes them to feel a mortal dread. They understand little of life, nothing of death. "We are the ones who resist merely passing through," they say to one another.

— What will take place, as an ordeal of love, between two beings who endeavor? — Ursula asks the *Younger One*, never concealing the scene: — Which way will they plummet: to the side of the nimbus or to the side of nothingness?

"To the 'There is' or to the not-'There is'?" I thought.

The Younger One does not know, and Ursula suggests he surround them with a penciled line to mark the place where they will plummet out of love.

— If, indeed, they love one another — she says to him.

— But what kind of love is that, who are they to risk their lives by doing this? — asks *the Younger One*, in an attempt at revolt.

— The ordeal does not lie in the risk. The ordeal lies in determining whether — in love — they are capable of not killing.

— So, lovers do not die. Lovers kill one another.

— Yes. Usually, there is one who kills.

"Signs and transparent rabbits," I thought.

"It is my abandoned house
— envisions my philosophical companion —
only there will I make a final return. I sense a dream: a
foggy house in the fog, where I go without knowing where I
entered; in that desert, only one bed has been prepared." He
was going to say grave, but he was restrained by the force of the
image.

"I do not want to lie down in it,
I am coming from it?
I am going toward it? I do not know. I know I think it is better to
fold the blankets,
take off my clothing, since I do not know for what finite or
infinite time I will yet be absent from that bed, where a new life
is awaiting me,
perhaps the all-encompassing embrace with the images of my
books.

How safe I would feel turning toward them,
knowing they are a spiritual autobiography   an indication, a
token of the sublime brought to my resting place,   which
I unravel. I observe that the blankets are thick, of a beautiful
quality which makes each of their colors bright and sharp,

folded brown and blue.

I foolishly long for the dog Mondego, the Magnificent, whom António killed, and who, in his youth, must have had some similarities to Gabriela's Jade. When I see her again, I will tell her we need a dog named Clamor, with a bark that will turn sorrow to its reverse, all this solitude where I have ended up,
which knows this about that.

Yes, I'm going to tell her, as soon as she arrives. But what if I don't see her again…?"

And he cried out, in distress and fear,
"Regina!"

The girl who came out of the text has the folded blankets on her knees. Each one is a letter, perhaps the unmaking of the poet who is being born. How to tell him Jade is not on that side? That it is good to have a Clamor who passes through the membrane?

The girl who came out of the text observes how the carpet of life has a fractured rhythm, increasingly shorter. She sees that the objects — all of them, without exception — rejoice in the weariness their companions feel for having run and shouted for as long as they did, and it is
now that they are allowed to slowly blue and
gaze up at the sky in a pure reverie of figures.

At the edge of the scene of the not-'There is,' the girl who came out of the text reflects _____ the ideas open up
a path,
move from one place to another. Like objects. Or furniture. Or

wind entering and leaving the trees. The physics of solid words
and feelings is interwoven with that of the mind's emotions —
and volatile liquids. Between her and the girl who feared the
imposture of language, there is a small physics laboratory,
beneath the roof. They both recognize that *roof* is a metaphor,
for in the world of expressing and desiring,
they pass alone through the 'There is';
that is, she thought

——————————— I am very fond of Philomena of the Knot.

It is a plant.

A plant from the nettle family, or Urticaceae, which I brought back from Belgium long ago, as a species. On the bus, I carried it on my lap, in a small pot. There were twenty-two migrants, and one migrant plant. And in Belgium, as a species, divided into small pots,
with an uneven size and development,
it had also been there with us for many years, its appearance dating back to the period in Herbais. It is a tender green, with sparse leaves that are in harmony with one another, with the sun filtering through the shadows, it periodically bears a small stem with blue blossoms. It is a humble variety.

In the provisional apartment we inhabit, it was planted crooked, and crooked grew, giving, from the beginning, its stem a little knot, which I thought would choke its sap and prevent it from growing. But that didn't happen. Philomena of the Knot was deft, it made a firm knot near the base, which served as a support, and among the Philomenas, it became a singular plant. I watered it often, having not yet established a regular schedule for watering all the plants.

My narrative text ends here, it now becomes a plant text.

Far too pliant,
Philomena of the Knot,

in autumn, it does not contemplate autumn. It stoops. The
green nettle no longer serves as its backbone, which unsettles
me. Is it because it is All Saints' Day? Is it because it is All Souls'
Day? The simple fact is that it is withering away, and losing the
color of its beauty. After talking to Leonarda, I decide to begin
my own fight for its survival, which I give a place of great
importance in my world.

> Philomena of the Knot, I cannot let you die,
> it is still the season of flowers. Do you
> remember Don Bush, the first *viator* bush?
> If you ask me what should truly characterize
> a human feeling, I would say, "Not allowing to die
> suddenly, and without consent."

I then observed, working the potting soil, that Philomena, a
plant which requires a great deal of dampness, was nonetheless
dying from an excess of water. I removed it from the pot. I lay it
down on a newspaper, so that it wouldn't lose *its heart* — the
soil that enfolds its roots. I fill the pot with new soil. I pick up
the plant and carefully try to accommodate it in its new habitat.
I return it to a drier soil, upon which I think it will once again
stand upright.

> It had a sentimental history with me,
> I felt it crying for help ————
> I gave it.

Philomena of the Knot will always be a beautiful paradigm
of affection. The affection I gave it, and which it used to

summon me.

And sitting in the armchair, between-doors, I let myself
meditate.

It isn't the first time I have failed to notice excesses of
water accumulating. Following this observation comes the
question
"Why did you feel that a crooked and knotted Philomena was
strange?" Once again, minutiae, they will tell me. Yet I have a
habit of letting thoughts and images float by as if I were
cherishing them, weighing their value in pleasure. I remember
being present at a conversation — long ago — during a lunch at
the restaurant at Ferme Jacobs. We were many, and I said
nothing. I listened to what was said. One of the guests was a
woman in her thirties, divorced. She spoke eloquently.

She said that when she fell in love with a man, the voice of a
singer singing *La bohème* sounded in her ears. She said that the
sweet attraction of the phallus (I think she had undergone
psychoanalysis) was mirrored in the man's voice just like a soul,
for — as she said — the soul had always been a bodily force —
full-bodied. The reference may have been evident, and it was in
some ways obvious, but the way she said it undermined that
evidence. You might instead think of a full-bodied wine, a
compact voice. She also said this was what led her to want to
make love to the man, "A love already devised," an expression
which I have never forgotten, because every time she repeated it
— and she said it any number of times — another "excess of
water" came to mind. The young woman was very explicit about
the desire she felt — a pure voice emerged from the phallus and
curled around the man like a rock of an ear; it all ensued slowly
— and suddenly disappeared. And she would yield, or

428

surrender. As if there was someone who wasn't familiar with the opera, she hummed melodic phrases for them, and a few lyrics, of a banality, incidentally, to dampen any passion. *Excess of water* was the name by which I came to know her in my memory, and perhaps because I felt there were strong knots in her way of loving, which were slow to loosen, and suddenly came undone (she confessed, moreover, that she often changed men),

I found myself trying to determine which man she loved above all things (or was it among all things?), what truncated form nature took in him, for whose use was the glory of the pure voice she had envisioned?

I am left with the memory of an overlaid being who, rather than using that overlaying, was using it to look for men, while I wrote a direct writing, one without fixed knots, or commonplaces.

This "while" indicates a difference and a parallelism. And nothing more. I recognize, in effect, that her search touched some kind of center of the flower of problematics. A center capable of blinding me, and not letting me see that an "excess of water" was destroying a plant, which not being inherently knotty, had been deft enough to use the knots with which it had been born. "We never choose indelibly," I thought. I could have been her — yet I didn't want to be, even ignoring the value of that rejected pleasure.

It's curious _____ the 'There is.' I almost have the desire to tell a Zen story, when I think about the "excess of water" woman. But right now, I'm not going to get up from this chair.

I do not understand why a problematic must always be philosophical, in a technical sense. I imagine a sequence of gestures, meaningless,   I would say *such that*, at a certain moment, they are interwoven with the beautiful, they luminesce, and the radiance projects a meaning. So — I keep both. The radiance of the gestures and the meaning. Making a bed can be a problematic, as well as taking notes on a book by Spinoza, Nietzsche, or Deleuze, putting flowers in a vase, washing the knives used for butter and fish, pouring a cup of coffee, translating Rilke or Rimbaud. Gazing at the 'There is.' If I were to say that everything is a problematic, it would be an imposture of language — an excess of water.

Not everything is a *problematic* or, moreover, *is able to be*.

But there are constants.
For example,
comparing incomparable things which pull us outside ourselves, leave us in another person — pulsating — like books strewn across the floor, near the blue glass vase _____

opening up the book of aging   the photograph album, the written books, the armoire of stored objects and, if they are not effulgences of others, leaving them lying there, like strangers

_____

the movement of lines that intersect, split in two, rise up, and suddenly create a desert space in the world; I looked at Ana's neckline, and my gaze was drawn to the way her face was tilted, coalescing with the brown wool texture of the fabric and, suddenly, only one pupil shone and, a colored marble, rolled toward the smell of toast _____

for as long as I let myself remain sitting in the armchair
I have the impression that, in any of the worlds of the 'There is,'
gestures are sequential
verbs, movable, and
that to remember is to move a foot and verify that it is upon;

I enjoy, as I have said, sitting in places in the house which
cannot be delineated by language, in stray places that are
between-doors, between meanings. Between curses and
murmurs, between turmoil and fire. "Nothing," Eckhart
reminds us, "is so firmly opposed to God than time." Or "In the
intellect man is ever young; the more active he is with that
power, the closer he is to his birth…"

And I gaze at two common teals, two web-footed
companions in a pattern awash in color. There is a scene poised
on my lips, a scene that asks me to let it come,
but does not want to come.
The neck of the teals is red — one is standing on a smooth
stone, the other is already in the water, but very near, almost
touching the first. Traces of river and pond grasses bring out the
background, a dazzling pastel blue. The girdle of time presses
against my stomach.

I get up from the chair to look for a synonym in the dictionary
open on the bed.

I turn the pages quickly, with the awareness of the entire book
in my hand.
Suddenly, the dictionary has become an abyss-book, where all
possibilities slumber, a kind of latent dream of the 'There is,'

an initial mass prior to the Big Bang.

I could not find the synonym, and consequently, the etymology
of the word I was looking for.

I give up, snip the small anguish of having abandoned what I
was meditating on, drying the damp earth that surrounded my
small roots.

I sit back down in the curved armchair, and look at the
dictionary,
mine no longer has a cover, it had a red cover that has been
removed, and has not been lost, it is among the precious objects
I envision,
which, very likely, only exist in my problematic _____

There are "orthopedic" and "non-orthopedic" texts, I now
remember. This impression came to me in the lode of a dream.
An orthopedic text is made of a search for language, for
a voice, an aria, for how to evade or correct a text that is not just
a text,
but a simple description of a body seen from the outside. A
non-orthopedic text would be what I attempt to comprehend
and do not understand _____
a swift breath which comes from the 'There is' of the dictionary,
distorts the words and tears out the pages, causing the meanings
and etymology of the words to overlap, leaving them with no
underpinning

and they should need no further scaffolding.

"My philosophical companion, don't be angry with me. Perhaps this won't be of any use, or perhaps it will. When in doubt, be understanding. Come a little closer, and read."

———————————————————— today I came across the name
for my dog — Clamor, the dog from Attica —
which I wasn't thinking about, but which, in my thinking,
I saw
was lacking — Jade, Trova, and Clamor. It could also be the title
of a book, or of a kinship based on the names of three dogs. I
would like to say that dogs are affectionate, but it would be so
time-consuming to leave this commonplace and return to it
with a new gaze that I prefer to write, for the moment, that
dogs, being contrary to men — accompany men; therefore,
and despite this,
contrary companions,
these three, following their own names,
had passed through the mirror of an unknown metal
and I, or rather my verb,
knowing something of the first — would know little of the
other
two,
beyond their names,
as these are not them.
      Complicated.

      Perhaps to put it another way ————————
      When I look at the world, I see with a certain clarity that
there are now many more beguines than we might imagine. In
human form, they persist. They are not hidden, but dispersed
and "overlapping." In my eyes, they are so, but they are not so in
my writing. There are realities I conceal from the text, just as
there are others it conceals from me. This respective mutual

concealment is not an imposture, but rather the shape of distance we have found in order to gaze at the 'There is.' If I were to name ordinary people, creators, people with banal professions — whoever — who, in my eyes, are beguines (women) and beguines (men),
my verb would introduce a strange enticement ("enticer") in their lives, which would, perhaps, alter the route of their trajectories. Accordingly, I gaze and do not write. I am not lying to them; I don't see myself as having the power to alter.

Take Vergílio, for example. He could be a beguine. He always has been. He has never seen himself with that gaze. I have never told him. But now that I will no longer see him face to face, the text is able to write him and vest him with the reality I have seen for him, which he never looked at himself — the route will not be altered.

_____ I and the text prefer the fluid verb — that, *the source they are looking for* — rather than the solid name, or the adjective with an excess of water;

that the spinning and the dance through the world are performed with a gaze all their own
and intensities are drawn together
at the points of intersection which appear
through intimate dynamics — and nothing else. This is, coinciding with the text, my view of the 'There is.'

There are dogs that are angels, but I would have to say how angels *verb* the 'There is.' Otherwise, the information is null, or pious. So enough is enough.

Today is Christmas — another commonplace.
Today is not a day for me to strike myself with words.
Tomorrow, I will depict.

Did you know? _____ commonplaces are the strange
"enticers" of our routes. Language futilely attempts to gather us
into a fold to which we do not belong.
Once again, enough is enough.
Before my pencil breaks.

_____ my dogs were as mysterious as
their names
but,

seen from the other side of the membrane,
this life was as mysterious as what was hidden in its reverse, or
mirror _____ without my knowing whether that mirror
reflected this world; but I believe it didn't. My dogs, for me, had
a dedication equal to their names,
they seemed to occupy the three states of the water in which I
floated, they were my serene guides, my equals without
thoughts and feelings parallel to my own.

I received, as a present, a bag — the shape and color of a
game bag, intended for my three dogs, who were absent from
my amble. Yet one ran ahead of me and became a guide, and
warrior, and multitude when I called him Clamor, a name that
was breathed to me, with a nose trained to evade the
commonplaces of my tongue; his, when he tires and runs, hangs
down; I put it in my mouth,
into my innermost mouth, for otherwise — I would bark.
When we arrived at the door of the house which Maria Isabel
lent us for several days, and climbed up the stairs to a small floor
that cannot accommodate the presence of dogs — he halted. It
was an autumnal winter's day, and I had passed through Cascais,
on Avenida Marginal. On the way back, I had returned amidst
dwellings of a beautiful abandonment, waiting for a better price,
and buildings without any beautitude, and I felt, looking at him,
that by parting _____ we would keep this journey

within us until the following autumn.   I then made sure.

Trova is a companion dog — the one who is closest to me. He speaks to me of Blue, of the beguines, of Aossê, of the dispersion of the 'There is.' Jade is a hound, red-haired and silent, he speaks to me of the poets, of Augusto, of the curious, and of the prelates who underpin the 'There is.' Clamor is white and a messenger, deft at passing through the membrane, he speaks to me of Vergílio, and all my other philosophical companions, Spinoza, Nietszche, Hamman, thinkers of the 'There is.' They are organized in relays, rather than a pack. If they encounter one another,
they are quite capable of snarling
but those who encounter all three will imagine that they are three of my buttresses and will wonder whether they have a fictitious or real existence. There are indeed such invented dogs
in the sense of encountered in an *imaginative compulsion* — as might have been said by Éluard, whom I am now translating.

And, after making sure _____ I sat down by the apartment window, reflecting on what is, in the end, a scrap of time — a remnant, or detritus, of time, a leftover going bad that Clamor wouldn't want, and that is thrown at someone. In the stronghold they form, these three dogs keep bones, actual hard, scavenged substances — never degraded remnants of time —
time neither essential nor intense, not acquired through a struggle. To be in danger of death is to be in danger of time, metamorphosis, and the mutation of an image. And that, these dogs do not allow. They fight. They bark at the scenes of my

reflection, run around mirrors in which they are reflected without ever giving up on keeping me alive, with an elucidated volition, in the storms of the 'There is.' "My dogs," I say. "Mine" for an instant, like all the signs here, waiting for attention and contention. "Keep your end of the bargain," they reply.

At last, we sit down around the basket of portraits which, once it has been fashioned into a table and covered in a world near and far
— here,
with a piece of cloth — became my table as well, a kind of communion of insistent and fleeting loves, in a place enclosed by a window.
Since, in Rilke, windows are of crucial importance, I thought of him. They saw the sign of a window forming. And suddenly, I felt I was a portrait, an image in which a feeling of eternity was reflected, levitating. I made an abrupt and violent gesture for the gaze to descend into the mind, the memory, the body, but all that portrait elicited was the unanimous growling of the three, as if to say, "Don't move, don't descend." Arrested by the sudden aggressiveness latent in all those images of the disappeared, and in the clenched jaws of the mastiffs, I spoke to them of Proclus, of the subtle hierarchy of the images, of how they descend and descend from the single tear God shed, of how I was alive, here, and not yet a portrait without a body, adding, however,
that images continue to descend and descend, but not from where Proclus imagined. To no avail. Clamor suddenly knocks me to the ground _____ me, to whom it is evident that this Earth encompasses so many worlds.

_____ we will learn;

I am at my desk, engaged in the harsh and illuminated craft of writing. I remove the *The* at the beginning of a sentence, instead of *The eyes loose flames*, it becomes *Eyes loose flames*. I have been told before that this was my craft. Then there is a knock at the door, it's the mail, I go down the stairs to retrieve a book sent to Augusto, and a letter for me.

In the meantime,

the passionate and impassioned daimon of writing sits on the table — the small icon raised for my nostalgia and contemplation. I contemplate that brothers love one another in accordance with the lineage from which they came, and the bed of writing from which both of us were born
has a dense rhythm,
a rhythm of a miracle descended into the world.

The rhythm I am speaking of is ineffable — it oscillates between absence and presence, it leaves, we know it returns, it returns, we know it leaves. I am, consequently, shadowless at this moment. The obligation to write burns my exposed side — an abiding and grateful responsibility. Despite my protests, I will always give thanks.

Now, in this instant, I contemplate the sentence that dissolves *Loving Cause* from the beginning, "My room is musical and windowless _____ ." Being born of writing dissolves pain _____ we will have to learn to be images that

traverse images, to accept as guides the dogs that bring us *a*
spoonful of solace
 "Drink, you have given thanks, it's for you."

  Elsewhere,
I wrote that I have always enjoyed writing in a place where
objects and goods are stored, because *writing is a storehouse of*
signs _____
or its scene; I am seeing, between seeing and waiting to see, the
storehouse of those signs, in a large or a small space — and my
philosophical companion comes in and says:
  — This is the storehouse of Rilke's signs; this is the
storehouse of Hölderlin's signs; this is the storehouse of your
Dickinson's signs; this is the storehouse of Fernando Pessoa's
signs. — And, at the end, he murmurs to no surprise of mine:
— This is the storehouse of my signs.

  Or, in a very small raised space, where there is a washing
machine, a blue bucket with a lid, a broom, baskets piled high
with manuscripts and traces of my childhood, he added, after
looking through a narrow window that opens onto a mass of
mountain treetops: — This must be the storehouse of Prunus
Triloba's signs. — Would that I could see the future world, and
the clear and legible signs that the worlds are transparent,
passing through here in our everyday lives.
  — We pass from image to image — I tell him: — From
signs to signs.
  — But we are not certain what we will find along the way.
  — Now it's your turn to go and see. — It's truly
extraordinary that we were born into a certain signography of
the 'There is,' where our biography is interwoven (and is so

often confused) with the geography of the worlds.

In this tiny storehouse, for example, slightly rectangular, slightly square, I sense — and I tell him this — that Pessoa's verses are lying on top of objects, perhaps a box, perhaps a dry cloth for cleaning, perhaps a simple thing, of the kind I will always see, and they write the new and also the rubbish of culture, used as if they were the new. The Pessoan verses by the broom give me great peace of mind, and even if it is sunny at the moment, they come from *Slanting Rain*. Also sleeping, at the core and in the incandescence of those signs, is the dog Clamor

("the dog who asked for me")

who, with the other two, are the three faithful, indomitable, contrary beings, who carry our everyday thinking on a spoon

_____ made of eating, sleeping, losing hope, finding hope, fading, persisting, lingering on the question

      why _____

    — Clamor will not die when I die — he says.

    — He is a long, vibrant dog, with no space that can enclose him.

    — He will live on after me.

This small storehouse with so many signs of human authors is his kennel. Here, there are meadows, a profusion of celestial and bitter books that beat their pages to fly, as in a dovecote.

    — I have within me, in this stronghold, a deferred expansiveness.

    — "Of myself," there is nothing. It is only the force of an enfolding, encompassing existence that is here.

Here,
the House of Salutation is deeply deep.

I move freely into it when I open the door; an emotion
never comes on its own, it comes tethered to a body; and I step
into the scene when the door is opened, it is the place par
excellence to be alone _____ when what is desired
is the 'There is'; a feeling of expansiveness spreads its breeze in
the lone house — a single large room, a single tonality — even
through multiple windows opened up the walls. I think, I think
again, I see the fingers written in the books, in all the
innumerable books strewn around the House.

The tablecloth has not been laid but the table is evident,
facing the window, just as evident is the appetite of my eyes to
absorb all the diffuse green scattered around it _____ it is
the outside being reflected within, it is the trodden light, it is
the plants underpinning, with a penetrating understanding of
us,
longings,
sorrows,
extreme hesitations.

I am sitting at the table where — at one point — Vergílio
sat down and said: — "I would write here." I remember here
_____ gazing at the wintry yellow that has settled on the
perpetual green. The last time we saw one another was at a
restaurant, in Sintra. The four of us, along with Lúcio and his
wife — Ana. The meal was running its course, but Vergílio, in
the use of his mind, was devastating. He had lost his belief in
everything. "We're doomed," he said. Augusto, in front of him,

was resigned. I simmered, until I impulsively put a teaspoon in front of his plate and said to him, as I had never said to him before, "Good Lord, this spoon is now here, and in the Edenic space." We gazed at one another,
our three dogs staring (the bone is between them, and they know it's serious. It's take it or leave it, or share it) _____
But it won't be a sharing of civilization. It is life against a desire. Or rather, it is a desiring of life, for there was no denying that, at that instant, the spoon was here, and it was also there. There was, of course, in my resolute act, a mute and pressing question: "Now that you're leaving, what does your body say about the color of the 'There is'?" And I longed for his gaze to answer, "The fact is bare, there's nothing to say."

When it's over, everything will be preserved in writing, with its own light. Writing could have been something else. Not looking for conformities, but attesting to an impact, as long as the will does not falter — and creates. What we did, in our own way, was to write *desire*
making it coincide with the blue of the green. We understand, in that confrontation-instant, that this association is a color in disequilibrium, which pulsates at the foundation of the 'There is,' attracting fragments which coalesce as they draw nearer to the door,
the one leading to the whirlwind.
We leave the gaze and, at long last, we enter.

_____ *The Younger One* returned with a
question on his lips:
— When are we going to Herbais-upon-Attica?

He foresaw astonishing revolutions in love (Rimbaud)
when he wrote, "He foresaw astonishing revolutions in love,"
and,
letting the imagination of the *drunken boat* (Hades) run wild, he
introduced those to come into the lucid nature of the
whirlwind:

I know skies torn by lightning, thunderbolts / swells,
currents; I know the close of the day / and the exalted dawn, as
well as the doves / and I've seen the man who thought he saw /
I've seen the blazing sun, sullied with mystic horrors, /
illuminating with long, steady streaks of violet, / like the actors
of ancient plays, / the waves rolling in the distance, their
shuddering swells! / In the green night, I dreamed of dazzling
snow, / a kiss rising slowly to the sea's gaze / circulation of
unheard saps, / the gold and blue awakening of phosphorus
songs!

At the same time,
I continue to see the procession of furniture and objects, which
pass by like a lady dragging her train. And yet, without them, in
my eyes, the house becomes insignificant, or, better written,
the house becomes questioning: "Why did you get rid of me?"
They pass through the door, facing backwards for the sake of
ease, say farewell with that mute question on their lips. I look at

their figures, their scenes, their faces. I focus on the fiber of the imperishable, slightly worn, for I am always the one who has to abandon the land which   I love as if it were
a sorrowless heaven

above a painting (it is a dream) that was over my parents' bed, its frame smooth, straight across the top, long. In the bedroom, the light came from the left; I longed for the moment I saw it to always be wintry and eternal. Two men (one of rare beauty) were face to face — the one of rare beauty leaning toward the other.

It was clear to me, like the shadow coming from the window, that this perfection of colors and features represented a reflection of inner beauty already attained by the position of the body and the gaze, and the silken skin of the face. I also sold and squandered it, and today it pains me as though I had sold and squandered my own gaze. All of them could have been the subject of elegies, depicting how the gaze departs and in what form, in its object materiality,
that gaze will be forever invisible to those who look at them. And yet, that blemish, and the visible contusions of aging, will belong to them — will be theirs — and their owners will say they are antiques.

If I care so much for these objects, often very simple and unremarkable, it is because where others see sedimented time, I see overlapping images, which gaze back at me, poised to continue their journey through the 'There is.'

I asked one of the men — but the question could be asked of them both — about the meaning of the scene in which the "beautiful one" was holding a coin in a hand ending in slender

fingers. I thought of wax because with them came the
possibility of light. One, or the other, maybe both,
told me that the painting depicted the moment when Jesus
— my Joshua in later years — uttered those words which
would later be found in the canonical gospels: "Render unto
Caesar the things that are Caesar's, and unto God the things
that are God's."   Are these objects
material furniture, seemingly innocent, shared between the
shadow and the dove, Caesar's,
or God's?

    Or both — in equal, or unequal parts?
    Or neither?

    — And if they are?
    — They will not be shared between shadow and dove.
    — They will be handed over to whom, then?
    — To no one — they have brought Power to the loss of
memory; they belong to the *atopic gaze*.

    Younger One, it is with this gaze that we will go to Herbais-
upon-Attica.

    — But if they divide the 'There is' among them, where will
we go? Is there a 'There is' left for us? Even a scrap of 'There is'?

    Clamor draws near, and lies at my feet. We are both certain
that *exodus*   ·
is the other name of the atopic gaze. Why tell him now?
Exodus is velocity,

you need a strong reason to set out on an exodus,

to be compelled to change with the force of those who arrive;
not to be forced to leave but to descend into the abyss and cross
the border.
Who cares about the place of being,
or of writing —
a board on your knees,
the branch of a tree,
the firm coverlet of a bed,
the back of a bird in your dreams,
the ancestral desk,

the body itself.

——————— it is only necessary for the body to have sufficient
velocity, to transform into it,
and stop

before leaving.

I see Joshua running through the holy books, running
ahead of the wind of the pages, as if fleeing from his own
shadow. Or from the intensity of the 'There is'?
But Caesar is not *as if*. I see the stones of Egypt falling from
the rooftops with his name inscribed. And the stones are not a
metaphor. They are the entire color of the A.

The letter you wrote me,
Vergílio, in your angular handwriting,
did not come in the mail,
it was on a small round table without a cloth, and
had a few words written on it:

                              "I am, at long last, going to see
what it is."

    And a door opened onto a small scene in a performance
— the performance of exodus,
like a scene opening onto the heart of those who write without
resentment.

                         "We have nothing, nothing was
                         taken from us.
                         We said, quite simply. And saying
                         was possible.
                              Nearly impossible was to find
                         where."

——————————————————————— It is the time of Ursula.

That book raised its hand, and said:
— Stop. — The hand fluttered in the middle of the path,
indicated the path of the music and the way out of the land
through the door of that road, which wholly enveloped the
hand in music until it said to itself:
— Stop. Stop on the path of being a hand but remain
musical, composing the end of the story.
— Everything I have said is true, or rather, not musical.
— Music, Ursula thought, and did not say, shatters what is true,
the true music of the whole does not exist, and the whole, as
soon as we climb up to the horizon, is a fragment.
— Perhaps. Still I say to you: Stop, eat your hand, unmake
it in the breeze, digest it in your ear.

But I,
Ursula,
I do not stop, I pass beyond my hand, I step across the threshold
of the landscape's consciousness of itself — I write its map in
the air; I soar without stopping, passing over steep mountains
echoing with the voices of animals lost in the glory of being
animals; I draw this map for *the Younger One*, who holds me
ever so tightly to the earth with the pins of his libidinal desire to
understand. With my thinking, or rather, stretching out my
thinking, I pick up *that book* — the Bible — and open it over
the entire surface of the landscape I can reach. The book
is exhausted, and rests upon so many pages; I wrap my fingers in
some of them; my spirit is far away, on a blank slate; my body is

with it — there — its heart receiving the torrent
of unheard dreams from the God who wrote it.
    — What a strange globe — exclaims *the Younger One.*
    — Yes. What a bitter way to enter the world.

    Scattered above the landscape are the Laws, the Historical
Books, the Prophetic Books, the Gospels, the Acts of the
Apostles, the Epistles, the Apocalypse, which swept the high
altar more thoroughly than the others, before entering the
armoire. In one book and in another, I scarcely find evil.

    "I cannot find it in your garden," I write in small letters.
    It seems abyssal that there are books with no gaps to let the
light through.
    I chase after

    the unreality which comes and goes — a small goldfinch
that came from Matthew when he recorded the virginal
conception of Jesus. As I open or close the wooden mouth that
someone secretly repudiated; the burning haste writes on the
chest, it is she who has wrists and fingers.

    I, Ursula,

having left my small room where the armoire protects me, sleep
and do not sleep, warm and do not warm, I feel as though I am
left over, I feel as though I am absent, the flame of the burning
haste has reached the room where *the Younger One* is paging
through *that book* — and all I desire is for the whirlwind to
increase its velocity.

For practical people
— and those instructed in stillness —
all these books in the epigraph, including the early history of
Genesis, are dead and exceedingly dead, even though they
stumble in that dust every day. What practice have those
practiced ones had? Practically, they have sundered the 'There
is' which is unbreakable. Practically, ever since they were born,
they have carried a coin and a ticket in their mouths _____ ;
with the coin they will pay the ferryman,
by the ticket, the guide from the hereafter will know who they
are — the accolades and prestige they have accumulated.
To retain their sight, they have departed and shared their
gaze.

And our fellow man?

They are the practiced ones who invented the hereafter.
There is always a hereafter for them.
But the fact,
the fact,

the fact is that those who are narrated stand in front of the
narrator, who relies on them.

And Ursula writes _____ "I sometimes want to ask
the realists if this world belongs to them — indeed, it belongs
to them — and if they recognize themselves in what it is."
But it was a slight and fleeting temptation, for she soon writes
her question, "Why do I rejoice or grieve with them, why do I
find them frustrating, magnificent, seeping out of the abyss of
images and ideas that drips from the teaspoon, or the teapot?"

Or else she writes, "Why do I consider them to be unfinished
men and women — bitter suggestions I must place on the
map?"

— Those who touch sin, defile it? — asked *the Younger
One*, before he left.

— Without a dog's eye, who has any hope of seeing what is
new? — asked Ursula in reply.

_____ if I consciously wanted
to fictionalize Ursula's life, I would be unable to, my
philosophical companion.

Ursula,
with whom you departed, along with the dog Clamor, no coin
in her mouth, no ticket between her teeth, she is only and solely
a fragment of a person,
her consciousness open like a fruit,
perplexed,
oscillating between "I can" and "I cannot,"
between "And if it were?" and "It isn't yet."

She encounters the different degrees of a shining
consciousness which urges her to encompass with her gaze the
alert spirit, asking herself: "If I were to stumble upon
another landscape behind this one, what consequent reality
would I discover?" Do not be fascinated by her vortex-like —
and restless — gaze. She says but does not know; she does not
start from certainties, but it's as though she is aspersing a
certain sense of strangeness around the house. She will,
however, be a good companion

for you. I tell you that it sometimes
disorients me — when I see her

enfolding her own desire in desire,
sundering it (which is very risky),
governing it without giving it governance.

    She will want to divide the events in your new world, ever
so complex, into terse stories with an abrupt ending, just as she
is telling the things inside her threatened house to set out, once
more, into the emptiness; and I see her suffer because she
believes it is futile to counterpose a large and a small reality, but
she — to my eyes — has the workings of a microscope that
produces very magnified images of small, extremely despised
fragments. There a curiosity in her, without anything of the
sublime. Your guide is — my companion — a figure who plays,
a funambulist, a dancer.

    To explain it more clearly, and so that you can understand
_____ the object that could advance my text (and
which she forgot to bring to me)
was absent in the red color I wore today
so as not to wear white,
the place where the blue days dwell _____ ; other objects
came, through the voices of friends on the telephone, brought
by their sorrows and nightmares, which I added to my own
sorrows and nightmares.
               Which Ursula would never do.

    While she forgets — and you leave —
my day blooms with counter-dreams, with powerless images
that vanish in us.
_____ inanely, utterly,
Ursula comes into my room, and not caring whether I'm busy

writing,
or reading the newspaper, tells me,
and insists,
that there are human beings with *palace* faces, and others with
shanty faces. I feel an enormous laugh well up in me — and I
don't contain it. She laughs as well. I ask her "if I had a shanty
face," but the laughter that erupted between us prevented her
from confirming it.

She sat down on the edge of my bed, but I could tell by the
hasty manner in which she did so that she had not come alone.
She intended to play a trick on me. In the palms of her hands,
she carried the images that horrify me
because of what they do,
and because they do not play a part in what I feel _____
eroticism and mysticism, subjects which are, at times,
appended to these texts.

She laughed, thought it was funny: "They put a coin in their
mouths, and a ticket."

I get up and sit down in front of the window, on a carpet of
scents.

— I'm not angry — I said, and I saw, I entered, I was the
local reality. The room was bare, coalesced in its fragments
_____ everything of the body, our letters, our maps, our
movements, the 'There is' we have chosen — there was no dry
branch separated from that desire for coalescence with the body
outside; the shadow was not mystical,
it was a bench which I climbed up and sat down upon,
naturally,
a person here;

in the end, it was *a day* like any other day, a day of a serene
cohabitation of the dispersed, without analytical frameworks,
or correspondences. An overlaying.

Ursula,
what is the name of a chair, a drawing, a vulture, a pigeon,
a wing?

What relationships do they have in this language?

I ended up writing at the bottom of the sheet of paper:
but what is this principle of reality, which is only
known inside itself, and — inside itself — is outside
itself?

Ursula laughed. She lifted up her skirts, and hid her fearless
palace face in them: — Are we going to play? — she asked.

— ...
— Gabriela, dance. If we're going to leave, why not leave
everything in disarray?

— *Everything you see here, you see somewhere else* — I
replied, and she understood it was my particular way of joining
in the game she was proposing.

— I don't see the cup here — she began.
— It's somewhere else, and the image is here.
— I don't see *the Younger One.*
— He's still in the study, and on the living room floor.
— I don't see dinner.
— It hasn't been made, but it's ready in some other place.
— I don't see the mirror.
— It's broken. But it's in the place I mentioned.
— I don't see you.
— I'm here where you see me. In the blue. There.

456

— How many walls are there?

— I don't see any. But if I look, I'll see there are three.

— Clamor is here.

— He's not in the study any longer.

— It's Vergílio, on the telephone.

— Tell him he's here. *This is the other place.*

FIRST CONFIDENCE:

There are real texts — they wear a crown in their humility.
There are real pieces of furniture — they have a loosening
           in their very being. They are
           exchanged for images.
There are cold threads on the windows, which keep them
           open.
There are unspeakable joys born of rings, which we bury in
           words, in lakes, high in the
           mountains.
There are certainties as true as uncertainties.
There are places we have already reached, without ever
           having inhabited them.
There is the exodus that consumes eras, one after another,
           like petals.
There is the perfectly bright unfathomable — in this
           libidinal moonlight.
There is the sex of reading.

I would like to see its face.

SECOND CONFIDENCE:

_____ passing through Herbais,

I went down a road that was precisely what connected the world
of representations to the world of the mind and forces; the
shortcut of representations to the forest of intensities; I had
passed through the modern world sans modernity, and I peered
at the blind eye with my eye, always striving to wield it — as
Ursula and Clamor incessantly told me. Joyous shadows of
lamps were prominent in their light; and at the doors, women
and men were thinking, others were writing, all were slaking the
hunger with which they had arrived, including those who had
come from the side of the news in the papers, but much more
alive than information and paper,
slaughtering us all   even the thinkers of the 'There is'; they
were the vagabonds with their suffering, which was real, near,
visible, and exuded a smell of sweat and human flesh. Looking
at it, thinking it, or writing it was like passing a scythe through
inhuman suffering. The first sensation is that of the suffering of
forces and intensity. The pain was so sharp that I constantly
wanted to shut my eyes because I had no words to open them.
Clamor barked at me and bit me, and I opened myself up to that
unheard intensity. There is no fire, but a cold that Dante did not
know.

Herbais is near a forest — that was where we guided our
steps. Even at a distance, I felt the pulsation of a heart and a

chest. And yet, in that forest which seemed unscathed, I could hear its cry for the fate of other forests that were burning, and the damp cry created a kind of music that circulated through the nature and the streets. This was the second sensation — that of an immeasurable number of animals howling for the destroyed forest and for a nameless pain that accompanies the being of animals. But I felt they were very close to the forces — which momentarily consoled me, though I didn't know why.

But I mustn't lose myself in circumlocutions, as if in the narrative of a novel. There we had brought our lives, unexpected, multiple, and inexplicable but, more than anything, ruptured, and we had woven, at the urging of the night in which we found ourselves, an immense fabric in which being oneself and being the other were equally important. "Don't take that feeling too far," Ursula told me. And indeed, we weren't supposed to shuffle the cards, indistinguishable; rather, we were supposed to recognize the suits passing through the human spirit, which doesn't confuse the devastated earth with a serene lake. Discernment, I realized, was vital, for life went on, although its nature needed to be rethought. "Gaze as I do," Clamor advised me, but my inexperience with *seeing as a dog* was utter. Yet I had the feeling he discerned forces and intensities, effortlessly. The cry of the forest struck me like no one or nothing else ever had, and it was no longer possible or natural to think sequentially, until, for the first time, I felt an indescribable uncertainty. Herbais seemed to be a slumbering place of desire. And I regretted that I had not trained myself to gaze at the bare facts, fearlessly and unthinkingly.

Ursula then told me that for us to bid farewell to the land, we needed to go to the center of the forest to unmake what is called "making love" and to divert the hearts of the trees, and their libido, to their bed; to say that trees have a libido destroys the meaning of this word as much as saying, in a low voice, that "to make love is to unmake it." So up we went. The night was still night. I was striding forward under a deep emotion, with the feeling of finding myself in the midst of a nameless catastrophe. To truly say what I felt, I would have to recognize that I was in the *detritus-reverse* of the world I had left behind. Ursula and Clamor's company would help me not to get dragged into this unusually compelling detritus, to coalesce with it and be — why not? — part of a kind of cosmic muck. Then I cried out for all the people I had left behind, for the books I had written, for the images that had staggered me. I wanted, that is to say, I wanted to remain myself, in another body, with the same consciousness. *Viscerally*, I knew I was not *that*, that I never had been, and never would be. I wasn't certain of anything, I had no idea what was going to happen to me, but at the core, I knew, as I had always known. I am a human. Everywhere in the world, I am a human. With a brain capable of understanding the universe, but without the information to understand it, with an imperishable sex of reading, swept up in feelings I rarely understood, I loved as I could and knew, little or nothing, I know, but I am not this, I shouted to the mountain, "I am not this," I want to understand, even if, to do so, I am only this — an open gaze like Ursula's, a gaze that smells, more than it knows, but sees. God, how cruel your creation is!

I felt like a lost child crying out in the valley, a child who knows it is eternally orphaned and responsible for the mountain and the river flowing down the mountain, for the ox that drinks, for the birds that fly, for the drifter who goes without bread. "I am," I cried, "I am the consciousness of all this. I will not surrender, my gift is to feel thinking and coalesce the diversity of all this. I wrote to exist, I wrote to hold in my inept hands what shone… and did not die."

Ursula then took me in her arms. Clamor rolled around us in a happiness I didn't understand, but it made me feel better. I know too little to describe our hesitant way of being together when hesitation follows certainty — and incandescence. It is like chasing after a brilliant rabbit (what force spoke to me of this?) that hides in an uncertain burrow, certain of itself and its haste; it is like an oscillation in which one speaks, reads, understands, forgets, takes on dimensions that elude hands and return to the dampness of the water and the ear.

That was how I saw it happen, however reluctant I am to express it, for in the new world, my legs are tied, and the nails with which I grasp on to my 'There is' are not yet claws.

    To gaze

    at lips

    to obey as one who commands

    to go with the dog

    to love the female figure

    are the deft and incandescent means

    conscious and unconscious

to be able to cast aside

any instrument of pleasure, of knowing, of losing

which is not this new body

and its music

receptive and liberated

which I will understand because

I am a human, in any world.

THIRD CONFIDENCE:

Our Enigma   how vivid is your
prominence within my house. Interwoven facts,
objects, the very continuity itself closes doors
and opens up precipices, but

                    there is

a fundamental tone that guides the restless children:
"You know this unforgettable river" — and a single
blue body of water running down to the gentleness of
the valley. Such indescribable emotion transforms into
a door or a path. It is morning, but it is growing dark.
Ahead of me, winding with silver precision, flows the
unforgettable river, which, uniting Ursula, Clamor, and
the Younger One, makes an unforgettable canopy over
my head, which, at times, entering into the old lost
thinking, seeps blood. But the miracle

is absolute, or rather, it fades because everything of everything, including the trees themselves, and the animals bound for the butcher, is amenable to learning.

I need to call Regina.

FOURTH CONFIDENCE:

_____ if one day there were a place — a
circus —

to depict the contents of the book — and its exterior — that
place would be Herbais. Herbais-upon-Attica. That is where the
School of the Valley (a name that seems obvious to me,
although I can't figure out why) should be located, next to the
memory of Jade, of Joshua found among the manure, and at the
stable. Luísa pontificates,
I will speak with her in the afternoon,
we will bring the cows to the circus, and we will milk them.
    Fragments of the known world are in attendance, but those
sitting in the stands are primarily the funambulists, who —
spectators and actors — will intervene on the stage. The
problem is determining which will be first.

    If I consult Spinoza, he will refer me to a musician, and the
musician to a poet, and the poet to a step on the staircase where
a child is sleeping on the lap of a resolute young woman who
has just arrived, and has a serene and determined dog at her
feet.

    The second problem is how to milk the cows,
for the dispersed figures, among them the funambulists, have
no particular or steadfast relationship with their hands.

The evening is characteristic of Herbais,
long,
with the seductive road indicating that the dream has traveled a
great distance.

I suddenly observe that one of us descends to the circus
and, with an earthly sweetness that fell from the sky, knows how
to milk the cows; a simple gaze guides the hands and the
movement — it is infinitely simple for those who plunge into
this night; the only secret is entering.

At times, it is painful, for someone suddenly collides with
an image they weren't carrying in their heart. They bring their
hands to their face to cover their eyes and not see, so that they
can go on without having to say "I didn't see it."
The repelled image appears to them at night and, since
everything is near and always functions, it takes them to the
circus, where new perceptions, different from those of the
wide-open world, are set alight.

The child who was on the young woman's lap awakes, and
asks to be taught what time is. Wrapped in her loose shawl, she
is exposed on the wheel of the orphans which, for any
experienced funambulist, is the wheel of moonlight. The
moonbeams halt her weeping,
they are real women singing   and only to her.
A man appears, and shows her what dancing is. The child
opens her eyes, forgets the sorrow of the world she left behind,
and hears all around her:
— I am *the Younger One.* — The child is an unconceived
idea, a new concept, a world to come, and where we are going.

467

She is utterly unprotected, only the shadow of the milk cows remains in the circus and roams in the space. It looks like the earth — but I could not tell you if it is this one, or another. But that matters little because earth is any place where a consciousness encounters the 'There is,' and learns to discern its colors. They, the students, sit huddled around these strange images, which use the night as if it were day — and the line of the drawing as if it were lead. They ask for nimbleness, and that the reticent night will not wane before they have learned.

— The first exercise is that of the interchangeability of places — said Luísa. Step forward into the libidinal moonlight. I hand her the book, which she reads as if it had been written in Attica. The children listen, and stop crying and, without noticing, pull the shawl up over their heads.

After

THE CONFIDENCE OF THE GIRL WHO CAME OUT OF THE
TEXT:

_____ for months I have sought a geography — not a
biography, still less a fiction — about the astonishing and
painful relationships between writers. I set out in pursuit of the
nature of the scriptural relationship between works — Vergílio's
and my own — which, as they are not actually grounded in the
same assumptions,
end up colliding,
each at their own velocity,
with the world, its meaning, and its evanescence.   At one
point, I even wrote that this geography was, more than
anything, a signography-upon-the-world.

In order to trace it, I sometimes came out of the text
_____ the writer acquiescing to be the girl clothed in
blue: to be someone who looks at the text after. From the
outside. Not from life or existence, but from another point of
view.

The text I have been writing for thirty-five years began as
short narratives of strangeness and then became identified with
the sequence of luminous scenes of the *interbeing*. I now want to
look at it from the point of view of the *libidinal moonlight*.

The world exists, and Vergílio is dead. I was not attempting
to create a reality where the world would cease to be un-
conformist, freeing us from our rebelliousness, which is *distance*

and responsibility, or reconciling us in a final embrace, as if
everything had been a mistake,
nor create the assumption he had died,
but as if he had not actually died.

No. What I am truly looking for is to see where the
continuity of the 'There is' fractures, where it changes register
and signs, and if it might be possible to speak it without hope,
or imposture. "Without hope" means without any guaranteed
illusion. When we realize that 'There is' is, we are not solely part
of it. We append a creational seeing _____ we create,
altering its landscape. No trace is ever lost, even if it tends to
fade away. My task today is to see signs, and convey them, with
all the force of impact I possess. To overlap them and
understand the consonances they develop among themselves.
To allow myself to be guided by the melodic direction I hear in
them, and accept the meaning or *sense* that results, if it results.
To begin *seeing* again every day, try to use the energy that
exhausts me to give me more energy, seek it out in the most
tenuous filaments of the reality I have at hand, not be afraid to
use the *strangeness* my body feels and thinks.

This strangeness is only an effect of the language of the
pervasive positivist cynicism within which I was raised. To *see* is
to make and unmake. Is to create language. And create myself.
To become a "puzzle," one day depicting a labyrinth, another
day a hill high in the landscape, another day a dark room dimly
lit by the outside noises, another day a passageway of serene
love that spans the street, where the hooves of horses can be
heard amidst melodies and rock beats. To not lose the thread,
without obsessing or worrying about losing it. And, at the
moment when the thread breaks, to let myself go, see where I

am taken, recapture the current again, accept the change in form and, from there, learn to see again. At that time, to reach out a hand and feel the figures. There are times when we will be pure volition _____ pure love of the 'There is.'

In any world,
I will be spoken and I will speak. The universe doesn't mean us any harm, it simply doesn't understand us. But it doesn't stop us from speaking ourselves. In time, it will accept our warmth. Our inability to live without affection, or the art through which we render ourselves noble and confused, will strike it as strange. We will not be its sovereign kings or its north, but rather the funambulists of its consciousness. Humans. Seeing.

I lived on a hill, *I will say*, on a tree-lined street in Lisbon — which was the first nature — next to a Basilica, next to a garden, and even a garden-cinema, next to a magnificent square where conveyances passed in a tile of life which was a faded and haunting spot,   among fathers and mothers who never tired of me.

And, suddenly,
when I walked into the restaurant O Canas the other day, I came across this phrase: "La vita è un cinema, baby."
That is my foreign country in Portugal _____ Campo de Ourique. You only have to arrive there to hear words in their own joy. Or in the joy that is expressed in this way. I don't know. The feeling of existing, in the place I passed through to arrive here, does not surface. The feeling of a paucity of force and intensity has already caused many swallows to die, including the first one I saw in a text — that of my Prince. I sit down on a

bench. Here, the swallow of the Happy Prince of my childhood,
if it lingered on the streets, would have much to do, going from
the newsstand to the benches in the Jardim da Parada where
pensioners sit, and drug addicts with their hallucination
acquired among the poorest.

   But this neighborhood comes from so far away for me,
and from a place that was so strong there,
because I believed it was the world in its natural state,
that these figures, still outside my books,
do not know whether they will roar ＿＿＿＿＿＿＿＿＿＿＿＿＿＿
or disappear.

   They arrive today in the mail,
coming from places I cannot imagine, from countries where my
books haven't even been translated into their languages. Where
I have never been — and will likely never go. José, who bears
my father's name,
wrote to me from South America; he is young, I suppose,
studious, and considers my art to be a gift, when in reality, it is a
point of view held by an artisan, in all her incandescence and
despair. But I understand what he wanted to tell me. And I
would find it easier to tell him,
if he knew that, when I read his letter,
I had a painting in front of me (perhaps Flemish),
depicting an open group of four women and an angel.

   It was another window that had opened up, days earlier,
on the wall in front of my desk. It was one of us; it was I.
It was I
who made Bira — my mother — frame this painting many
years ago, who gave it shelter in her room, at the foot of her bed,

who asked for it — when she passed away — who kept it in the
House of Salutation and, finally, brought it here, where I
reopened the story,
causing it to receive the light which, because of the angle
between the window and the wall, is cast onto the mirror on my
desk. Where I placed it. Because

beguines use a mirror to exist, they smile with an intense
brightness at their own image. Before they give it away to
whoever comes along, they make it eternally their own
_____ it is the path that, according to their own art, they
have chosen in the 'There is'.

I'm going to have to interrupt the reading of the letter, as
my livelihood is calling me,
although the sorrowful beguine with the deep gaze in the
painting continues to read the book of hours in her hand, at
long last illuminated and filled with unimaginable
incandescence, I envision. I see her reconstructing the book in
her creational imagination, with her thinking present in her gaze
upon her own life; the other, who I would say is more practical,
and less involved in the gazes exchanged with the book of
hours,
simply reads,
in the first stage of reading, fulfilling an obligation of the
monastic rule. Yet she reads faithfully, and her hands, one with
an invisible finger, bent over the brown cover of the book —
where she conceals her sex of reading — are beautiful, in their
acquired, and innate, faithfulness.
    I sense it is she for whom the angel is saving the music of
his lute, and the kiss — the kiss coming from outside the

painting; the other, she doesn't need. What am I doing,

> where have I disappeared to being so present,
always seated, pressing my closed fist against my mouth? At
times, I think about Vergílio ——————— I feel he is being
made, at a distance, in Ursula's heart. It is only natural that the
event of his life and death should come to join the beguines,
color their days with an outward, and altogether inward,
anxiety. I return to *Joshua, Companions and Lovers*, which I was
writing, which brought me back to Portugal, in 1985. It is as if
their great solitary house, in the midst of the cold and the early
blossoms before the arrival of summer, was assailed by the face
of the same texts, slightly older, more defined, more altered.
They found their hollow,
their bifurcated intensity.

Between the inside and the outside is the window of the
painting,
and someone climbs into the same text
where the Virgin Mary was a hairdresser, and Joshua inhabited
the apocryphal gospels
from which the beguines sought to draw the spirit of non-
hypocrisy.

And that's all for today,

and I said little, in the fragility I am traversing — it is the eve of
an unexpected and surprising event. I will correspond with this
young man — José; I will write him letters. I will receive them;
I will answer them; I will create a companion in friendship by
writing to him directly; he will be far away from us, but we will
ponder his questions as if they came out of a book. Indeed, all
important events come out of books. That is to say, out of letters

that store up,
accumulate,
and squander. Gold is abolished, but its shine and reflection in a
mirror
are treasured. They lose substance, retain meaning, take on
virtuality. This is the treasure I wanted to cultivate here; I feel as
though the meditating beguine in the painting has retreated
into it, gazes at it, thinks of it when she raises her eyes from the
book.

I will therefore continue to unravel sensations and
memories,
until the event makes itself known. What is most interesting in
these scattered notes is not, in my opinion, the similarity of
structure they all reveal, but the fact they come into contact, or
consonance,
and the new, if it exists,
responds to the new,
until the information they convey settles in the sediment of the
gaze.

And yet, they were not written by the same author. The
woman who walks through the neighborhood of her childhood
is not the one who receives the letter. The former has, in truth,
passed through a fragment of the metanight, and the latter has
let herself be swept away by an instant of libidinal moonlight. It
is true that she wonders about

the physical appearance of the young man who wrote the
letter. She says she will never recognize him, that she has never
seen him, but what troubles her is that she will never be able to
tell the others — the younger ones, the ones who read God's
plans in the book of hours. What force of reflection, through

day and night, from sunrise to sunset,
    will exist in the conjunction of that room and that painting?
What is the nature of what causes it to pulsate? Imagine, she
says,

imagine the libidinal young man coming to me out of the waters
of his own image, a young man scarcely known to himself,
carrying a face turned back in his hand, for I feel, she says,
as though the burgeoning atmosphere of progress has slowed,
in him and in her. And she also says _____ .
I will undress him in the water of the reciprocal sorrow of
which affections are made. Starting with myself, she says. He is
not surprised and, innocent or not, he will quietly enter my
arms,
and lie down,
wherever he pleases,
in one of my shadows.   Anywhere he touches, that will be
my lap. Yes,

I am a collector of blue. And I turn to the Book of Hours to find
out where he is blued. Yes, I know the libidinal young man will
fulfill all his promises, will bring pulsation to his chosen blue
_____   — And then what? — asks the girl who hates
useless conversation, for the sake of pure seduction. In this way,
the authorship of the text is delineated. Leaving aside the
reference to the water of sorrow,
what information will the libidinal young man bring,
what is its value in pleasure?   At this question, a slight
shudder

ran through all the objects that wanted to inquire into their own color, superseded, just as the arrested yet needful image of their own usefulness; the girl who came out of the text thought about the *love-object* of her reverie and noticed that, as such, it was no longer useful to her; the usefulness of things, she says,

tires me, not that it doesn't exist
but I don't want to let the idea die — which seems accurate to
me — that things live
in deep or tenuous layers,
in themselves; and whoever possesses the blue nature certainly
has a secret affinity with me; as the armoire, at the height of its
grandeur, had a great affinity with the blue carpet on the floor,
and where the Book of Hours, finally fallen from the painting,
had plummeted; to live,

you must delve into the darkness;
to continue living, you must delve into the blue, even though
the square room with two old windows is full of a gratuitous
nostalgia I chase Trova away from, when he approaches them.
He ignores the Book of Hours entirely, but has a good nose for
blue_____ because I taught it to him. In the imagetic,
imaginary blue, we both long to know where the heart of the
world beats.
        — Will I confuse him with the libidinal young man?
        — You won't.

        — And with the mad cows?

    And I fell pensively
into the heart of the mad cows   of humans, Ltd, a
company specializing in holocausts. I read the news,

announcers talk on the radio and television, I am not surprised
by the permeability that exists between species, but I am left
with the bitter, perplexed, receding image
that the life of those who appear to be humans is gold dust,
while that of animals — in the context of their own nature — is
nothing.

Living animals are degraded monetary values, objects
traded impassively and impossibly, declining profits; they have
fallen into the depths of slavery, reached such a degree of
unreality that a piece of meat, at our table, has become a
specter; we ingest nightmares — our own cold attitudes. They
will be the final remnant of the cosmic landfill we have been
constructing. And how
luminous and
seductive
it is!
   At the heart of the world,
parts are diverging. The heart is threads. Threads made of
landscape, humans, animals and plants, atmosphere, language
and meanings which purport to be both system and coherence.
That was, broadly, the 'There is' we constructed. We are leaving
Attica. Parmenides goes unheard. Spinoza continues to read his
Ethics at the door of the slaughterhouse. Bach plays in the
streets, mixed with jazz and rock, and deafening drum beats. All
is well. Is this the heart of the world we speak to the universe?
   Do we speak of power, or compassion, Frederick N.?
   My concern is not whether there will be a catastrophe
_____ because there will.
   There always has been.
   But which one, this time? _____

Which myth are we writing? O blind singers of this age, our fatal melody, and what we say expels us from this land, any land. May funambulists ascend to the heavens, to the blue sky, may they guide our steps _____ .

_____ when Heart of the Bear,

following the laws of nature, left the land of the living, a tree stood in his place. A seed of a southern tree, which in a garden to the north, became an enormous pine, with outstretched, distant branches, where I could clearly see that he, as an animal, as a tree, or perhaps later, as a man, would never let fall helplessly to the ground the body of Thomas Müntzer
— the decapitated —
which once,
long ago but always in the same book I am writing,
he had held in his paws.

Just like today, I was mistaken for compassion, in concept and in human deed   in the end, I was the one who had baptized that tree, born out of instinct, and planted it in Luísa's courtyard-clearing, in Herbais-upon-Attica. It had become ink, a drawing in motion, brilliant color spattered with blood. I would climb that garden platform to bury in the ground, with a prayer, all that weighs on the light crust of the divine nature. In the center of the clearing — one of my passions in the forest, which was, despite appearances, a highly elaborate garden — there was a circular fountain, perhaps a meter in diameter, made of stone, where water did not spout or flow but, if it did, it would well up in the center.

_____ very often, without being aware of it, I carry with me, to the places I go, paintings by painters who, to my observing eye, emerged with the reality of dreams and, in that acquired nature, expand my life by opening doors or suggesting transformations, which must already be taking place without my knowing it. The inspiration for this painting, by a Portuguese artist from the eighteenth century, came from the north; but as I am convinced that nationalities only exist to give names to streets, and because I believe that knowing something we will never come to know is arid and wasted time, what was left of that painting, on the stage,

was everything which, unclassifiable,
remained of it, that is to say, the vision _____
the scene of the ancient painter in the raised clearing of the garden.

Fons vitae. First, the name. Source of Life. A crucified Christ, which I took for a banal Joshua seeping blood on the side pierced by a spear, stood precisely in the middle of the circular fountain. Standing at its edge, on either side of Joshua, his mother, dressed in black, and the beloved disciple, John, with an ardent, somber appearance, like that of the dog Clamor. This is the composition Ursula has before her eyes as she educates the child to be a prodigious uncrucified funambulist.

She teaches him to say
"Ecce homo" with his own mouth,
not allowing others to say it
as if they were speaking of him in an absent third person.

Seated on a crude bench, she does not reveal why she is

teaching him to dance in the air, in front of an empty, quiet fountain in the garden. For an instant, all was calm. Then, the tranquility was swiftly filled with images and motion, a creational breath passed through the place, and the arc of compassionat struck the metanight of language, in plain sight. And, through an unforeseen and surprising return of that image,
Fons Vitae ceased to be the symbol of compassion — or not only that — in order to also be the symbol of the prescient and fearless funambulist — the Ecce Homo of compassionate discernment.

When I plummeted into myself, and was able to meditate on the transmutation of the painting, I understood the funambulist to be a human, to be compassionate _____ but I understood neither the fountain, nor the object of discernment, nor, more than anything, the relationship
        between being compassionate and making yourself known in knowledge.

_____ he returned today, and asked me to write down my life in the same direct tone with which one looks into a mirror; I felt a scratch covering this surface, and a kind of breathlessness made me want to go downstairs, and breathe better oxygen, as here, the gardens look out onto the sidewalks, and are the frequent landscape of the streets. To remember the "overwhelming suffering" this journey sometimes brought me. I stop to meditate, to look at the typewriter two or three times, and feel the attenuated sorrow in the place where breathing fails. I breathe — and go with the dancing *Younger One* to the far end of the gazebo, next to the tree, by the ogival doors of the Palácio.

I'm going.

The night is dark and transparent, the slanting rain strikes
the lampposts, people pass by with masked faces, there is
trouble, there is elucidation, there are forms that emerge from
the substance of beauty and become spiritual. I am looking for
the proper name for the graceful young dancer who
accompanies me — who calls himself *compassionate discernment*
— and I see, in the lights of the horizon falling over the sea,
the degree to which the spirit is also the name of the body.
He suddenly grabs me and leaps up onto the rooftops,
makes a spire with his feet, hurling his head over the mountain
of ordinary houses, dotted on the hill; the head that had been
on his shoulders faltered in the dance but remained balanced,
always whirling, until it made my intelligence, my libidinal
moonlight, and my heart ache. Flying, I doubt that I am
flying,
walking, I wonder about the steps I take. But it was impossible
not to feel as though he was greater than Bach's music, and all
the choirs that had moved him. He, too, disbelieved what he
had seen. Heavens! At every moment, he made me feel as
though I was falling. And yet, the sharpness of the movement
was so peaceful. I felt as if I was on the edge of the rooftops,
carried away by the wind.

"What can we do _____ *when the pure love of
dancing overwhelms us?"*

I understood then that,
just as Ursula, in order to extricate Sebastian, the Don, from his
kingly doom, had given him a place in her garden, where he had

become Don Bush,
in order to extricate *the Younger One* from his hesitant mind, she
pointed him to his fate as a source, in the middle of the in-
combustible forest. A source, at once real — water — and as
mysterious as a source — cognizant of slaking the physical
thirst for knowledge in anyone who drank from it. That had
been his purpose in life,
that would be, if he so desired —
as, indeed, he was desiring —
his way of being a funambulist in the new world.

He then asked me
if he was permitted to steal the contents of the Book of Job,   or
the water, or the phenomena of nature. I looked at him,
astonished, for I could not conceive that he would ask about me
what his volition could accomplish in a flash. But I understood
it was his Ursuline way of establishing an alliance with me for all
eternity. It is on the back of such questions that I travel through
life. That I grow younger. Or grow older. "The chandelier no
longer writes," I tell him, "The path no longer moves forward, it
has multiplied, and it has split." He pulled me, in response,
higher, laughed, in a thunder that must have been heard, and
shouted at me:

"Let's go back to the beginning that leads to the end,"
and cast the vision he was carrying over the valley

The liquid in the cup — the tea — is now teeming with the
bubbles of dreams.
Gonçala and Leonarda are playing as children; they
suddenly rise and fall from the places where they are, their skirts

gleam, and they play, unknowingly, that the books are clothed in a sacredness which can uplift them, or destroy them; hesitating over the choice of an image can either create a dove or a hunter; choose a third image: exhale them. One of them runs away, and arrives at the village overlook, where she can see the place — the house on the second floor — where the other one stayed with us.

The dancer says to her: — Look! There in the distance, Gonçala is at the overlook, gazing at us.

Leonarda replies:

— There in the distance, is the interior of the world. The house I live in.

The dancer then grasps all the people he had trapped in his libidinal obsession, prisoners of his art of creating problematics, from the smallest to the largest who were struggling in the darkness,
and pulls them into the image that *forms* his complete, and never seen body. They all let him travel through the image he shows them,
until he is prominent,
and alone with it.

It is his final act, before he departs for millions of years. Unveiling his compassion, in the simplest, most human way. He goes into the small house. It is evident that he loses many of his body's references, and his spirit opens up to the adventure of transforming and being transformed
as he settles in the armchair,
sitting there watching — still watching the young woman of his love. There is nothing he wants to steal from her. He has come

— always and only — to give to her. He gazes at the complex loving
energy,
so complex and in motion,
that it begins to become infinitely simple to be with the young woman,
in the presence of her animals and the Creator who taught him to demultiply in any attempt to divide.

We see him moving forward, deeper into the image. Humble and unrelenting. This is the room of the fire, although we see no stove, no fireplace,
only a long bench with a backboard. He stares at the coloring substance of libidinal energy and, because he already knows it without ever having experienced it,
and considers it free and compulsive,
he has no fear of dulling the young woman's profile.   She recognizes only that there is, before her, a force that comes from far away, and even though the power of its impact is incalculable, it will do her no harm,
it has come from immeasurably far away to tell her how much he loves her. As the Angel had done with the Virgin. There is, in him, who is pressing ahead toward the core of language, an onslaught that rushes from the Mount of psychic energy which presided over the Creation of the World, regardless of its object,
but that young woman is its object and its recipient. The entire fire of life is made for her. We see her baring her mind. Even in the incomprehensible, her movement through language is relentless. He feels a blue, diffuse emotion that tunes his body to give her precisely what she will accept, and suddenly an unparalleled pleasure engulfs him — creational and immense.

And this is what he tells her, when she asks him: — What?
— I received an immense pleasure. — He feels like a bird
stumbling because it is walking on land. Without a book and
outside it. We see this is the image he is showing us, but we do
not see what, in the universe, is extraordinary about this image.
He looks at us, slightly startled. He has shown us what he
himself had never seen, and the extent of his compassion eludes
us.

He then sits down for the last time on the edge of writing,
in the lap of his profound love. He sees those passing by shining
in the eyes of the animals lying there.

"The lack of oneness saddens me," he writes.

And he begins the first steps of his dance. He turns back
upon himself. He slowly picks up velocity. He gradually
becomes a whirlwind of light. In the solitude of his corner, he
seemed to dance wreckage. The rain fell on the image and, by
and by, everything took on the appearance our mind demands
— a slanting rain strikes the light of the lamp, shines, and
creates an optical illusion. We return to our human mission as
blind singers creating the myths of its condition.

The world exists and Vergílio is dead, but
one more word is pleading for me to write it.

He passionately loved this language, this arid and chaotic
culture. What he thought, he thought against the frustrated
positivism pervasive here. He was this land, he was Portuguese.
Which always astonished me, because of my insurmountable
failure of identification. Many loved him for this. Others hated

him for it. What is done is done. I will not find it strange, however,

if, on rainy nights, many see an aerial funambulist giving them faith in knowing, and in the bare and incomprehensible fact of being human — men and women. No, it isn't the slanting, radiant rain striking the light. No. It is he, the blind singer, in the love he had for you. In the "compassionate discernment" he was capable of. It isn't, it isn't

a small rain, but a hesitant source dusting us with lucidity.

— Gabriela!

— Yes!

— We will see each other again, millions of years from now.

— Yes!

— Do your part! Fearlessly, fearlessly, fearlessly.

Notes on Quotations
in Llansol's Diaries

Llansol was reading many different authors while writing her diaries, most often in their French translations, but it is not always possible to determine who or what she is quoting. There is no definitive list of these quotations, nor have they been identified in other editions of the diaries beyond Llansol's own textual references, leaving it up to the reader to identify them (or not). For this edition, an attempt was made to track down as many of the quotations as possible and reproduce their English translations. The one exception is Rimbaud—those passages have been translated directly from Llansol's own Portuguese, being attentive to the differences in her phrasing compared to other English versions.

DIARY I: FINITA

p. 17–18: "The European princes should really ask themselves whether they can do without our support. We immoralists — today we are the only power which needs no allies to reach victory: that makes us by far the strongest among the strong. We do not even need lies: what other power could dispense with them? A strong seduction fights for us, perhaps the strongest there is: the seduction of truth...of 'truth'? Who put that word into [our mouths]? [...] No, we don't need even that, we would gain power and victory even without truth. The magic that fights for us [...] is the *magic of the extreme*, the seduction that every extreme exercises: we immoralists, we are extreme [...]"

Friedrich Nietzsche, *Writings from the Late Notebooks* 10[94], tr. Kate Sturge. Cambridge University Press (2003), p. 189-190.

p. 21: "What do you want me to tell you about myself? I don't know anything about myself; I don't even know the date of my own death"

"Jorge Luis Borges: 'No estoy seguro de que yo exista en realidad.'" El País, 26 September 1981.

(Llansol encountered this quotation in a French translation, which is slightly different than the Spanish-language original. The translation has been based on the French version reproduced by Llansol.)

p. 21: "I owe the discovery of Uqbar to the conjunction of a mirror and an encyclopedia."

Jorge Luis Borges, "Tlön, Uqbar, Orbis Tertius" in *Collected Fictions*, tr. Andrew Hurley. Penguin Books (1999), p. 68.

p. 40: "In taking this path, then, love does not become happy."

Søren Kierkegaard, *Kierkegaard's Writings, VII: Philosophical Fragments*, tr. Howard V. Hong and Edna H. Hong. Princeton University Press (1985), p. 29.

p. 40: "Nature itself comes up with many terrifying devices and many subterfuges in order to disturb."
Søren Kierkegaard, *Kierkegaard's Writings, VII: Philosophical Fragments*, tr. Howard V. Hong and Edna H. Hong. Princeton University Press (1985), p. 44.

p. 41: "The human mind so often aspires to might and power"
Søren Kierkegaard, *Kierkegaard's Writings, VII: Philosophical Fragments*, tr. Howard V. Hong and Edna H. Hong. Princeton University Press (1985), p. 30.

p. 42: "one's greatest suffering and one's highest hope"
Friedrich Nietzsche, *The Joyful Wisdom*, no. 268, tr. Thomas Common. T.N. Foulis (1910), p. 209.

p. 44: "A muddiness of mind in which earthly distinction ferments almost grossly."
Søren Kierkegaard, *Kierkegaard's Writings, VII: Philosophical Fragments*, tr. Howard V. Hong and Edna H. Hong. Princeton University Press (1985), p. 12.

p. 44: "Because the truth in which I rest was in me and emerged from me. Not even Socrates would have been capable of giving it to me, no more than the coachman is capable of pulling the horse's load, even though he may help the horse do it by means of the whip."
Søren Kierkegaard, *Kierkegaard's Writings, VII: Philosophical Fragments*, tr. Howard V. Hong and Edna H. Hong. Princeton University Press (1985), p. 12.

p. 45: "Viewed Socratically, any point of departure in time is *eo ipso* something accidental, a vanishing point, an occasion."
Søren Kierkegaard, *Kierkegaard's Writings, VII: Philosophical Fragments*, tr. Howard V. Hong and Edna H. Hong. Princeton University Press (1985), p. 11.

p. 45: "then the moment in time must have such decisive significance"
Søren Kierkegaard, *Kierkegaard's Writings, VII: Philosophical Fragments*, tr. Howard V. Hong and Edna H. Hong. Princeton University Press (1985), p. 13

p. 48: "But how are we to raise *the defunct languages* of nature from the dead?"
Johann Georg Hamann, Writings on Philosophy and Language, tr. Kenneth Haynes. Cambridge University Press (2007), p. 85.

p. 66: "No longer to write anything which does not reduce to despair every sort of man who is 'in a hurry.'"
Friedrich Nietzsche, *Daybreak*, tr. R.J. Hollingdale. Cambridge University Press (1997), p. 5.

p. 67: "Are we then without pity?"
Friedrich Nietzsche, *Daybreak*, tr. R.J. Hollingdale. Cambridge University Press (1997), p. 92.

p. 67: "the need for little deviant acts"
Friedrich Nietzsche, *Daybreak*, tr. R.J. Hollingdale. Cambridge University Press (1997), p. 97.

p. 67: "Hitherto, the subject reflected on least adequately has been good and evil."
Friedrich Nietzsche, *Daybreak*, tr. R.J. Hollingdale. Cambridge University Press (1997), p. 2.

p. 68: "Which is why we need first to adjust and justify the goal of a Shakespearean drama, that is to say, not to understand it."
Friedrich Nietzsche, *Daybreak*, tr. R.J. Hollingdale. Cambridge University Press (1997), p. 141.

p. 70: "what one desires of life is rest and silence"
Friedrich Nietzsche, *Daybreak*, tr. R.J. Hollingdale. Cambridge University Press (1997), p. 228.

p. 70: "The snake that cannot slough its skin, perishes. Likewise spirits which are prevented from changing their opinions; they cease to be spirits."
Friedrich Nietzsche, *Daybreak*, tr. R.J. Hollingdale. Cambridge University Press (1997), p. 228.

p. 70: "This authority of morality paralyzes thinking."
Friedrich Nietzsche, *Daybreak*, tr. R.J. Hollingdale. Cambridge University Press (1997), p. 62.

p. 70: "in bright daylight the ear is less necessary. That is how music acquired the character of an art of night and twilight."
Friedrich Nietzsche, *Daybreak*, tr. R.J. Hollingdale. Cambridge University Press (1997), p. 143.

p. 71: "the timid man does not know what it is to be alone"
Friedrich Nietzsche, *Daybreak*, tr. R.J. Hollingdale. Cambridge
University Press (1997), p. 143.

p. 73: "You have, four or five miles from here, a corral for your
domesticated animals. These animals need to be taken care
of. Will you allow me to live there with them?"
Jules Verne, *The Mysterious Island*.

p. 93: "He would feel so distinctly the soul of his mistress rising
to the surface of her face that he could not refrain from
touching it with his lips."
Marcel Proust, *Swann's Way*, tr. C.K. Scott Moncrieff and Ter-
ence Kilmartin. The Modern Library (1992), p. 342.

p. 95: "The union of close blood-relatives...is yet the prerogative
of kings."
Carl Jung, *The Psychology of the Transference*, tr. R.F.C. Hull.
Princeton University Press (1966), p. 56.
(In the French translation reproduced by Llansol: "...kings and
gods.")

p. 101: "I could tell you so much that is fine about it. Sometimes
it seems to me I could die when it is done: so to the very end
do all difficulty and sweetness come together in these pages,
so finally does it all stand there and yet so boundlessly capable of the transformations inherent in it that I have the feeling of transmitting myself with this book, far and surely, beyond all danger of death. [...] And if I think so calmly of no
longer existing after this work, it is because I do not yet dare
at all to promise myself the fullness I am gradually achieving

with it: for now I am training for myself [...] a massive, enduring prose, with which it will be possible to make absolutely everything. It would be glorious after that to continue or daily to begin anew with life's whole boundless task..."

Rainer Maria Rilke, *Letters of Rainer Maria Rilke, 1892-1910*, tr. Jane Bannard Greene and M.D. Herter Norton. W.W. Norton & Company (1945), #201.

p. 102: "sadly and bewilderingly"
Rainer Maria Rilke, *Letters of Rainer Maria Rilke, 1892-1910*, tr. Jane Bannard Greene and M.D. Herter Norton. W.W. Norton & Company (1945), #193.

p. 102: "No friend have I, I must live with myself alone; but I know well that God is closer to me than to others in my art, I go about with him without fear, I have always recognized and understood him; I am also not at all afraid for my music, that can have no ill fate; he to whom it makes itself intelligible must become free of all the misery with which others are encumbered."
Rainer Maria Rilke, *Letters of Rainer Maria Rilke, 1892-1910*, tr. Jane Bannard Greene and M.D. Herter Norton. W.W. Norton & Company (1945), #293.

p. 103: "If one *single* truth like the sun prevails, it is *day*. If you behold, instead of this one truth, as many as the sands of the seashore, and then behold a little light which excels in brightness a whole host of suns, it is a *night* beloved of poets and thieves...The *poet* at the beginning of days is the same as the *thief* at the end of days."
Johann Georg Hamann, Writings on Philosophy and Language,

tr. Kenneth Haynes. Cambridge University Press (2007), p. 78.

p. 121: "Full of sympathetic old things..."
Rainer Maria Rilke, *Letters of Rainer Maria Rilke, 1910-1926*, tr. Jane Bannard Greene and M.D. Herter Norton. W.W. Norton & Company (1948), #149.

p. 128: "We must all seek our own combination, our own personal balance point between art's life and life's art."
Rainer Maria Rilke and Lou Andreas-Salomé, *Rilke and Andreas-Salomé: A Love Story in Letters*, tr. Edward Snow and Michael Winkler. W.W. Norton & Company (2008), p. 75.

p. 143: "At that moment when day and night mingle their light"
Dominique Fernandez, *Porporino, or the Secrets of Naples*, tr. Eileen Finletter. William Morrow (1976), p. 28.

p. 143: "I felt the same emotions I was later to feel as an adult, both deepest despair because I was excluded from life as a man, and marvelous beatitude because I was spared from it."
Dominique Fernandez, *Porporino, or the Secrets of Naples*, tr. Eileen Finletter. William Morrow (1976), p. 31

p. 144: "but all things mingled, eternally one and limitless"
Marie Delcourt, *Hermaphrodite: Myths and Rites of the Bisexual Figure in Classical Antiquity*, tr. Jennifer Nicholson. Longacre Press (1961), p. 69.
(This is part of a quotation attributed to Rufinus, fourth century AD.)

p. 145: "and presupposes an ability to experience events which are enacted in a reality other than the physical reality of daily life, events which spontaneously transmute themselves into symbols"

Henry Corbin, *Creative Imagination in the Sufism of Ibn Arabi*, tr. Ralph Manheim. Princeton University Press (1969), p. 32.

p. 156: "But in the presence of such complexity, of a Figure that discloses so many associations and undergoes so many metamorphoses...we must lay bare the implicit intentions of the mystic consciousness, discern what it shows itself of itself"

Henry Corbin, *Creative Imagination in the Sufism of Ibn Arabi*, tr. Ralph Manheim. Princeton University Press (1969), p. 58.

p. 157: "This mantle is for us indeed a symbol of confraternity, a sign that we share in the same spiritual culture."

Henry Corbin, *Creative Imagination in the Sufism of Ibn Arabi*, tr. Ralph Manheim. Princeton University Press (1969), p. 65.
(In the French reproduced by Llansol: "...the same spiritual geography.")

p. 158: "...That the Form under which each of the Spirituals knows God is also the form under which God knows him, because it is the form under which God reveals Himself to Himself in that man."

Henry Corbin, *Creative Imagination in the Sufism of Ibn Arabi*, tr. Ralph Manheim. Princeton University Press (1969), p. 62.

p. 188: "for love's sake, rate ourselves too highly"
Baruch Spinoza, *Ethics*, tr. R.H.M. Elwes. Prop. XLIX.

p. 195: "The Soul selects her own Society _____
    Then _____ shuts the Door _____ "
Emily Dickinson.

p. 238: "It is from the reading of books — not necessarily philosophical — that these initial shocks become questions and
problems, giving one to think. The role of national literatures here is perhaps very important. Not just that one
learns words from it, but in it one lives 'the true life which is
absent' but which is precisely no longer utopian. I think that
in the great fear of bookishness, one underestimates the 'ontological' reference of the human to the book that one takes
for a source of information, or for a 'tool' of learning, even
though it is a modality of our being."
Emmanuel Levinas, *Ethics and Inifinity*, tr. Richard A. Cohen.
Duquesne University Press, (1985), p. 21-22.

p. 247: "outside there is a stillness as if nothing existed"
Fernando Pessoa, *The Complete Works of Alberto Caeiro*, tr. Mar-
garet Jull Costa and Patricio Ferrari. New Directions (2020),
#44.

p. 247: "Pass, bird, pass, and teach me how to pass"
Fernando Pessoa, *The Complete Works of Alberto Caeiro*, tr. Mar-
garet Jull Costa and Patricio Ferrari. New Directions (2020),
#43.

p. 317–318: "Loving those who are like this: when they enter a
   room they are not persons, characters or subjects, but an atmospheric variation, a change of hue, an imperceptible molecule, a discrete population, a fog or a cloud of droplets."
Gilles Deleuze and Claire Parnet, Dialogues, tr. Hugh Tomlin-
son and Barbara Habberjam. Columbia University Press
(1987), p. 66.

p. 357–359: "The mares that carry me, as far as impulse might
   reach,
   were taking me, when they brought me and placed me
   upon the much-speaking route
   of the goddess, that carries everywhere unscathed the man
   who knows
   thereon was I carried, for thereon the much-guided mares
   were carrying me,
   straining to pull the chariot, and maidens were leading the
   way
   ...Daughters of the Sun were hastening
   to escort me, after leaving the House of Night for the light,
   having pushed back with their hands the veils from their
   heads.
   There are the gates of the paths of Night and Day...
   and for these Justice, much-avenging, holds the keys of
   retribution.
   Coaxing her with gentle words, the maidens
   did cunningly persuade her that she should push back the
   bolted bar for them

swiftly from the gates; and these made of the doors
a gaping gap as they were opened wide,
swinging in turn in their sockets the brazen posts...
straight through them at that point
did the maidens drive the chariot and mares along the
broad way
...and the goddess received me kindly, and took my right
hand with her hand,
and uttered speech and thus addressed me:
Youth...
it is no ill fortune that sent you forth to travel
this route (for it lies far indeed from the beaten track of
men),
...and it is right that you should learn all things,
both the steadfast heart of persuasive Truth
and the beliefs of mortals, in which there is no true trust."
Parmenides of Elea, *Fragments*, tr. David Gallop. University of
Toronto Press (1984), p. 49-53.

p. 366: "Come, I shall tell you, and do you listen and convey the
story,
what routes of inquiry alone there are for thinking."
Parmenides of Elea, *Fragments*, tr. David Gallop. University of
Toronto Press (1984), p. 55.

p. 366-367: "The one - that is and that cannot not be,
is the path of persuasion,
for it attends upon Truth.
The other - that is not, and that needs must not be,
that I point out to you to be a path wholly unlearnable,
for you could not know what-is-not."

Parmenides of Elea, *Fragments*, tr. David Gallop. University of
 Toronto Press (1984), p. 55.

p. 383: "I never lost _____ as much but twice _____"
Emily Dickinson.

p. 389–390: "When a person dies,
 there arises
 this doubt —
 he still *exists*, say some
 he *does not*, say others —
 I want you to teach me the truth:
 this is my third boon,"
The Upanishads, tr. Eknath Easwaran. Nilgiri Press (1987).

p. 431: "Nothing is so firmly opposed to God than time."
Meister Eckhart, *The Complete Mystical Works of Meister Eckhart*,
 tr. Maurice O'C. Walshe. Crossroad Publishing Company
 (2009), p. 452.

JOÃO BARRENTO is an essayist and literary translator, formerly a Professor of German and Comparative Literature. He has published more than twenty books, two of them dedicated to the work of Maria Gabriela Llansol. His translations encompass a wide range of works since the Middle Ages, particularly of major authors such as Goethe, Hölderlin, Musil, and Walter Benjamin, as well as twentieth-century poetry. Since 2008, he has been the director of the cultural association Espaço Llansol, responsible for the preservation, cataloging, and dissemination of Llansol's literary estate and archives. In 2023, he was awarded the Prémio Camões, the most prestigious literary prize in the Portuguese language.

MARIA GABRIELA LLANSOL (1931–2008) is a singular figure in Portuguese literature, one of the greatest writers of the 20th century, yet never before translated into English. Although entirely unknown in the United States, she twice won the award for best novel from the Portuguese Writers' Association with her textually idiosyncratic, fragmentary, and densely poetic writing; other recipients of this prize include José Saramago and António Lobos Antunes. Upon her death in 2008, she left behind twenty-seven published books and more than seventy unpublished notebooks, all of which evade any traditional definitions of genre. Deep Vellum published her trilogy *Geography of Rebels*, in English translation by Audrey Young, in 2018.

AUDREY YOUNG is a translator, researcher, and archivist. She received a Fulbright grant to research non-theatrical film in Portugal and studied Portuguese language and culture at the University of Lisbon with a scholarship from the Instituto Camões. She has worked at the Getty Research Institute, the Cineteca Nacional México, and the Arquivo Nacional do Brasil, among other archives.